Sponsored by
the Center for Policy Research in Education,
a consortium of
the Eagleton Institute of Politics at Rutgers University,
the University of Wisconsin, Madison,
Michigan State University,
and Stanford University;
funded by
the Office of Educational Research and Improvement,
U.S. Department of Education,
under grant number
OERI G008690011

Restructuring
Schools

*Richard F. Elmore
and Associates*

Restructuring Schools

The Next Generation of Educational Reform

 Jossey-Bass Publishers

San Francisco   •   Oxford   •   1990

RESTRUCTURING SCHOOLS
The Next Generation of Educational Reform
by Richard F. Elmore and Associates

Copyright © 1990 by: Jossey-Bass Inc., Publishers
                     350 Sansome Street
                     San Francisco, California 94104
                              &
                     Jossey-Bass Limited
                     Headington Hill Hall
                     Oxford OX3 0BW

Library of Congress Cataloging-in-Publication Data

Elmore, Richard F.
   Restructuring schools : the next generation of educational reform/
   Richard F. Elmore and associates.
       p.   cm. — (Jossey-Bass education series)
   "Sponsored by the Center for Policy Research in Education" — Series
t.p.
   Includes bibliographical references (p.   ).
   ISBN 1-55542-234-9
   1. School management and organization — United States.   2. Public
schools — United States.   3. Education and state — United States.
4. Education — United States — Aims and objectives.   I. Center for
Policy Research in Education.   II. Title.   III. Series.
LB2805.E46   1990
371.2'00973 — dc20   89-49292
                                                          CIP

Manufactured in the United States of America

The paper in this book meets the guidelines for
permanence and durability of the Committee on
Production Guidelines for Book Longevity of
the Council on Library Resources.

JACKET DESIGN BY WILLI BAUM

FIRST EDITION

Code 9034

The Jossey-Bass
Education Series

Contents

Preface

Since the late 1970s, America has been engaged in a far-reaching debate about the purposes, organization, and performance of its schools. The debate has been carried out in state legislatures, governors' offices, and local school boards across the country and has included topics ranging from the qualifications and preparation of teachers to student learning and the content of the curriculum to testing and the performance of schools. Lately, part of this debate has begun to focus on a variety of issues regarding the organization and governance of schools that pertain to school restructuring.

State and local policymakers, researchers, teachers, and administrators confront a variety of conflicting points of view and prescriptions in the debate over school restructuring. One line of argument, for example, states that schools can improve only by introducing teaching and learning practices based on systematic, scientifically validated knowledge. Another point of view is that schools will improve when educators are given greater opportunity to exercise skill and judgment and more control over the conditions of their work. And a third point of view states that schools must become more accountable to their main clients—students and parents—if they are to become more effective. These points of view, and others represented in the restructuring debate, present conflicting perceptions of the problems of American schooling and prescriptions for solving them. Policymakers will be under increasing pressure to choose among these points of view when designing school improvement policies. Educators will be under increasing pressure to provide their own perspectives on the need for organizational reforms and to implement prescriptions expressed in policy. Researchers will find themselves increasingly dealing with the consequences of school restructuring policies as they study the conditions of teaching and learning in schools.

Restructuring Schools is designed to help policymakers, educators, and researchers develop a deeper understanding of the issues of school restructuring and to give greater conceptual clarity to the terms of the current debate. The authors are experienced analysts of educational policy and organization who have studied a variety of attempts at school reform from a variety of perspectives. They were asked to examine the current debate on school restructuring as sympathetic critics: to "unpack" the main ideas behind school restructuring, to anchor these ideas in current research, and to analyze the consequences of the ideas for organization and practice in schools. This book is not designed to provide a simple blueprint for school restructuring. Indeed, the authors share a distrust of easy solutions and a genuine interest in the problem solving that must accompany serious and sustained efforts to improve the conditions of teaching and learning in schools. The book is predicated on the assumption that a clearer understanding of the issues underlying the school restructuring debate and an exploration of the intellectual roots of current attempts at school reform will give policymakers, educators, and researchers insight into the possible course of reform.

Writing about school restructuring has to date been confined to current periodicals and published proposals by school reform advocates. While periodicals and reform proposals provide valuable material for historical accounts of this period of school reform, they make no pretense to being reflective or analytical, nor are they necessarily concerned with the conceptual roots of the debate. In this book we attempt to open up the conceptual side of the debate and to introduce an inquiry into the nature and effects of school restructuring. We intend for this inquiry to be accessible not just to an academic audience but also to those who have a more immediate and practical interest in the issue.

Audience

Restructuring Schools should serve various purposes for different audiences. For those who operate in the policymaking

arena—legislators, school board members, and policy staff—
the book should serve as a source of ideas to inform policy and
a source of critical reflections to be used in the design of reform
proposals. Deeper understanding of these issues, we believe, will
ultimately lead to more sustained and effective policies toward
school organization and governance. For practitioners—teachers, administrators, and allied school personnel—the book should
serve as a source of ideas for broadening and deepening the role
of educators in school reform. One message that cuts across all
the chapters is that educators will be central actors in school
restructuring. For researchers, the book should serve as a stim-
ulus for inquiry into the central issues of restructuring. All
chapters demonstrate the need for further systematic inquiry
into the premises and effects of changes in school organization
and governance. Overall, we believe the book represents an important convergence of the interests of policymakers, educators,
and researchers.

Overview of the Contents

The chapters of the book are organized into two main
parts. I believe that the combination of micro and macro
perspectives presented here is unique in the literature on school
reform. Following an introductory chapter detailing the political
rationale and theoretical basis for school restructuring, Part One
presents school restructuring from several perspectives, focusing on proposals to change the nature of teaching and learning, teachers' working conditions, and the relationship between
schools and their clients.

In Chapter Two, Brian Rowan argues that different views
of teaching and learning—inspirational as opposed to routinized,
for example—lead to different forms of school organization and
control. In order to choose an appropriate structure, Rowan
contends, school reformers must decide what view of teaching
they want it to reflect.

In Chapter Three, Gary Sykes suggests that professionalism (as predicated on the authority, regard, resources, and
knowledge that practitioners command) may serve as a basis
for school restructuring, provided that there is an increase in

teachers' collegial accountability, cooperation in the construction of curriculum, access to sources of information, and latitude in defining the terms of their own work — and at the same time, a decrease in pressures and mandates originating outside the school itself.

In Chapter Four, Hendrik Gideonse asks how the internal structure of schools might be different if they were organized as places where teachers and students alike engaged in active inquiry as the main method of teaching and learning. Such a change, he argues, would result in greater flexibility in scheduling, curriculum structure, and student grouping practices, as well as more frequent consultations among parents, students, and teachers.

Susan Moore Johnson, in Chapter Five, takes a critical look at such recent attempts to reform teachers' work as the career ladder and merit pay programs. Most reforms, she argues, fail to take into account either teachers' own conceptions of effective practice or the practical conditions required to make schools function effectively. Changing the conditions of teachers' work, she concludes, is of necessity a school-level process, whose outcome will vary widely from one school setting to another.

In Chapter Six, Mary Anne Raywid examines two different approaches to decentralized decision making in schools: site-based management and client choice. Site-based management, she argues, derives essentially from a traditional bureaucratic model of control, with modest variations in the assumptions about where the responsibility for certain decisions should rest. Client choice models, by contrast, represent a significant change in the locus of responsibility, because they effectively create different avenues of access to and influence on school decisions than the bureaucratic models do.

The discussion of restructuring in Part Two takes into account the perspective of state and local policymakers and analyzes the actual experience of selected states and localities. In Chapter Seven, Jane David reviews the preliminary results from school districts that have embarked on ambitious restructuring efforts. She finds, among other things, that districts have started their restructuring efforts with the serious intention of changing the conditions of teaching and learning in schools, rather than of designing special programs for limited impact. And she observes that restructuring requires both considerable outlay of resources and creation of broad-based local coalitions of unions, community activists, and district administrators, as well as school-level practitioners.

In Chapter Eight, Michael Cohen examines the strategic problems confronting states that are undertaking restructuring initiatives. He argues that in order to succeed, state restructuring initiatives must be tailored to conditions at the school, district, and state levels. Schools must focus more clearly on goals and instructional strategies; districts must focus on increasing the schools' responsibility for learning, and states must critically assess overall performance and the capacity to introduce new practices at the district and school levels.

In the concluding chapter, I consider three possible scenarios for the future of school restructuring, ranging from complete transformation of the basic conditions of public schooling, to adaptive realignment of schools that accommodates new knowledge and new political forces, to insignificant changes and a co-optation of restructuring reforms. The outcome of restructuring efforts, I conclude, will hinge on the degree to which political, community, and professional interests coalesce around a common agenda.

Acknowledgments

These papers were written for the Policy Forum on New Roles and Responsibilities in the Public Schools, sponsored by the Center for Policy Research in Education (CPRE). CPRE is a unique consortium of four institutions—the Eagleton Institute of Politics at Rutgers University; the University of Wisconsin, Madison; Stanford University; and Michigan State University—funded by the U.S. Department of Education's Office of Educational Research and Improvement to conduct research on state and local educational policy. The CPRE Policy Forum was conceived as a means of drawing the leading scholars in the country into serious discourse and writing about emerging issues in educational policy. Participants in the policy forum New Roles and Responsibilities in the Public Schools convened first in the spring of 1987 to discuss the underlying themes and problems of school restructuring and again in the fall of 1987 to discuss initial drafts of papers on these themes. In addition to the authors represented in this volume, other participants made significant contributions to the forum discussions. William Clune, Linda Darling-Hammond, William Firestone, Dean Honetschlager, Martin Orland, Penelope Peterson, Stewart Purkey, Richard Rossmiller, Karen Seashore-Lewis, Marshall Smith, Joan Talbert, and Arthur Wise shared their ideas. Two individuals in particular made contributions far beyond their formal roles: Susan Fuhrman, director of CPRE and a senior researcher at the center, provided extraordinary intellectual and managerial support for the forum; and James Fox, a senior staff member at the Office of Educational Research and Improvement, has served not only as a first-class intellectual colleague but also as an exemplary project officer for CPRE. Special thanks are also due to Lesley Iura from Jossey-Bass, who is the world's most patient and supportive editor.

East Lansing, Michigan   Richard F. Elmore
February 1990

The Authors

Richard F. Elmore is professor of education and political science at Michigan State University and senior research fellow with the Center for Policy Research in Education, a federally funded policy research center that is a joint venture of the Eagleton Institute of Politics at Rutgers University; the University of Wisconsin, Madison; Stanford University; and Michigan State University. His current research focuses on the effects of state and local policies on the structure and content of public schooling, and on policies directed at the labor market and educational problems of disadvantaged youth. He also maintains a professional involvement in education programs for public sector executives.

Before assuming his position at Michigan State University, Elmore was associate dean and associate professor in the Graduate School of Public Affairs, University of Washington, Seattle, where he was on the faculty for eleven years. He received the University of Washington's Distinguished Teaching Award in June 1985.

Elmore received his B.A. degree (1966) from Whitman College in Walla Walla, Washington, in political science, his M.A. degree (1969) from Claremont Graduate School in government, and his Ed.D. degree (1976) from Harvard University in policy.

Elmore has held consulting and advisory positions with the U.S. Department of Education, the National Academy of Sciences, the Executive Office of the President of the United States, the State of Washington, the City of Seattle, and the Port of Seattle. He has also worked as a legislative analyst in the Office of the Secretary of Health, Education, and Welfare and the Office of the Commissioner of Education in the federal government.

Michael Cohen is director of education programs at the National Governors' Association (NGA), where he assists education policy leaders in designing strategies and policies for restructuring schools. Before joining the NGA staff in May 1987, he worked at the National Association of State Boards of Education as director of policy development and planning and directed the State Education Policy Consortium, which worked to determine the information needs of state education policymakers and strengthen ties between policymakers and researchers.

While working at the National Institute of Education (NIE), from 1973 through 1983, Cohen created and directed the Effective Schools research program for the federal government. He has written numerous articles and book chapters, has lectured widely, and has worked with state and local policymakers, teachers, and principals across the country, using the effective schools research in school improvement and reform efforts.

Cohen received his B.A. degree (1972) from the State University of New York, Binghamton, in sociology.

Jane L. David is director of the Bay Area Research Group in Palo Alto, California. Her research and consulting activities focus on the connections between school change and education policy at all levels. Current clients include the National Governors' Association, Apple Computer, Inc., SRI International, and several districts and state agencies. She received both her B.A. degree (1966) in French and her M.A. degree (1969) in mathematics education from the University of Oklahoma, and her Ed.D. degree (1974) from Harvard University in education and social policy.

Hendrik D. Gideonse is University Professor of education and policy science and former dean (1972–1986) of the College of Education at the University of Cincinnati. He received his B.A. degree (1958) from Amherst College in political science and his Ed.M. (1959) and Ed.D. (1963) degrees from Harvard University in the history and philosophy of education. He is a member of the Unit Accreditation Board of the National Council for the Accreditation of Teacher Education and of the in-

structional staff of the knowledge-base workshop sponsored by
the American Association of Colleges of Teacher Education.

Susan Moore Johnson is associate professor of administration, planning, and social policy at the Harvard Graduate School
of Education, where she is also on the research staff of the National Center for Educational Leadership. She received her A.B.
degree (1967) from Mount Holyoke College in English literature
and her M.A.T. degree (1969) in English and Ed.D. degree
(1982) in administration and social policy and planning from
Harvard University. She is the author of *Teachers' Unions in Schools*
(1984) and *Teachers at Work* (1990).

Mary Anne Raywid is professor of administration and
policy studies at Hofstra University, where she also directs the
Center for the Study of Educational Alternatives. She has been
active in education organizations, has served on the editorial
boards of a dozen professional journals, and has published widely
in the broad area of school-society relationships. School reform,
restructuring, and choice are her current major interests. She
received her B.A. degree (1949) from the University of North
Carolina, Greensboro, in history and English, her M.A. degree
(1950) from the University of Illinois in political science, and
her Ph.D. degree (1959) from the University of Illinois in foundations of education.

Brian Rowan is associate professor of education and sociology and chairman of the Department of Educational Administration at Michigan State University. In addition, he is a
research associate with the Center for Research on the Context
of Secondary School Teaching, a federally funded research and
development center at Stanford University and Michigan State
University. Rowan's research focuses on the application of organization theory to the study of school systems, on school effectiveness, and on the management and delivery of compensatory
instruction to disadvantaged students.

Before assuming his position at Michigan State University, Rowan was senior research director at Far West Laboratory

for Educational Research and Development in San Francisco. He received his B.A. degree (1972) from Rutgers University in sociology and his Ph.D. degree (1978) from Stanford University, also in sociology.

Rowan has been a consultant or adviser to numerous organizations and government agencies. He currently is a member of the Program Effectiveness Panel of the U.S. Department of Education.

Gary Sykes is an assistant professor of education at Michigan State University, where he also serves on the staff of the Holmes Group, a consortium of research universities pursuing a reform agenda in teacher education. He conducts research through the Center for Policy Research in Education and consults regularly with the recently formed National Board for Professional Teaching Standards. His research interests include the effects of policy on teachers and teaching, teacher education, and the assessment of teaching.

Before assuming his position at Michigan State, Sykes worked as a research associate at the National Institute of Education and as research director of the California Commission on the Teaching Profession. He received his B.A. degree (1969) from Princeton University in history and his Ph.D. degree (1988) from Stanford University in the design and evaluation of educational programs.

Restructuring
Schools

✳ ONE

Introduction:
On Changing the Structure
of Public Schools

Richard F. Elmore

The idea of restructured schools has become increasingly important in recent debates on educational reform. In the current political language, the "first wave" of recent educational reforms, extending from the late 1970s to the present, was designed to focus public education on academic content and to introduce higher standards for students and teachers. The "second wave," extending from the present onward, focuses on fundamental changes in expectations for student learning, in the practice of teaching, and in the organization and management of public schools. Behind the idea of restructured schools is a fragile consensus that public schools, as they are presently constituted, are not capable of meeting society's expectations for the education of young people.

The motive for restructuring schools is often couched in the language of economic competitiveness and material well-being. A recent issue of *Business Week* ("America's Schools . . . ," 1988, p. 129), for example, observed: "A new call for school reform is ringing across the land. This one is different. The nation's economic problems are being placed at the schoolhouse door. Economic growth, competitiveness, and living standards depend heavily on making investments in human capital. That means attending to the state of America's schools." In order to sustain our present standard of living and regain our competitive

1

position in the world economy, it is argued, we will need a better educated work force, which will, in turn, mean that schools will have to dramatically improve the way they educate all children.

At other times, the motive for restructuring schools is stated in the language of demography, equity, and social justice. The proportion of children living in poverty is increasing, the argument goes, and these children will have to be well-educated if they are to attain economic self-sufficiency and support a growing population of elderly, or our society will face unacceptably high levels of poverty and dependency. The Carnegie Task Force on Teaching as a Profession (1986, p. 14) puts the problem this way: "While it was once possible for people to succeed in this society if they were simply willing to work hard, it is increasingly difficult for the poorly educated to find jobs. . . . [In addition], the proportion of the population in the prime working years will decline steadily in the years to come. . . . This makes it imperative that all those who are able to work make the maximum contribution to the economic well-being of the nation."

Still another motive for restructuring schools arises from what many perceive to be an emerging crisis of quality in the teaching force, which will lose a large proportion of current teachers through attrition or retirement in the next decade. This teacher turnover will occur during a period of broad changes in the labor force. Education is losing its claim on the labor pool from which teachers have traditionally been drawn — college-educated, largely female, often minority, upwardly mobile young people — who now have access to other professional occupations. If teaching is to regain its competitive position in the labor market, it is contended, schools will have to become more attractive places to work and the economic rewards of teaching will have to become competitive with those of other professional occupations. "The traditions of recruitment, norms of preparation, and conditions of work in schools have severely hindered efforts to improve the quality of teaching," the Holmes Group argues (1986, p. 31).

Taken together, these positions represent a potentially powerful coincidence of political, business, professional, and academic interests that could dramatically affect public education if they were to act in concert. But this coincidence of interests does not necessarily guarantee a well-articulated policy agenda for restructuring schools, much less any significant change in the nature and outcomes of schooling. Not since the late nineteenth century, when the present organizational contours of mass public education emerged, has the political rhetoric of school reform been so broad and comprehensive. During the last major period of school reform, in the 1960s, for example, policies were designed to secure the benefits of equal access for excluded minorities. These policies were based on the assumption that most schools were generally effective in preparing students for the demands of full participation in society, even if they often operated in a discriminatory fashion. The present school reform agenda potentially runs much deeper. Reformers argue that schools are deficient in certain respects for *all* students, though they may be worse for some.

While the present reform agenda is potentially more far-reaching than any other since the emergence of mass public education, it is also more susceptible to failure for at least three reasons. First, the very breadth of political support may mean that the reform movement will lack sufficient specificity and coherence to have a significant and lasting impact on schools. The political constituency for restructuring schools is a diffuse collection of state and local political leaders, local educators who have managed to change the way schools work in a few exemplary settings, a few leading business executives, a few leaders of teacher organizations, and a few leaders of major university schools of education. These groups bring very different political interests to bear on the question of reform, operate on different assumptions about the ends to be achieved through reform, and represent very different constituencies.

Second, past efforts at school reform give little cause for optimism about the current agenda. Some scholars have observed that school reformers have never had difficulty creating small islands of exemplary organization and practice or sustaining these small experiments for relatively long periods of time (Cohen, 1987, 1988; Cuban, 1984; Elmore, 1987; Elmore and McLaughlin, 1988). The main problem educational reform faces is that fundamental changes in the conditions of teaching and learning seldom reach beyond the islands where they are tried, into the broader educational system. An irony of education reform is that during certain periods of history "restructured schools" have been everywhere and nowhere at the same time. Public schools have had little difficulty deflecting or co-opting the best efforts of school reformers.

Third, the current attractiveness of restructured schools as a theme for educational reform may stem largely from the lack of definition of what "restructuring" means. School restructuring has many of the characteristics of what political and organizational theorists call a "garbage can" (Cohen, March, and Olsen, 1972; Kingdon, 1984, 75–94); that is, the theme of restructuring schools can accommodate a variety of conceptions of what is problematical about American education, as well as a variety of solutions favored by certain interest groups in search of problems. As long as the theme of school restructuring is fluid and unspecified, it functions well as a rallying point for reformers. But once the theme is defined, it may begin to divide rather than unite diverse political interests. A major policy question in the debate over restructured schools, to paraphrase Gertrude Stein's famous line about Oakland, California, is "when you get there, is there any there there?" That is, is there enough substance behind restructuring proposals to constitute a reform agenda, and if there is, what political and practical problems does the agenda raise?

This book is an attempt to define more clearly what restructured schools would mean conceptually, politically, and organizationally. The chapters in this volume subject the idea of restructured schools to close analysis, first, by asking what school restructuring is "about" in fundamental terms; second, by specifying the assumptions underlying various points of view about restructuring; third, by speculating about the implications of different points of view for school organization and teaching practice; and fourth, by identifying where varying political interests conflict or converge regarding the meaings of school restructuring. Our objective in writing these chapters is to give conceptual and practical depth to the current debate on school restructuring, rather than to provide a manifesto for the

restructuring movement or a recipe for those who would undertake restructuring. Indeed, the main message of this book is that
school restructuring is "about" many things, and if the restructuring movement is to have an impact on American education,
its advocates must focus more clearly on the problems raised
by various proposals for restructuring.

These chapters were originally papers written, following
preliminary discussions, for the Policy Forum on New Roles
and Responsibilities in the Public Schools, sponsored by the
Center for Policy Research in Education in 1987. From the first
series of Policy Forum discussions emerged general agreement
that school restructuring was "about" at least three types of
changes: (1) teaching and learning in schools, (2) conditions of
teachers' work in schools, and (3) the governance and incentive
structures under which schools operate.

In the remainder of this chapter I introduce the major
themes in the political debate over school restructuring, sketch
out the three models of restructuring that emerged from the Policy Forum, and provide an overview of the chapters that follow.

Political Discourse About School Restructuring

Political debate about school restructuring has centered
on the themes of empowerment, accountability, and academic
learning. *Empowerment* is a term most often used in connection
with teachers (Maeroff, 1988), but also with some frequency
in connection with schools, or with students and parents. Underlying the rhetoric of empowerment is the idea that the growth
of school bureaucracy and obtrusive regulation by federal, state,
and local government has undermined the authority of teachers,
blurred the responsibility of schools toward students and parents,
and deflected attention from the central tasks of teaching and
learning. School restructuring, then, is partly about empowering teachers, students, and parents to play a more influential
role in determining what schools do.

The idea of empowerment raises serious difficulties, which
may explain why it seems to be losing favor as a theme of restructuring. One difficulty is the question of who empowers whom.

There seems to be an assumption that people who currently hold power — state and local bureaucrats, for example — should give it to someone else — teachers, for example — in the interest of making schools work more effectively. Many of the people who are thought to hold power, however, perceive themselves to be just as powerless as those who are thought to be the beneficiaries of empowerment. Furthermore, the conditions under which the transfer of power is to occur are never specified.

A more serious difficulty with the theme of empowerment, as many people have observed, is that it does not address the more fundamental question of responsibility. If people are to be empowered to do things they have not previously done, to whom are they responsible in the exercise of that power? Teacher empowerment, for example, implies responsibility to some broader collectivity, but which? To the "profession" of teaching? If so, how will the profession organize itself to assert its authority? To parents and students? If so, how will parents and students exercise their responsibility in a way consistent with the broader interests of the community? To the community at large? If so, how is this responsibility to be expressed institutionally without recreating school bureaucracy?

As problematical as the idea of empowerment is, it exposes an important problem underlying school restructuring. As public policymaking affecting schools has increased dramatically over the past two or three decades, schools and school systems have become more complex, organizationally and politically (Cohen, 1982). The chief source of this complexity has been the creation of new teaching and administrative roles and the growth of organized political interests. These roles and interests have become increasingly institutionalized; they have become a stable, legitimate presence in policymaking. Hence, policy choices have increasingly become choices about which of a variety of institutional interests to empower to solve a problem (Clune, 1987). Any fundamental change in school organization will reverberate through these institutionalized roles and interests, altering their positions relative to one another. Whether school restructuring is politically and organizationally feasible, then, will depend on how clever the advocates of reform are in reckoning with those affected by restructuring.

Another major theme of restructuring is accountability. Here the underlying assumption is that school bureaucracy has become so large and complex, the purposes of schooling so diffuse, and the curriculum so sprawling and unfocused that schools are no longer accountable for what they accomplish with students. It has now become commonplace for reformers to cite as evidence of a looming crisis in American education drop-out rates of 25 to 60 percent, low academic achievement for a large proportion of those who remain in school, and the failure of American schools to keep pace with their European and Japanese counterparts in the teaching of academic content. School restructuring, then, is partly about holding schools more accountable for the results they produce with students.

As long as the accountability argument is kept at a high level of abstraction, it has strong political appeal. The more specific it becomes, however, the more problematical it is. One would be hard pressed, for example, to say that American students are underevaluated or undertested. Standardized testing is an enormous economic enterprise in the United States and a very visible fixture at all levels of schooling. In addition, the practice of teaching in American schools typically includes regular assessment of student learning through examinations composed by teachers and through regular grading of student progress. In fact, American schools probably test and grade students more frequently than European schools that produce higher levels of academic achievement. American schools are also accountable in other ways. Organized community interests routinely mobilize to influence course content in local schools (Boyd, 1979). Individual parents routinely intervene with their children's schools to change teacher assignments or gain special treatment. Federal and state special education laws mandate specific plans and accountability for students with physical and emotional impairments. In many states, school financing systems require periodic votes of the citizenry to raise operating revenue for the schools. These votes usually affect whether a school district will be able to offer specific academic content or extracurricular activities. Over the past decade, almost all states have increased their use of standardized testing as a way of monitoring the performance of local schools (Richards, 1988; Selden, 1988). Considering these multiple sources of accountability, it is difficult to say that schools are not held accountable for results. It is probably more plausible to argue that schools are buffeted and pulled in conflicting directions by numerous forces demanding accountability, and that their very responsiveness to these forces makes a coherent internal structure problematical.

Many current reformers seem to assume that schools have beome less accountable as they have become more complex. It is just as plausible to argue that schools have become more complex by being more accountable to splintered and conflicting demands. Whichever of these propositions turns out to be more accurate, there is an underlying kernel of truth to both accountability arguments. If school restructuring does not address the conflicting demands of accountability, it will probably merely reproduce the structure that it seeks to ameliorate.

A final theme of school restructuring is academic content. The scholarly critiques of American schooling that have fueled the restructuring debate are surprisingly unanimous on a single point: American schools do a poor job of engaging most students in serious learning of academic content (Goodlad, 1984; Sizer, 1984; Powell, Farrar, and Cohen, 1985; Sedlak and others, 1986). According to these critiques, classroom activity for the average student is dull, perfunctory, and disconnected from what goes on in other classrooms or in the larger community. Teachers accommodate to the essentially impossible task of engaging large numbers of students with varying abilities and motivations in serious learning either by reducing their own expectations for student learning to minimal levels or by maneuvering themselves into positions where they are able to teach select homogeneous groups of students with high academic ability. Students accommodate themselves to the boredom and fragmentation of academic life by disengaging from it and seeking engagement in the social life of the school or in work outside of school. School administrators and teachers, the critique continues, have distanced themselves from any collective responsibility for defining what every student should know because conflicting external pressures and difficult internal working conditions make any sustained attention to coherent academic objectives impossible. School restructuring, then, is partly about orienting schools and the people who work in them toward serious, sustained engagement in academic learning.

An important subtheme of engagement in academic learning is the notion of "higher-order knowledge" or "teaching for understanding." Critics argue that powerful institutional forces have combined to reinforce a very limited model of teaching and learning in most schools. This model has come to be characterized as "Teaching is telling, knowledge is facts, and learning is recall" (Cohen, 1988). For most advocates of restructured schools this model is obsolete, both in terms of what schools should aspire to in a democratic society and in terms of the kind of knowledge required to participate in an advanced postindustrial economy. The existing model of teaching and learning, reform advocates argue, should be replaced by one that views teaching as engaging students in active problem solving, knowledge acquiring both facts and problem-solving strategies, and learning as deep understanding and active engagement in the acquisition of new knowledge. This model, the argument continues, will require very different knowledge and skills on the part of educators and very different conditions of work in schools.

As a theme of reform, teaching for understanding has great appeal, since it captures what many philosophers have described as the purposes of education from Socrates and Aristotle, through Rousseau and Jefferson, to Dewey. It is a difficult idea to oppose in principle. In practice, however, it is highly problematical. As its advocates freely admit, teaching for understanding requires a transformation not only of educational practice but also of knowledge about teaching and learning that underlies practice. We know only at a rudimentary level, for example, how to teach basic academic subjects in ways that promote problem-solving skills rather than factual recall. Furthermore, even at its present rudimentary level, inquiry suggests that problem-solving skills probably differ significantly depending on the subject matter area. This difference means that teaching for understanding is not a unitary phenomenon, but one that has very different manifestations in different areas of knowledge. If reform advocates are correct in their estimate that most current teaching practices do not approximate teaching for understanding, then one might ask how we will get from this state to one in which most teachers are equipped with a new model of practice. The answer in the minds of most reformers involves simultaneously changing the way teachers are educated, the conditions in which they work, and the relationship between research and the practice of teaching. The present reform agenda is not much more explicit than this, though it will probably become more so.

An additional problematical aspect of teaching for understanding is its implications for reform of the curriculum in the typical elementary or secondary school. The idea clearly implies a major consolidation and restructuring of the sprawling and fragmented curriculum that characterizes most elementary and secondary schools, where the day is divided into a welter of twenty- to fifty-minute segments devoted to separate subjects. Teaching for understanding will presumably require more sustained attention to fewer discrete subjects. This transformation will have different implications for elementary and secondary schools. But at both levels it will readily become apparent that the existing structure of the curriculum is nested in a complex web of state regulations, local rules and conventions, community norms, traditional texts and materials, and special interest politics. Restructuring the school curriculum, in other words, may lay bare underlying conflicts about the purposes of schooling in communities.

Despite these practical problems, the theme of teaching for understanding captures an important source of public malaise regarding American schools. In many critics' judgment, American educators have become increasingly inarticulate about what they are trying to accomplish in schools and increasingly indifferent to public concern about what students need to know in order to function effectively in a democracy and an advanced economy. The notion of teaching for understanding is potentially a persuasive way for educators to explain themselves to their patrons and clients.

Models of Restructured Schools

Political discourse about school restructuring, then, is organized around at least three main ideas: focusing schools on

teaching academic subject matter in ways that promote understanding and problem solving, shifting power toward schools
and the people who work in them, and ensuring the accountability of educators to their clients and to the broader public.
These purposes have led reformers to focus on three main dimensions of restructuring: (1) changes in the way teaching and learning occur, or the core technology of schooling; (2) changes in
the occupational situation of educators, including conditions of
entry and licensure of teachers and administrators, and school
structure, conditions of work, and decision-making processes
within schools; and (3) changes in the distribution of power between schools and their clients, or in the governance structure
within which schools operate. Advocates of restructured schools
seldom distinguish between these three aspects. In fact, most
school reform proposals include combinations of changes on
more than one dimension. The Carnegie report, for example,
proposes changes in teaching designed to increase the professional stature, autonomy, and material rewards of teachers, with
changes in the governance structure of schools designed to devolve decision-making authority onto schools (Carnegie Task
Force on Teaching as a Profession, 1986). The National Governors' Association proposes many changes, including increases
in teacher compensation, greater parental choice, more independence from state and local control for schools that meet performance targets, and state takeovers of failing schools (National
Governors' Association, 1986).

   While reform proposals frequently address more than one
of these dimensions, it is useful, for analytic purposes, to treat
them separately. (For other examples, see Elmore, 1978, and
Schlechty and Joslin, 1981). As we shall see, changes on one
dimension are not necessarily consistent with changes on others.
Furthermore, choosing one dimension over the others as a point
of departure for school restructuring can have very different implications for both the process of reform and the results one can
expect. If school restructuring is to work, reformers will have
to confront the tensions between these dimensions.

   To provide an analytical treatment of school restructuring, I shall define three models corresponding to the three leading
dimensions of current restructuring proposals. I shall outline

the key assumptions behind each model and discuss the implications of each model for the nature and process of restructuring. After treating each model separately, I shall discuss the problems of design and implementation associated with comprehensive restructuring proposals that attempt to combine models.

Model 1: Reforming the Core Technology of Schools. If a major purpose of restructuring is to transform teaching and learning, then restructuring can be thought of as bringing the structure of classrooms and schools into conformity with the best available knowledge about teaching and learning. At the center of this model are the following assumptions:

- Teaching and learning should be structured by scientific knowledge, which consists of theories subjected to empirical verification using agreed-upon methods of inquiry.
- Teaching and learning entail certain predictable technologies — types of adult-student interaction, definitions of subject matter, grouping practices, ways of organizing time, and so forth — which can be defined, translated into practice, and deployed in a variety of ways to achieve certain types of results for certain types of students in certain types of settings.
- At the classroom level, restructuring consists of finding the appropriate combination of technologies for a given set of conditions and implementing those technologies through changes in teaching practice.
- At the school level, restructuring consists of managing resources and organizational structures in order to increase the likelihood that the most effective technologies will be employed.

In the technical model, then, restructuring consists of deploying scientific knowledge in the service of educational objectives. It is not necessary to assume, as reformers often do, that there is a single best technical model, or a single set of generic skills that characterize "good" teaching regardless of type of student, community setting, subject matter, and the like. It is simply necessary to assume that the relevant aspects of technology, setting, student attributes, and content can be defined, so that reasonable cause-and-effect relationships between them can be established through inquiry.

The technical view holds out the prospect that relatively straightforward changes in specified factors — use of time, grouping practices, sequencing, and so forth — can result in major changes in student learning. Hence, the technical approach carries an implied or express critierion of efficiency; that is, a belief that classrooms and schools can be managed to produce much greater results for a given level of input. The technical approach also carries an implied or express view of knowledge as a formal process of production and utilization. Production involves empirical verification through accepted modes of inquiry, and utilization involves translating general patterns of effective technology into specific practices for individual teachers, students, classrooms, and schools. Expertise in education, then, consists of mastery of theory and method, as well as knowledge of the results of empirical inquiry.

The technical view can take several forms. One view expressed by Brian Rowan (Chapter Two) is that technologies of teaching and learning are socially constructed by interactions between practitioners, policymakers, and communities. A particular view of the technology of teaching and learning corresponds to a particular form of organization and control. A highly routinized view of teaching and learning, for example, leads to strong control of input, process, and output, while an inspirational view leads to strong control of inputs, but weak control of process and output. In this variation of the technical model, then, policy can be changed to reflect different conceptions of teaching and learning, but such changes carry with them very different approaches to organization and control.

A second form of the technical approach, represented by "process-product" research on effective teaching, is that certain teacher behaviors can be reliably associated with certain student outcomes. As these relationships are specified and tested empirically, they can be translated into patterns of practice and modes of organization. For example, the major findings of process-product research have stressed the importance of spending adequate time on learning activities, building on students' prior knowledge, providing adequate practice of new skills, and eliciting regular feedback as attributes of effective teaching (Brophy and Good, 1986). In this view, teacher behavior can be changed to reflect reliable patterns of successful practice, though the research does not address the question of how these changes occur and how they are, or are not, sustained in classroom and school organization.

A third variant on the technical model is what Smith and O'Day (1988) call holistic approaches to teaching and learning, which are distinguished from process-product approaches by the fact that they focus less on teacher behavior and more on modes of classroom interaction as determinants of student learning. Included in this category are such approaches as individualized instruction, which stresses tailoring teaching and content to the individual child; mastery learning, which stresses progress through clearly defined stages of content in either group or individualized settings; and varieties of student-assisted learning, including peer tutoring and cooperative learning. In this view, the mode of classroom interaction can be changed to promote improved learning by students. Again, though, the research does not address how such changes can be introduced and sustained on a broad scale.

One can also see evidence of the technical model in proposals to change instruction through the introduction of information-processing technology and new forms of instructional material. These proposals frequently stress the effects of new technologies on the engagement of students in learning and on the teacher's role in managing student learning. Thus, for example, computers are often promoted as "more efficient" ways to manage student learning because they allow students to learn at a faster rate and teachers to focus more on individual student learning.

From the perspective of the technical model, then, school restructuring is accomplished by importing the best available knowledge about teaching and learning into schools and transforming the structure of schools to correspond to that knowledge.

This model requires a steady supply of new knowledge, mechanisms for translating that knowledge into practice, and constant adjustments in the structure of schools to reflect new knowledge.

Model 2: Reforming the Occupational Conditions of Teaching. Another approach to restructuring schools takes its point of departure from the occupational conditions of teaching. At the core of this model are the following assumptions:

- Knowledge of teaching and learning is composed of at least equal parts of systematic knowledge and judgmental knowledge, where the former is based on well-established canons of inquiry and the latter is characterized by a high degree of uncertainty.
- Because of the uncertain and contingent nature of judgmental knowledge, the determinants of effective teaching lie in the skills, values, and predispositions of teachers. These attributes can be encouraged in teachers through professional education, selection processes, and occupational structures.
- A key condition of school restructuring, then, is changing routes of entry and promotion in the profession of teaching to reward higher levels of systematic knowledge and judgmental skill.
- At the classroom level, the appropriate structure is one that maximizes teachers' access to new knowledge and teachers' influence over the basic elements of instructional practice (time, materials, student engagement, and so forth).
- At the school level, the appropriate structure is one that promotes teachers' access to systematic knowledge and to the judgmental knowledge of other teachers, and one that rewards the acquisition of knowledge with higher status, higher material rewards, and greater autonomy in practice.

The dominant version of this model suggests that schools should be organized to approximate the conditions of professional workplaces. Among these conditions are a well-defined occupational hierarchy based on knowledge and competence, collegial control of hiring and evaluation, regular access to the

knowledge required to cultivate higher levels of competence
in practice, and strong lateral ties to professional associations
rather than dependence on bureaucratic hierarchy for status.
While advocates readily acknowledge that these conditions are
often not met in the established professions of medicine and law,
and that a "profession" of teaching would necessarily look very
different from these established professions, they nonetheless
argue that certain conditions of a professional workplace are
necessary ingredients for the improvement of public schools.

Gary Sykes (Chapter Three) defines the underlying problems of professional work in teaching by referring to what he
calls the ark of the professional covenant — authority, regard,
resources, and knowledge. He argues that schools will not function effectively as professional communities until they introduce
structures of professional accountability, strengthen relations between teachers through the construction of the curriculum,
enhance teachers' access to external sources of knowledge, create
opportunities for informal leadership among teachers, broaden
the range of legitimate activities in which teachers can engage,
and decrease the pressure of external mandates on teachers.

Hendrik D. Gideonse (Chapter Four) takes a complementary perspective, defining the work of teachers as the conduct
of inquiry about teaching and learning, and defining teachers
as inquirers. In his view, schools that take seriously the notion
of inquiry would be organized and would operate in very different ways from traditional schools. They would, for example,
be much more flexible in the use of time, in the structure of
the curriculum, and in grouping practices. They would rely more
on consultation between key parties — parents, teachers, and students. And they would involve greater use of immediate feedback and self-correction as sources of accountability.

Susan Moore Johnson (Chapter Five) takes a more skeptical view of attempts to change the conditions of teachers' work
by examining the failures of past attempts and deriving advice
for future reformers. Most reform proposals, she argues, fail
to take account of either teachers' own conceptions of the conditions for effective practice or the practical conditions entailed
in making a school work effectively from the teachers' perspec-

tive. Changing the conditions of teachers' work requires a high degree of school-level problem solving, and problems are likely to differ from one school to another.

The differences between the professional model of restructuring and the technical one are subtle but important. Systematic knowledge—that is, knowledge based on established methods of inquiry—plays an important role in both models. In the technical model, the accumulation of systematic knowledge is a separate activity from the practice of teaching, which is the domain of specialists, though inquiry must inform practice. In the professional model, as Gideonse reminds us, the teacher is the central figure in the application of knowledge and an important figure in its creation. The teacher's judgment and discretion are the key factors determining what gets taught in the classroom. In the technical model, systematic knowledge is outside the teachers' province. In the professional model, systematic knowledge has no effect until, in conjunction with judgment, it is applied by teachers. In the technical model, systematic knowledge serves as the basis for changes in school structure. In the professional model, changes in school structure are designed to enable teachers to employ systematic knowledge in the highly discretionary, judgmental activity of educational practice.

Another distinguishing feature of the professional model is its emphasis on knowledge and competence as the chief determinants of rewards and status in the organization. If the professional practice of education is based on a body of systematic and judgmental knowledge, then, as Sykes reminds us, the competence to make decisions about rewards and status in the organization must reside with those who have that knowledge; otherwise there will be few incentives to cultivate skill in practice. If the knowledge required for good practice can be gained by anyone, without extensive study, inquiry, and experience, then there are few incentives for skilled practitioners to continue to practice.

In the professional model, as the chapters in this volume suggest, the central problem of restructuring is how to create an organization in which teachers will assume responsibility for cultivating their own teaching practice and for evaluating the practice of their peers. Several conditions are central to this cultivation of responsibility. One is that teachers must have access to knowledge — from outside their organization and from their peers within the organization — if they are to be held responsible for what they know. Another is that teachers must have repeated legitimate opportunities to observe and evaluate one another's teaching. Most schools are organized to minimize contacts between teachers in the routine practice of teaching and to limit teachers' access to outside knowledge, except that provided through state-run certification mechanisms or through the administrative hierarchy. Yet another condition for cultivating responsibility is that teachers must have access to resources commensurate with the importance and complexity of the tasks they are asked to perform. In most instances, as Sykes suggests, the tasks of teaching are defined broadly, but the resources are narrowly circumscribed. A final condition is that teaching must have public legitimacy, or *regard* in Sykes's terms, commensurate with the social importance of the task.

From the perspective of the professional model, then, school restructuring is accomplished by changing the organization of schools to reflect the high-level expertise and judgment embodied in teachers' work. This model requires a steady supply of highly skilled practitioners, a reward system that values knowledge and competence, and an occupational structure that places heavy emphasis on collegial interaction on problems concerning practice and access to outside knowledge.

Model 3: Reforming the Relationship Between Schools and Their Clients. A third approach to restructuring schools takes its point of departure from the relationship between schools and their clients. At the core of this model are the following assumptions:

- Since the control of public education ultimately resides with the electorate, the success of public schools should be judged by how well they meet the purposes specified by their clients, where clients are both the immediate consumers of the service (students and parents) and the community at large.

- Schools, like other organizations, respond to signals from their environment. Hence, changing the rules and incentives under which schools operate will change what schools teach and how well they teach it.
- At the classroom level, the appropriate structure is the one that favors teachers' responsiveness to individual students and to the preferences of parents for what students should learn.
- At the school level, the appropriate structure is the one that rewards educators for making decisions consistent with the preferences of clients.

The client model underlies restructuring proposals that recommend greater parent and student choice and school-site management. The argument states that organizations that have a direct connection with their clientele and a high degree of influence over their resources will produce results that are more in line with what their clients want and will be perceived by their clients as more successful. Because the model attaches great significance to client preferences, it has relatively little to say about what the internal structure of schools should be. In fact, a school system that ran on the principles of the client model would have a wide variety of schools representing the prevailing range of client preferences for things like subject-matter emphasis, discipline policy, school-community relations, and teachers' roles. Hence, the "appropriate" structure at the classroom and school level is the one that provides the greatest client satisfaction.

Mary Anne Raywid (Chapter Six) argues that there is a fundamental difference between restructuring proposals derived from parental choices and those derived from site-based management. The difference is that parental-choice proposals are designed to change the incentive structure of public schools from an essentially bureaucratic model to one more closely attuned to client preferences, while site-based management models propose ways to adapt the existing bureaucratic structure of schools by decentralizing some functions.

The main difference between the client model and the previous two models lies in the role assigned to expert knowledge and professional judgment. Expertise and professional judgment play an instrumental role in the client model; that is, the educator in a school operating under the client model is in much the same position as a market manager in a consumer service firm (for example, a private health clinic or a financial services firm). The educator's expert knowledge lies in discerning what clients want, which of those wants can be accommodated within existing resource constraints, and which package of services will attract a clientele sufficient to support the organization on the scale at which it chooses to operate. Raywid argues that, even given these differences, client choice is not necessarily inconsistent with professionalism in public schools, and in fact the two may reinforce each other in cases where there is convergence between educators and their clients on specific strategies of teaching and learning. Nonetheless, the client control model takes a "demand-side" perspective on professional knowledge; knowledge is seen as existing to satisfy client preferences. The technical and professional models take a "supply-side" perspective on professional knowledge; experts are believed to understand, in some senses, what clients need better than clients themselves.

The client model also has important implications for the governance structure of education. If client preferences are the ultimate determinant of the success of schools, then most regulations that are predicated on uniform standards of practice for all schools are suspect — uniform testing, curriculum, textbook adoptions, and so on. Uniform standards create inflexibilities in schools' responsiveness to clients' preferences. Hence, if the client model were in effect, it would require a very different school regulatory structure from the one currently in place. Advocates of increased client influence are clearer, however, about the regulatory constraints they would remove than they are about what kind of regulation would be appropriate under a new regime.

From the perspective of the client model, then, schools will change their internal structure in response to changes in their external incentives. The "best" or most appropriate school structure is the one that is most responsive to client preferences. Expert knowledge and judgment consist of adapting internal operations to client preferences within resource constraints and according to general operating objectives.

The Internal Tensions of School Restructuring

This brief account of models for restructuring schools is sufficient to suggest some of the major tensions that are likely to occur in the newest generation of school reform. The success of restructuring will depend, to a large extent, on how well these tensions are managed and the degree to which the proposed solutions are responsive to the central themes of restructuring identified earlier: empowerment, accountability, and engagement in academic learning.

Empowerment. The three models expose a tension between sources of power in and around schools. The technical and professional models stress specialized knowledge — both systematic and judgmental — as a source of legitimate power in schools. The client model stresses the clients' interests and preferences as the source of legitimate power. The technical and professional models would first empower people with expertise in education; the client model would first empower parents and students, the consumers of the educational product.

Some argue that there is no necessary contradiction between expertise and clients' interests as sources of power (see Chapters Three and Six of this volume; also Gutmann, 1987, 75–78). As a practical matter, though, tensions over sources of power will probably arise in at least two ways. First, parents and educators will inevitably disagree over content and pedagogy. The stronger the educators' claim to legitimate expertise, the less likely they will be to compromise on issues where parents' interests and preferences contradict prevailing ideas of good practice. The stronger the clients' hand in matters of choice and governance in schools, the less accommodating clients will be on issues where educators assert a claim of expert knowledge. This tension is even more troublesome when clients want to have a say in an area central to the expertise of educators — for example, curriculum content — but assert their claim on moral or political, rather than educational, grounds — for example, when parents object to the way a biology curriculum treats human reproduction. If teaching and learning can be improved signif-cantly by strengthening connections between systematic knowl-edge and practice, then we are altering the balance between the claims of experts and clients. This tension suggests that as the claims of expertise increase, so too should the obligations of ex-perts to make expertise accessible to clients. Also, as clients' ex-pression of interests and preferences increases, so too should the obligation of clients to grant authority to those with expert knowledge.

A second, and potentially more serious, tension will oc-cur when certain schools seize the opportunity to restructure themselves, and in doing so, achieve significant gains for their students, while others develop more slowly or not at all. In this case, the tension is between, on the one hand, educators and clients who have formed a common bond and, on the other, educators and clients who have been excluded from the benefits of successful restructuring. Empowerment, in other words, does not guarantee equal results. School restructuring, if it works, will create serious inequities between schools. The traditional solution to such problems in public education has been to im-pose uniformity from a central bureaucratic source, even at the expense of quality and innovation at the school level. This solu-tion, of course, runs completely counter to the idea of empower-ing educators and clients to form and govern schools. Clearly, central administrators will have to develop new ways of han-dling diversity and variability in school systems (see Elmore and McLaughlin, 1988, pp. 38–52, 61).

Accountability. The technical model suggests that account-ability must rely on systematic knowledge about what schools can do and on the development of technically sound measures consistent with this knowledge. The professional model suggests that, because teaching requires the exercise of judgment, ex-ternal evaluation and accountability are difficult, and the most important mechanisms of accountability are collegial. The client model suggests that accountability is a matter of political and market control, not of expert knowledge or collegial influence.

It is possible that these models could converge in accountability mechanisms that are theoretically and technically sound, that provide for strong collegial judgment, and that satisfy external clients and decision makers. On the other hand, it is possible, as noted above, that the problem with schools is not lack of accountability but accountability to too many diverse interests. If this is the case, then a convergence of the technical, professional, and client models of accountability increases the fragmentation of schools, which defeats the objective of increased focus on the central tasks of teaching and learning. There is a danger that restructuring could result in another layer of accountability on top of the existing ones, along with still more complications for the schools.

The tensions over accountability suggest that school restructuring should consist in large part of inventing individual and school-level indicators of performance that reflect what teachers and administrators are trying to accomplish, rather than what external authorities think they should be accomplishing. If technical experts, professionals, and clients differ over accountability, then standards of accountability should be determined in the schools, where they affect student learning most directly.

Considerations of coherence and frugality should also weigh significantly in the selection of individual and school-level indicators. Attempting to reconcile technical, professional, and client interests in constructing accountability measures increases the likelihood that different schools will be drawn in divergent directions. In the absence of some mutually agreed-upon principles of coherence and economy, schools will probably recreate the incoherence of the existing system.

Academic Learning. The focus of school restructuring on the improvement of student learning may be both its major strength and its major weakness. It is a strength because student learning is presumably the central reason schools exist. It is a weakness because schools are expected to do many more things than promote student learning, including provide custodial care of children and, increasingly, serve as the location for social services for children and youth. The tensions that are likely to develop regarding academic learning, then, will have to do first with differences in the meaning of academic learning as perceived by technical experts, professionals, and clients and second with disagreements over the range of functions schools will be expected to perform and the relationship of those functions to academic learning.

Successful resolution of the tensions seems to require at least two conditions. First, as in the case of empowerment, sustaining a focus on academic learning in restructured schools depends heavily on the creation of settings and modes of discourse in which experts, professionals, and clients debate and construct the meaning of academic learning. In the absence of such a dialogue, academic learning will become a political issue by which each interest group attempts to assert control over the others: academic experts over teachers, teachers over parents, parents over teachers, and so on.

Second, sustaining a focus on academic learning will require that schools develop strategies for managing their relationships with other institutions that serve children and youth and that can protect schools from becoming the chief provider of noneducational services. Schools have typically resolved tensions between their academic and nonacademic purposes through accommodation and improvisation, rather than by drawing clear distinctions between what they provide and what can be provided through alliances with other organizations. In the absence of explicit strategies for managing these relationships, tensions over the centrality of academic learning in schools will persist.

Issues of Policy and Practice

These, then, are the systemic tensions that will probably characterize attempts to restructure public schools. Whether school restructuring has anything more than a passing influence on American education will depend on how well the tensions are worked out in policy and practice. As noted above, decisions about restructuring will be made within established state and local governance structures through the orchestration of established political interests with competing objectives. Engaging these structures and interests in the practical tasks of restructuring is a major problem of school reform. Another problem, as noted above, is how to sustain school restructuring on a large enough scale so that it affects more than an isolated collection of schools with special objectives and conditions. The solutions to these problems will be determined at the local and state levels.

Jane L. David (Chapter Seven) examines local problems of policy and practice from the perspective of school districts that have begun ambitious restructuring efforts on their own. She finds three common themes in these districts. First, the movement to restructure schools has grown out of key local constituencies' interest in making schools more stimulating environments for teachers and students. Restructuring in these districts is more than just another district initiative or special program designed to inspire public confidence. It is a long-term commitment to changing the basic conditions of teaching and learning. Second, districts undertaking restructuring dedicate resources (staff time and money) and authority to the creation and support of new ideas for instruction, new roles within schools, and new opportunities for professional growth and development among educators. Third, restructuring school districts have actively forged new political coalitions to support school reform and have negotiated new terms of accountability that relax external controls on schools in return for demonstrated high performance.

Michael Cohen (Chapter Eight) looks at restructuring mainly from the perspective of the state. He argues that restructuring, if it is to amount to anything concrete in schools, must focus on a discrete set of school-, local-, and state-level themes. At the school level, these themes include: more focused goals, greater attention to conceptions of knowledge represented in the curriculum, and greater acumen in the management of instructional tasks, student-grouping practices, and the use of time. At the district level, the main theme is redefining the relationship between district- and school-level actors to stress the importance of school-level responsibility for learning. At the state level, the themes are focusing state efforts on goal-setting, assessment of overall performance, and development of capacity at the district and school level.

Both David and Cohen emphasize the interdependence of school-, district-, and state-level actors in restructuring efforts. David uses the metaphor of a jigsaw puzzle to describe the problem of interdependence. School-level decisions about personnel and curriculum content, for example, interlock with district-level hiring practices, collective bargaining contracts, curriculum guides, and testing protocols, which in turn interlock with state policies on teacher certification and course requirements. Changing one piece of the puzzle requires alterations in all the other pieces. Cohen likewise argues that restructuring schools requires restructuring the entire system of organization, governance, and accountability that concerns schools.

The Plan of This Book

School restructuring, then, is a complex compound of specialized knowledge about teaching and learning, organizational structure, administrative organization, and political decision making. In organizing this book, we have tried to portray this complexity in a useful and comprehensible way. Using the framework in this introductory chapter, contributors discuss in turn the technical, professional, and client models of restructuring. Rowan provides the background for understanding the relationship between the technology of teaching and the structure of schools. Sykes, Gideonse, and Moore Johnson provide three complementary perspectives on the implications of professional models of restructuring. Raywid explores two different versions of the client-control model — parental choice of schools and school-based management. Finally, David and Cohen present the perspectives of local and state governments on the problems of policy and practice involved in restructuring schools.

References

"America's Schools Still Aren't Making the Grade." *Business Week,* Sept. 19, 1988, 129–136.

Boyd, W. "The Changing Politics of Policy Making for American Schools." In J. Schaffarazick and G. Sykes (eds.), *Value Conflict and Curriculum Issues.* Berkeley, Calif.: McCutchan, 1979.

Brophy, J., and Good, T. "Teacher Behavior and Student Achievement." In M. Wittrock (ed.), *Handbook of Research on Teaching.* New York: Macmillan, 1986.

Carnegie Task Force on Teaching as a Profession. *A Nation Prepared: Teachers for the 21st Century.* New York: Carnegie Forum on Education and the Economy, 1986.

Clune, W. "Institutional Choice as a Theoretical Framework for Educational Policy." *Educational Evaluation and Policy Analysis,* 1987, *9* (2), 117–132.

Cohen, D. "Policy and Organization: The Impact of State and Federal Educational Policy on School Governance." *Harvard Educational Review,* 1982, *52* (4), 474–499.

Cohen, D. "Educational Technology, Policy, and Practice." *Educational Evaluation and Policy Analysis,* 1987, *9* (2), 153–170.

Cohen, D. "Teaching Practice: Plus Ça Change . . . " Issue Paper 88-3. East Lansing, Mich.: National Center for Research on Teacher Education, Michigan State University, 1988.

Cohen, M., March, J., and Olsen, J. "A Garbage Can Model of Organizational Choice." *Administrative Science Quarterly,* 1972, *17* (1), 1–25.

Cuban, L. *How Teachers Taught: Constancy and Change in the American Classroom, 1890–1980.* New York: Longman, 1984.

Elmore, R. "Organizational Models of Social Program Implementation." *Public Policy,* 1978, *26* (2), 185–228.

Elmore, R. "Reform and the Culture of Authority in Schools." *Educational Administration Quarterly,* 1987, *23* (4), 60–78.

Elmore, R., and McLaughlin, M. *Steady Work: Policy, Practice and the Reform of American Education.* Santa Monica, Calif.: Rand Corporation, 1988.

Goodlad, J. *A Place Called School.* New York: McGraw-Hill, 1984.

Gutmann, A. *Democratic Education.* Princeton, N.J.: Princeton University Press, 1987.

The Holmes Group. *Tomorrow's Teachers: A Report from the Holmes Group.* East Lansing, Mich.: The Holmes Group, 1986.

Kingdon, J. *Agendas, Alternatives, and Public Policies.* Boston: Little, Brown, 1984.

Maeroff, G. "A Blueprint for Empowering Teachers." *Phi Delta Kappan,* 1988, *69* (7), 473–477.

National Governors' Association, Center for Policy Research and Analysis. *Time for Results: The Governors' 1991 Report on Education.* Washington, D.C.: National Governors' Association, 1986.

Powell, A., Farrar, E., and Cohen, D. *The Shopping Mall High School.* Boston: Houghton Mifflin, 1985.

Richards, C. "Indicators and Three Types of Educational Monitoring Systems." *Phi Delta Kappan,* 1988, *69* (7), 495–498.

Schlechty, P. and Joslin, A. "Images of Schools." *Teachers College Record,* 1981, *86* (1), 156–170.

Sedlak, M., and others. *Selling Students Short.* New York: Teachers College Press, 1986.

Selden, R. "Missing Data: A Progress Report from the States." *Phi Delta Kappan,* 1988, *69* (7), 492–494.

Sizer, T. *Horace's Compromise.* Boston: Houghton Mifflin, 1984.

Smith, M. S., and O'Day, J. "Teaching Policy and Research on Teaching," unpublished manuscript, Stanford University, 1988.

※ *Part One*

Approaches to Restructuring Schools

The idea of restructured schools suggests fundamental reform of the way schools are organized and the way they operate. The papers in this section explore some of the possible meanings that restructuring might have for schools. Brian Rowan (Chapter Two) discusses how different conceptions of the task of teaching can lead to different forms of organization and control. Gary Sykes (Chapter Three) analyzes the consequences of teacher professionalism for school organization. Hendrik Gideonse (Chapter Four) asks how the introduction of teacher-initiated inquiry into educational practices would change the structure and operation of schools. Susan Moore Johnson (Chapter Five) examines current restructuring proposals from the perspective of earlier attempts to reform teaching and deduces lessons from these attempts. Mary Anne Raywid (Chapter Six) analyzes two different proposals for restructuring the relationship between schools and their clients — school-based management and parental choice of schools. Taken together, these papers constitute a variety of perspectives on how school restructuring might work and what problems school practitioners will face in attempting to change the structure and operations of schools in fundamental ways.

※ TWO

Applying Conceptions of Teaching to Organizational Reform

Brian Rowan

As proposals to reform the organizational structure of schools grow in number, education analysts are beginning to speak of a new wave of educational reform — the "restructuring" movement. Unlike past reform movements in education that have had a certain measure of coherence and unity, a perplexing aspect of this latest reform movement is the lack of common ground among supporters. Rather than consisting of a set of coherent demands for change, the restructuring movement instead consists of various reform initiatives which, in the aggregate, contain conflicting accounts of what is wrong with schools and conflicting proposals about how school structures should be changed.

Consider the three major lines of reform that dominate current discussions about "restructured" schools. On the one hand, there are a set of proposals grounded in early research on effective schools, a body of work that sees today's schools as loosely coupled organizations in need of further rationalization and bureaucratization. Based on this research, the effective schools movement has tended to advocate bureaucratic reforms such as frequent evaluation of student achievement outcomes and stricter administrative supervision of teaching. More recently, an alternative to this approach has been gaining support. Advocates of teacher professionalism have begun to argue that schools are already highly bureaucratized and tightly structured and that this situation stifles the professional autonomy of teachers. Based on this analysis, this group has railed agbainst the overbureaucratization of schools, calling for the design of workplaces that give teachers greater authority and power within the educational system and high levels of professional autonomy. Still a third segment of the restructuring movement is disillusioned with both these proposals. Since at least the 1960s, this group has called for "decentralization" and "community control" of schools on the premise that schools are already highly professionalized *and* highly bureaucratized, a situation this group argues insulates schools from parental control. Most recently, this group has coalesced around the banner of "schools of choice," believing that this new design represents the most practical way of reasserting parental control of education.

This chapter develops a theoretical perspective on school organization to help policymakers and social scientists sort through these conflicting proposals. The major argument is that proposals for the reform of school organization need to be based on a careful analysis of the nature of teaching and learning in classrooms and of how these processes can best be organized and managed. To accomplish this type of analysis, a theoretical perspective based on more than twenty years of research on organizations is applied to schools. A major finding from this research is that organizational structures, particularly arrangements for coordinating and controlling work, vary according to the type of "technology" used within organizations (for reviews, see Scott, 1975; Simpson, 1985). The major theme for this chapter is to develop various models of the "technology" of teaching and to illustrate how these different models suggest different paths to school improvement.

The perspective developed here is not new. An analysis of teaching as a technology was at the core of Bidwell's (1965) seminal analysis of the school as a formal organization and more recently of perspective-informed research on teacher evaluation (Darling-Hammond, Wise, and Pease, 1983), collective bargaining in education (Mitchell and Kerchner, 1983), and decision making in schools and universities (March and Olsen, 1976). The perspective that this chapter takes is also grounded in current research on teaching and debates about the relevance of this research to the practical problems of teacher training and professional development. This literature can also be seen as a set of inquiries into the nature of teaching as a technology (Gage, 1978; McKeachie, 1974; Cronbach, 1975).

At the core of our inquiry are two critical assumptions. The first is that technologies are socially constructed (Berger and Luckmann, 1967); that is, the creation and institutionalization of new technical knowledge shapes the perceptions of workers and administrators and defines the nature of the tasks undertaken as work within an organization. Thus, the nature of teaching is not fixed and immutable. Rather, teaching can be conceived as having a variety of dimensions or properties, and the implementation of these different conceptions of teaching ultimately lead to different instructional outcomes. A second assumption is that socially constructed task knowledge has important consequences for the design of organizational structures, particularly structures that coordinate and control work. Thus, different conceptions of teaching imply different strategies of school management. A purpose of this chapter is to demonstrate that the nature of teaching as a "technology" is currently under debate and that the various positions in this debate can serve as the basis for deriving alternative designs for the organization of schools.

Technology and Structure

We begin our discussion with a general overview of research on technology and organizational structure. In this research, "technology" is defined broadly as the actions individuals perform on objects, with or without tools or mechanical devices, in order to effect changes in those objects (Perrow, 1967). Using this definition, different organization theorists have conceptualized different dimensions of technology (Scott, 1975). However, one dimension has proven remarkably robust in predicting variation in organizational structure. Studies of factory

work, office work, and work in professional settings all show
that structural arrangements for coordinating and controlling
work are closely associated with task certainty (Simpson, 1985).

Task certainty occurs when the properties of inputs are
relatively well understood and are perceived as homogeneous
and stable. Under these conditions, worker behavior becomes
routine and can be centrally planned and supervised. As a
general rule, when task certainty is high, organizations develop
a "mechanistic"control structure that features high levels of centralization, formalization, and routine bureaucratic procedure.
On the other hand, when tasks become more uncertain, control structures become more "organic." Formalization and centralization decrease, and more flexible and loosely structured
administrative patterns develop. Technical uncertainty occurs
when inputs are imperfectly understood and perceived as
unstable or heterogeneous in character. Under these conditions,
work requires flexibility, and a set of standardized routines is
inappropriate. As a result, workers gain autonomy, and informal and consultative arrangements among workers replace central planning and supervision (Perrow, 1967).

Types of Technologies

It is possible to develop a richer discussion of the effects
of technology on structure by following Thompson's (1967) thinking about organizational decision making. Thompson assumed
that organizations operate under norms of rationality and strive
for technical closure. But closure can occur only when organizations develop clear goals and a certain understanding of how
cause-and-effect relationships link technical means to those goals.
Thus, for example, in models of rational choice, actors are
assumed to have both a clear preference order regarding outcomes (goals) and a thorough understanding of the extent to
which alternative courses of action (means) yield these outcomes.
In Thompson's conceptual framework, this kind of rationality
is implied in a technology that has clear goals and certain means.

Using these ideas, Thompson (1967, chapter five)
developed a classification scheme for types of technical decision
making. Table 2.1 shows these major types.

Table 2.1. Types of Technologies.

	Goals	Means
Routine	+	+
Judgmental	+	−
Diagnostic	−	+
Inspirational	−	−

+ = Certain
− = Uncertain

The Routine Task. The first type of task is one which has both clear goals and clear means. Such jobs are found in settings where inputs are relatively homogeneous and well understood and where task environments are perceived as stable. Under these conditions, organizations can define clear technical goals and utilize narrow and repetitive procedures to process inputs. Assembly-line work is perhaps the best example of this type of task.

The Judgmental Task. A second means-end configuration introduces a measure of uncertainty into technical decisions. In this type of task, clear goals exist, but there is little codified knowledge about how to achieve these goals. Such tasks arise in environments where the tasks are stable (for example, where there is a stable demand for outputs) but inputs are relatively heterogeneous and imperfectly understood. In research on organizations, craft work is often cited as an exemplar of this type of work. For example, consider the craft of editing. The goals of an editor are reasonably clear—to produce a manuscript that will sell well, usually in an identified market. Yet the means for achieving this goal are only partially codified, and the editor must exercise considerable judgment in improving the work of a variety of authors.

The Diagnostic Task. A third type of task also introduces uncertainty into the productive process, but here the source of uncertainty is the lack of clear and stable goals. These tasks emerge in settings where a clear understanding of cause-and-effect relationships exists, but inputs have high variety and low stability. Under these conditions, a major problem for workers and managers is the diagnosis of technical problems in terms of goals, and managers and clients place considerable trust in the ability of workers to identify important and valuable goals for action. Physicians in general practice provide one example of workers who perform this type of task.

The Inspirational Task. A final type of task is the most uncertain, lacking both clear goals and well-developed knowledge of means-end relationships. Artists, research and development scientists, and other types of workers who rely on creativity for direction in their tasks are examples of workers using an inspirational technology. The task environments of these workers are so dynamic that goals for work are continuously emergent and techniques are continuously modified.

Types of Control Structures

Having discussed four types of technologies, we shift our analysis to a discussion of control structures. Organization theorists typically denote three principal forms of control—input controls, procedural controls, and output controls. Table 2.2 presents the overall control structure expected to govern the types of tasks described above.

The table assumes that all organizations are subject to input controls, either in the form of market constraints or public financing, with the result that virtually all tasks within organizations are subjected to budget controls. What differs from type to type is the extent to which workers are subject to output and

Table 2.2. Control Structures Associated with Types of Technologies.

	Input	Process	Output	Control Strategy
Routine	+	+	+	Total control
Judgmental	+	−	+	Outcome-based control
Diagnostic	+	+	−	Process control
Inspirational	+	−	−	Social control

+ = Control present/strong
− = Control absent/weak

process controls. The predictions about control structures presented in this table are based on the following general principle: Certainty in a particular dimension of technology (that is, goals or means) yields tighter control over that dimension; correspondingly, uncertainty in a particular dimension yields looser controls. Thus, when ends are certain, output can be measured, and output measures can be used to evaluate and control worker performance; when technical means are certain, task processes can be codified in great detail and supervision of worker behavior can be used as a method of evaluation and control.

Consider further the four types of control structures listed in Table 2.2. When tasks are *routine*, organizations pursue a strategy of total control. Task behavior is highly prescribed, outputs are directly measured, and inputs are allocated to subunits on the basis of measured efficiency. When tasks are *judgmental*, organizations measure outputs, but workers are allowed conditional autonomy in the selection of task processes. Under norms of rationality, inputs are allocated to subunits on the basis of measured goal attainment. When tasks are *diagnostic*, organizations implement procedural controls but there are few output controls, since selection of purposes cannot be routinized. Under norms of rationality, inputs are allocated to subunits on the basis of measured conformity to procedural rules. Finally, when tasks are *inspirational*, organizations pursue a strategy of social control. Workers are allowed to set goals and develop procedures; however, they must perform their work within fixed budgetary constraints. In this setting, workers spend much time establishing the legitimacy of their claims to organizational resources (Meyer and Rowan, 1977), and these resources are allocated on the basis of what Thompson (1967) called "social" criteria and Ouchi (1980) called "clan" controls. In this type of system, expressive rather than instrumental or procedural criteria determine resource allocations.

Reform Strategies

The purpose of this chapter is to apply these general ideas about technology and control to the case of current school reform movements. This task is complicated by the fact that American public schools are professional bureaucracies. Because of this, tasks within schools are potentially subject to two different control systems. One is the set of organizational rules developed and enforced by the state and local bureaucracies in education. The other consists of controls developed and enforced by professional associations. It is often assumed that professional and organizational control systems are in conflict, and that growth in one control system necessarily entails a weakening of the other. However, recent work by Freidson (1984) suggests that bureaucratic and professional controls can expand simultaneously, in part because professional controls respond to changes in technology in much the same ways as organizational controls (Simpson, 1985).

An additional complication arises because the educational profession is becoming increasingly differentiated, not only vertically, into a hierarchy, but also horizontally, into subspecialties (Kerr, 1983). The analysis in this chapter focuses on vertical differentiation, that is, the development of a hierarchy within the educational profession. Freidson (1984) argued that professions whose members are employed in bureaucracies often divide into three distinct sectors; a knowledge-producing sector (for example, university elites), an administrative sector (for example, state and local education administrators), and a rank and file sector (for example, teachers). Extending the work of Perrow (1967), it can be argued that stratification within a profession, as well as within an organization, is affected by socially constructed definitions of task technologies.

Table 2.3 summarizes the types of control systems likely to develop in educational organizations as a result of efforts to institutionalize various conceptions of teaching. The table also summarizes a set of predictions about power and dominance within organizations and professions. In the following paragraphs, the information in this table is discussed in terms of strategies for reform and their likely consequences for school structure.

Strategy 1: Maintain the Status Quo

We begin by describing the current status quo in education. For over two decades, organization researchers have argued

Table 2.3. Technologies of Teaching and
Organizational and Professional Controls in Schools.

	Organizational Controls	Professional Controls	Dominant Sector
Routine	I, P, O	I, P, O	Administrative Sector
Judgmental	I, O	I, O	Rank-and-File Sector
Diagnostic	I, P	I, P	Knowledge Sector
Inspirational	I	I	Public

I = Input controls
P = Process controls
O = Output controls

that the task of teaching is inspirational (Bidwell, 1965; March
and Olsen, 1976; Weick, 1976; Meyer and Rowan, 1978). Indeed, this view of teaching seems inevitable given the inherent
variability in aptitudes and interests of students within classrooms and the pluralistic and sometimes conflicting goals for
education held by the American public. A number of teacher
educators and researchers of teaching have reached similar conclusions about teaching. Gage (1978, p. 15), for example, argued
that good teachers rely on "intuition, creativity, improvisation,
and expressiveness" in performing their tasks. This view of
teaching has led some teachers to question the relevance of a
science of teaching to educational practice and to reject the rationalized evaluation of teaching in favor of more subtle and
particularistic standards of connoisseurship (Eisner, 1978).

To the extent that this view of teaching is institutionalized
in society, a ready explanation exists for the relative weakness
of bureaucratic and professional controls in the American public
school system. It is well known that bureaucratic control at all
levels of the American educational system is decentralized and
weak, and that this is especially true of controls over the core
technology of schools—instruction (Meyer and Rowan, 1978).
It is also the case that professional controls over teaching are
relatively weak in the United States. Compared with many other
professions in society, the teaching profession has relatively weak
barriers to entry and few standards of practice. This lack of professional controls might account for a number of findings about
teaching. For example, Jackson (1968) found that teachers' dis-

course about teaching was conceptually simple and largely de-
void of elaborate words and ideas, and Dornbusch and Scott
(1975) found that teachers were more likely than nurses to attribute success on the job to personality characteristics rather
than professional training. Both these findings suggest the lack
of highly codified professional standards of teaching and a reliance by teachers on personal, rather than scientific, resources
in the performance of teaching tasks.

The inspirational nature of teaching gives rise to a strategy
of social control in education. Due to technical uncertainties,
neither output nor process criteria can be used to evaluate worker
and organizational performance, and educational administrators
find it difficult to justify claims to resources on rational grounds.
Instead, administrators resort to social criteria of evaluation,
such as prestige or tradition, to mobilize resources. At the same
time, the general lack of rationality within the technical core
equalizes organizational and professional power relationships.
Since no one sector can make claims to rational expertise, there
is little stratification within the profession and within organizations there is much shared decision making and little hierarchical authority (Meyer and Rowan, 1978). At the same time, the
general lack of rationality in teaching works against the power
and prestige of educational professionals within society. By lacking a well-defined claim to rational expertise, educators sometimes find it difficult to exercise technical authority over parents;
the occupation of teaching remains a semiprofession and citizens
retain nominal authority over the enterprise of education.

The countless reform initiatives that have been targeted
at tightening the organizational and professional controls within
this sytem will be discussed below. For now, however, we consider how reform typically takes place within a system that maintains an inspirational technical core. Rowan (1984) proposed
that inspirational reform initiatives function much like revitaliza-
tion movements in which charismatic leaders mobilize the energy
and resources of supporters through appeals to powerful expressive symbols. As Meyer and Rowan (1978) noted, such
movements have the capacity to alter fundamentally the ideology
of schooling and enhance the legitimacy of education's claim on

societal resources. They also can change teachers' definitions of work and the meaning derived from it. Nevertheless, no matter how much schools change along these expressive dimensions, the inspirational nature of teaching will prevent administrators and teachers from demonstrating improvement on rational grounds.

Strategy 2: Routinize Teaching

Although there is much evidence for the inspirational nature of teaching, an important theme in educational reform is the search for a routine technology of instruction. At the turn of the century, this theme motivated the initial bureaucratization of schools (Callahan, 1962; Tyack, 1974), and in recent years the theme has served as a rallying point for movements that advocate centralized educational programming and strengthened professional controls. Thus, for example, the current wave of educational reform involves not only the development of centralized output and process controls for schools but also calls for pervasive reform of the professional system of training, licensing, and control.

These current rationalizing reforms are grounded in a tradition of "process-product" research on teaching, although alternative theoretical perspectives on the routine nature of teaching exist (see Greer, 1983). From this research a model of teaching known as "direct instruction" has crystalized (for a review, see Rosenshine, 1979). According to Rosenshine (1979, quoted in Darling-Hammond, Wise, and Pease, 1983, pp. 294–295), direct instruction

> refers to teaching activities where goals are clear to students, time allocated to instruction is sufficient and continuous, coverage of content is extensive, the performance of students is monitored, questions are at a low cognitive level . . . and feedback to students is immediate and academically oriented. . . . The goal is to move students through a sequenced set of materials or tasks. Such materials are common across classrooms and have a relatively strong congruence with the tasks on achievement tests.

The direct instruction model of teaching has been seized by administrative elites in education as a justification for strengthening organizational controls over teaching. It is evident from the above quotation, for example, that the model endorses the development and measurement of highly specific instructional objectives and that it can provide fairly detailed descriptions of teaching behaviors that consistently meet these objectives. As a result, state and local policymakers often are urged by reformers to rationalize instruction through the development of clear instructional objectives and a better definition of effective practices (Murphy, Hallinger, and Mesa, 1985).

Enough school systems have taken this path to reform for us to be able to describe in some detail the consequences for organizational control systems. In a recent survey of school districts involved in instructional improvement, Rowan, Edelstein, and Leal (1983) found a pervasive pattern of increased input, process, and output controls. In the name of "curriculum alignment," input and output controls increased, as districts standardized texts and implemented criterion-referenced testing programs. Districts also developed more stringent behavior controls. Teachers were provided with in-service training on techniques of direct instruction and principals were required to become more active in the supervision and evaluation of teaching. The net result was a centralization of administrative authority over instruction through the development of more stringent input, output, and procedural controls.

It is more difficult to predict the consequences of this movement for the structure of professional controls in education. On the one hand, it is tempting to believe that the centralization of organizational control will lead to the "deprofessionalization" and "proletarianization" of teaching (see Haug, 1975; Oppenheimer, 1973). However, this view seems unlikely, both on theoretical grounds and as a reflection of current circumstances in the educational reform movement. First, as Freidson (1984) and Simpson (1985) have shown, professionalization and bureaucratization often occur concurrently when tasks become more rationalized. Moreover, this seems to be the case in the current educational reform movement. Initial calls for administrative centralization have been accompanied by calls for the further professionalization of teaching, and currently on the books or in the making are proposals to change professional controls over entry, licensing, training, and standards of practice (see Darling-Hammond, Wise, and Pease, 1983).

Finally, consider how a commitment to the development of a routine technology of teaching could alter the delicate balance of power that now exists between professionals in education. The case of controls in large bureaucratic engineering firms is particularly instructive here (Freidson, 1984, p. 15). In these firms the bureaucratic and professional hierarchy are intertwined, and administrators, who are themselves members of the profession, are granted authority to control the work of rank-and-file engineers. A similar control structure could arise in education. First, administrative elites would gain greater authority over teachers. In addition, administrators would gain authority over parents, in part because claims to resources could now be made on rational grounds. However, in gaining this power, administrative elites would be critically dependent on knowledge elites for the development of expertise. Thus, a coalition of administrators and knowledge elites would gain professional dominance.

Strategy 3: Pursue Output Controls

Although many educationists endorse the trend toward the routinization of teaching, to many others the search for a routine technology of teaching appears futile. For example, in research on teaching, the "process-product" approach was challenged by research on "aptitude-treatment interactions" (ATI). Both ATI and process-product researchers embrace the new technology of domain-referenced testing and thus believe that clear learning goals can and should be specified, but there is a critical difference between the approaches in their assumptions about students. ATI research is based on an assumption of variability between students in aptitudes, whereas the literature on direct instruction and its school-level equivalent, research on effective schools, largely underplay the effects of aptitude on achievement in order to emphasize egalitarianism.

Although ATI research has succeeded in highlighting variability in student aptitudes, it has failed to achieve certainty about the effectiveness of different teaching strategies for students of varying aptitudes. It is thus most useful to our argument as a line of research that supports a view of teaching in which goals are clear but means are uncertain. Uncertainty about means arises because of the complex statistical models used in ATI research. The empirical confirmation of ATI theories requires an analysis of statistical interactions, a process that has been likened to "a hall of mirrors that extends to infinity" (Cronbach, 1975, p. 199). In ATI research investigators are drawn into a consideration of ever more complex interactions, even though it is difficult enough to conceptualize and talk about simple interaction effects. At its best ATI theory is likely to lead to very narrow generalizations, applying only to "circumscribed local instructional situations for relatively small segments of the educational population" (Snow, 1977, p. 12). Thus, ATI research suggests a technology of teaching in which goals can be fixed but means to these goals remain uncertain.

This model of teaching as a judgmental task suggests a reform strategy that holds workers accountable for the achievement of prescribed goals but grants conditional autonomy in the choice of means to these goals. In a situation where there is a consensus of all constituencies about instructional goals — for example, the importance of basic skills in reading and mathematics — it is possible to allocate resources to schools and teachers on the basis of student achievement. Indeed, a number of state and local agencies have already established "recognition" programs based on this principle. Generally, these programs award formal recognition and/or extra funds to schools that perform above expectations on achievement tests (for a description, see Rowan, 1987). The interesting feature of these programs is that they do not impose process controls over schools, unlike many "effective schools" interventions, which ask schools not only to improve achievement but also to use a particular organizational/instructional strategy.

Little research has been done in schools with this kind of control system, so caution must be exercised in discussing the likely consequences of this reform strategy. Nevertheless, it makes some sense to assume that teachers would gain power in this situation, especially in the domain of instruction. After all, it is teachers who must act in the absence of certain knowledge to resolve the critical uncertainty of how to attain organizational goals. And the absence of knowledge and authority over this problem implies a corresponding decrease in the relative dominance of administrative and knowledge elites, both organizationally and professionally.

It also seems reasonable to assume that rank-and-file members, upon assuming power within the profession, will become concerned with issues of distributive justice. This issue already produces conflict in the area of student competency testing, where performance is related to race and socioeconomic status, and it is a potential problem in the measurement of instructional effectiveness at the classroom and school level, where aggregate achievement scores also are highly correlated with pupil status. Moreover, in the absence of technical certainty, it makes sense to assume that the teaching profession will take a keen interest in the level at which performance standards are set. Research in industrial settings has shown that workers paid on the basis of outputs often manipulate control systems by imposing social controls on workers that define a fair day's work and that discourage initiative. The teaching profession, as a formal and collective entity, might react similarly and attempt to restrict performance standards to a fair level. In this setting, knowledge elites will play a minor role, having failed to provide education with meaningful process standards and remaining largely irrelevant to the major issue of the day, the equitable distribution of resources among members of the profession.

Strategy 4: Continue the Search for Expert Teaching

A final strategy of reform represents a vision of tomorrow's schools rather than a viable strategy for immediate reform. It is based upon a view of teaching that assumes teachers have available both technical expertise — that is, knowledge of how to teach — and moral expertise — that is, the authority to evaluate and act upon alternative task goals. In this vision of

teaching, the issue of effective teaching processes is not problematic since the means of teaching are well known. Instead,
what is at issue are the very goals of instruction, which are seen
as diverse and continuously varying. Brophy and Evertson
(1976, quoted in Darling-Hammond, Wise, and Pease, 1983,
p. 298) aptly summarize this view.

> Effective teaching requires the ability to implement a very
> large number of diagnostic, instructional, managerial, and
> therapeutic skills, tailoring behavior in specific contexts and
> situations to the specific needs of the moment. Effective
> teachers must not only be able to do a large number of
> things; they must also be able to recognize which of the
> many things they know how to do applies at a given mo-
> ment and be able to follow through by performing the
> behavior effectively.

The vision of teaching that emerges here is sensitive to
the variety of goals in teaching. A teacher is seen as acting not
simply to further instructional ends but also to maintain classroom order and provide social and emotional support to students. Moreover, these multiple goals change frequently,
depending on both students and situations. Nevertheless,
teachers are seen as having a broad set of known techniques
and skills to draw upon in their work. Hence this view seems
to accord well with our description of the diagnostic task.

Clearly, this vision of teaching requires further development of the science of teaching, and as the review of ATI research shows, this will be a complex problem. The technically
expert teacher will need a very large number of technical routines, and these will need to be adapted to specific local circumstances if they are to have empirical validity. Under these
conditions, it makes sense to assume that knowledge elites will
gain power, both organizationally and professionally. From
organization theory, it is known that the technical complexity
of diagnostic tasks leads to increased specialization. From the
perspective developed here, this specialization will occur both
organizationally, with the growth of a technical support staff

in schools, and professionally, with the differentiation of the profession into specialties in the knowledge elite (Smart and McLaughlin, 1982; Kerr, 1983).

As knowledge of cause-and-effect relationships increases, control structures should begin to emphasize process controls. In this scenario, professional standards and practices boards will develop (for a discussion of such trends in education, see Darling-Hammond, Wise, and Pease, 1983), and educational resources will be mobilized based on the teaching processes used within schools. This precedent is already established in education. Schools now are reimbursed above and beyond normal costs for providing "special" forms of instruction to students (for example, special education or compensatory education). With growth of specialization, the types of well-defined educational treatments might further increase. At the school level, administrators will come to depend on staff personnel to direct and assess the work of rank-and-file teachers engaged in specialized tasks (Perrow, 1967; Freidson, 1984). Finally, it seems reasonable to assume that teachers will respond to increased procedural controls by attempting to soften their blow, and teacher organizations can be expected to lobby for rules about due process for evaluation of teachers.

Within this arrangement, teachers will retain considerable autonomy in the task of teaching. After all, it is teachers' diagnostic skills that resolve a critical uncertainty for the schools: the setting of educational goals. Sykes (1987, p. 19), following Barber (1983), argues that the legitimacy of this type of professional autonomy is based partly on an expectation of "fiduciary responsibility, the expectation that service providers demonstrate a special concern for others' interests above their own." This grant of moral and diagnostic authority to workers is an important characteristic of the most prestigious professions in society (lawyers, ministers, physicians, architects), and a grant of such authority in schools would probably contribute to an enhancement of the status of teaching as a profession. Moral autonomy would also give teachers a unique role within the politics of education. Lacking control over technical expertise, rank-and-file members could nevertheless serve as the moral conscience of the profession and develop the power to direct educational resources toward either progressive or conservative ends.

Analysis of Reform Strategies

The problem is to judge the relative merits of these alternative reform strategies. A convenient way to approach this problem is to discuss the expected effects of the strategies on the clients of schools and on the workers in schools.

Effects on Clients

A prime consideration for judging the merits of a reform effort should be the empirical and normative validity of its view of teaching as a "technology." At present, much empirical research suggests that schools operate an inspirational technology. Yet much educational reform has been driven by a vision of teaching as a routine task. A major concern about this movement is that it may prove to be hyperrational (Wise, 1979). Certainly the narrow focus on basic skills and the highly standardized instructional treatments advocated by the movement seem fundamentally at odds with the conventional perception in education of students as a diverse and spontaneous lot. This perception appears to call for a more organic approach to managing teaching in which teachers have considerable autonomy in the setting of goals and the use of means.

A more realistic strategy of reform treats teaching as a judgmental task. In fact, a transformation from today's control system to one based on a view of teaching as a judgmental task could be accomplished easily in today's policy environment. For example, among the many goals of schooling, there is a consensus that students should master certain basic skills. Moreover, a measurement technology for evaluating educational basic-skills outcomes exists and is largely in place. Thus, one appealing aspect of the judgmental approach is that it does not require much investment, especially costly investments in the slow growth of professional knowledge about cause-and-effect relationships in education. Instead, existing structures of outcome measures can be activated to gain more control over teaching. The problem, however, is that this measurement system currently stresses a narrow set of short-term goals that do not correspond to all of the public's desires for students, and a focus on narrow goals might draw the attention of educators away from other valued goals, for example, vocational training, higher order thinking, or affective development. A recommended tactic for this movement, then, would be to broaden the types of tests used as outcome criteria to assure that a variety of goals are assessed.

Yet another reform strategy is to embrace the diagnostic approach to teaching. This approach is consistent with assumptions about student diversity and with the notion that the American public has diverse goals for schooling. However, this reform strategy requires substantial investments in research and teacher training if it is to produce teachers with sufficient knowledge of how to meet a variety of educational ends. Increasingly sophisticated research on teaching is beginning to develop this kind of knowledge, especially in the areas of subject and skill-specific teaching and classroom management. However, the approach is not without problems. In the short run, even the advocates of this approach admit that more knowledge is needed to implement reforms. Moreover, in the long run, the successful implementation of this strategy, by enhancing the power and status of both knowledge elites and teachers, might result in greater social distance between educators and the lay public and increasing control of the educational system by professionals.

From the point of view of the clients of public education, the question is not whether it is possible to reform schools, but rather whether or not an inspirational view of teaching should be abandoned. There are a number of sound reasons for maintaining the current system, with its weak organizational and professional controls. By doing so, the public can guard against the development of potentially costly barriers to entry into the profession and maintain more direct public authority over the operations of schools. At the same time, one potential improvement to this system warrants attention. This is the introduction of market controls and the development of schools of choice.

In such a market, where the product was produced inspiration-
ally, education could not be rationally valued, but evaluation
could be based on normative or cultural grounds. The trend
toward magnet schools and the more limited trend toward open
enrollment and voucher schemes represent plausible approaches
to reforming an inspirational system. Taken to the extreme,
however, support for such a market might result in radical decentralization of the school system, perhaps even privatization, and
it would probably turn schools into specialty shops that served
narrow communities of interest. Indeed, such a trend is already
in evidence in many areas of the country, where the growth of
Christian schools has been extraordinary.

Effects on Workers

It is also possible to judge the various reform strategies
on the basis of their effects on workers within education. For
now, discussion is restricted to teachers, the largest segment of
the education profession. Observers of the current wave of educational reform, especially those with an interest in the professionalization of teaching, have begun to question whether the
present structure of schools can foster the retention of good
teachers and their personal development throughout a career
(for example, Gideonse, 1982).

Fortunately, a number of organization theorists have considered the effects of task structure on worker satisfaction and
development (for a review, see Beer, 1976). Their research is
often based on an assumption that individuals strive for self-
actualization, a state of broad and self-directed personal growth
that fosters high need satisfaction, and that job satisfaction increases as this need is satisfied. In research on many types of
occupations, for example, the following task characteristics have
been found to increase employee satisfaction: performing a variety of skills, performing a complete task, performing an important task, having discretion or latitude in decision making to
perform tasks, and receiving feedback on task performance
(Hackman and Lawler, 1971). Walton (1978) labeled tasks with
these characteristics "high commitment" work systems. In these

systems, effective performance requires workers who have high needs for personal growth and improvement of skills. Workers who perform effectively in this system also develop a high commitment to the organization, and employee absenteeism and turnover are low.

The control structures associated with various reform strategies could affect the job satisfaction and personal development of teachers differentially. Currently, the vast majority of practicing teachers have high job satisfaction (Meyer and Rowan, 1978). However, many of those recruited to education leave, and there is a legitimate concern among policy analysts that the most academically talented recruits too frequently leave the profession (Vance and Schlechty, 1982). This seems consistent with a view of teaching as an inspirational task. There is much autonomy and variety in this type of teaching, which should account for the high levels of job satisfaction among practicing teachers. However, the low level of rational knowledge about teaching means that the reward structure of schools is not based on rational mastery of facts and procedures, a factor that could discourage teaching recruits who strive to develop intellectually. Instead, rewards in an inspirational system are expressive in character, and job satisfaction is related to intrinsic and personal motivations (Lortie, 1975).

It is questionable whether the routinization of teaching would be an improvement over the current situation. In this reform, restructured schools would develop along mechanistic lines, which would reduce teacher satisfaction and might discourage the academically committed from staying in teaching. Increased input, output, and behavior controls would substantially reduce teacher autonomy and centralization of planning would place responsibility for the pursuit of rational knowledge about teaching in the hands of administrative elites and knowledge workers. This need not result in the deprofessionalization of teaching, as some alarmists have warned. Indeed, increased controls over teaching could create barriers to entry into the teaching force and thus improve the professional standing of teaching. Still, the most satisfying and rewarding jobs in education would be in administrative and knowledge-producing sectors of the profession rather than in rank-and-file positions.

The encouragement of a judgmental approach to teaching offers teachers more autonomy on the job than the routine approach, but less than that afforded by an inspirational approach. Teachers would have procedural autonomy but be held accountable for specific outcomes. The measure of autonomy afforded by this control arrangement should foster medium levels of job satisfaction. The major threat to worker satisfaction in this kind of outcome-based control system lies in underinvestment in organizational knowledge. If the level of task knowledge provided organizationally is insufficient to meet goals on a regular basis, teachers would not expect much success, and this kind of system could respond in only two ways: either lower the output standards in order to shore up expectations of success or withdraw rewards from the majority who are performing below standard. The latter approach almost certainly would produce even more job dissatisfaction, especially if the vast majority went unrewarded. Unfortunately, a lowering of output standards also might lower satisfaction. Recall that industrial workers have often engaged in informal and social controls, such as quota-restriction and goldbricking, in response to output controls. Were this to happen in education, we might expect those who thrive in high commitment work settings to flee schools for more challenging work.

The final approach to reform, which sees teachers as diagnosticians, can only succeed after substantial investments in knowledge production. As we have seen, this system would spawn organizations with larger support staffs composed of knowledge specialists, and this group could gain rights to format teachers' work. However, the dynamic view of students and goals contained within this approach would mitigate against routinization and spawn organic forms of management. Teachers would have autonomy to set task goals and would seek assistance and support from specialists. Obviously, this kind of system could produce very high levels of job satisfaction. Not only would it offer opportunities for rational mastery of procedures, and thus perhaps attract the academically talented, but also it would give teachers opportunities for expressive growth and intrinsic rewards by allowing them choice of educational goals. The only threat to this sytem is recruitment. If education cannot attract a workforce that thrives in this kind of high commitment work setting, a vision of teaching as a diagnostic task has little chance of practical success.

Conclusion

This chapter has considered alternative strategies for "restructuring" schools. An argument based on organization theory was developed to make predictions about how the structure of controls over teaching might vary according to socially constructed definitions of teaching as a "technology." A brief survey of research on teaching located four distinct theories of teaching that correspond to the theoretical logic of the chapter and, more importantly, that are presently endorsed by one or more constituencies in education. Using the theoretical perspective, a set of four "restructuring" proposals were then derived.

A control stategy based on a vision of teaching as a routine technology seemed consistent with much of the rhetoric of the effective schools movement, which endorses the direct instruction model of teaching and advocates a mechanistic form of school management that includes frequent monitoring of instructional outcomes and close supervision of teaching. While this model has many supporters, a number of educators and policymakers have come to realize that this routine and mechanistic system of management may be inappropriate given the diversity of students and educational goals that characterizes American education. Moreover, there are sound theoretical reasons to believe that this mechanistic control strategy would lead to decreases in the job satisfaction of teachers. Thus, when compared to other reform strategies, this restructuring proposal seems to have the least chance of producing favorable outcomes for students or teachers.

A view of teaching as a judgmental task can be found in research that rejects the search for a single best way of teaching but which endorses the development of clearly specified learning objectives (for example, research on aptitude-treatment interactions). When taken to its logical limit, ATI research appears to imply that teachers need autonomy on the job because they need to adjust procedures to variability in student inputs. Given the variability of students in American schools and classrooms, this represents a major advantage over a control system grounded in a conception of teaching as a routine technology. Moreover, if the right performance evaluation standards can be developed, this kind of outcome-based control system can provide high levels of job satisfaction for teachers. The major concern that policy analysts should have about such a control system is its potential to narrow the range of educational goals. Were this to happen, this system, like the one discussed above, could end up being unresponsive to the diversity of legitimate goals in American education and thus not serve the public well. From a practical standpoint, however, the outcome-based control system has a major advantage. Given the sophistication and availability of measurement technologies in most states and local districts, this type of control system could be implemented with little additional investment in schooling. Moreover, since the control system is based on a logic that does not require additional knowledge about teaching, it could be (and has been) implemented quickly in response to calls for educational accountability.

The inspirational view of teaching was argued to be the status quo in education. On the basis of the theoretical perspective developed in this chapter and on existing research on schools, we would expect this type of control system to provide teachers with high levels of autonomy and to allow schools to accommodate the diversity of students and goals in American education. It also provides for little social distance between educators and parents and for relatively direct citizen control. In fact, this system of controls has proven amazingly viable and has led to high levels of teacher and parent satisfaction. However, a major political vulnerability of the system is its lack of an explicitly rational view of teaching. This makes the system continually vulnerable to rationalizing reform movements. It may also be a reason the system is failing to attract an academically talented workforce. In an inspirational system, the talented teacher succeeds because of personal, not intellectual, resources and seeks expressive rather than rational satisfaction from the job.

A final strategy is consistent with emerging views of teaching as a complex "professional" task. This view of teaching as a diagnostic task, and the control structure consistent with it, appears to be one of the more appealing alternatives to an inspirational view of teaching. Like the inspirational model, this model of teaching can accommodate student diversity and multiple educational goals. Moreover, calls for the professionalization of teaching could encourage the recruitment and retention of an intellectually oriented and morally committed workforce. The problems with the strategy are that it would require substantial investment in the production of scientific knowledge of teaching and could create social distance between educational professionals and the public. Moreover, since knowledge of cause-and-effect relationships in teaching is presently uncertain, support for this approach to reform requires substantial faith in a scientific approach to education.

Thus, among the various reform strategies discussed in this chapter, one appears unrealistic (the routine approach), one is potentially narrow in scope but relatively inexpensive to implement in the short run (the judgmental approach), and two have enough strong points to be considered viable options for policymakers (the inspirational and diagnostic approaches). The last two alternatives suggest very different organizational and professional designs for education, and a policymaker's support of one approach over another will be based on dissatisfaction with the current status quo in education and/or willingness to invest in the science of education.

A larger message of this chapter is that educational reform proposals can be theoretically derived from assumptions about the nature of teaching and learning in classrooms. In fact, the main contribution of this discussion has been the application of a well-known and empirically robust theory of organizational technologies to the conceptualization of teaching. We have demonstrated that different theories of teaching as a "technology" exist in education and that considerations of how teaching and learning occur are basic to proposals for the reform of school organization.

References

Barber, B. *The Logical Limits of Trust.* New Brunswick, N.J.: Rutgers University Press, 1983.

Beer, M. "The Technology of Organization Development." In M. Dunnette (ed.), *Handbook of Industrial and Organizational Psychology.* Chicago: Rand McNally, 1976.

Berger, P. L., and Luckmann, T. *The Social Construction of Reality.* New York: Doubleday, 1967.

Bidwell, C. "The School as a Formal Organization." In J. G. March (ed.), *Handbook of Organizations.* Skokie, Ill.: Rand McNally, 1965.

Brophy, J. E., and Evertson, C. *Learning from Teaching: A Developmental Perspective.* Newton, Mass.: Allyn and Bacon, 1976.

Callahan, R. E. *Education and the Cult of Efficiency.* Chicago: University of Chicago Press, 1962.

Cronbach, L. J. "Beyond Two Disciplines of Scientific Psychology." *American Psychologist,* 1975, *30* 116–217.

Darling-Hammond, L., Wise, A. E., and Pease, S. R. "Teacher Evaluation in the Organizational Context." *Review of Educational Research,* 1983, *53,* 285–328.

Dornbusch, S. M., and Scott, W. R. *Evaluation and the Exercise of Authority.* San Francisco: Jossey-Bass, 1975.

Eisner, E. "On the Use of Educational Connoisseurship and Criticism for Evaluating Classroom Life." *Teachers College Record,* 1978, *78,* 345–358.

Freidson, E. "The Changing Nature of Professional Work." *Annual Review of Sociology,* 1984, *10,* 1–20.

Gage, N. L. *The Scientific Basis of the Art of Teaching.* New York: Teachers College Press, 1978.

Gideonse, H. D. "The Necessary Revolution in Teacher Education." *Phi Delta Kappan,* 1982, *64,* 15–18.

Greer, R. D. "Contingencies of the Science and Technology of Teaching and Prebehavioristic Research Practices in Education." *Educational Researcher,* 1983, *12,* 3–9.

Hackman, J. R., and Lawler, E. E. "Employee Reactions to Job Characteristics." *Journal of Applied Psychology,* 1971, *55,* 259–286.

Haug, M. R. "The Deprofessionalization of Everyone?" *Sociological Focus,* 1975, *3,* 197–213.

Jackson, P. W. *Life in Classrooms.* New York: Holt, Rinehart, & Winston, 1968.

Kerr, S. T. "Teacher Specialization and the Growth of a Bureaucratic Profession." *Teachers College Record,* 1983, *84,* 630–651.

Lortie, D. C. *Schoolteacher.* Chicago: University of Chicago Press, 1975.

McKeachie, W. J. "The Decline and Fall of the Laws of Learning." *Educational Researcher,* 1974, *3,* 7–11.

March, J. G., and Olsen, J. P. *Ambiguity and Choice in Organizations.* Bergen, Norway: Universitetforlaget, 1976.

Meyer, J. W., and Rowan, B. "Institutionalized Organizations: Formal Structure as Myth and Ceremony." *American Journal of Sociology,* 1977, *83,* 340–363.

Meyer, J. W., and Rowan, B. "The Structure of Educational Organizations." In M. W. Meyer and Associates, *Environments and Organizations.* San Francisco: Jossey-Bass, 1978.

Mitchell, D. E., and Kerchner, C. T. "Labor Relations and Teacher Policy." In L. Schulman and G. Sykes (eds.), *Handbook of Teaching and Public Policy.* New York: Longman, 1983.

Murphy, J., Hallinger, P., and Mesa, R. P. "School Effectiveness: Checking Progress and Assumptions and Developing a Role for the State and Federal Government." *Teachers College Record,* 1985, *86,* 615–641.

Oppenheimer, M. "The Proletarianization of the Professional." In P. S. Halmos (ed.), *Professionalism and Social Change.* Keele, U.K.: Keele University Press, 1973.

Ouchi, W. G. "Markets, Bureaucracies, and Clans." *Administrative Science Quarterly,* 1980, *25,* 129–141.

Perrow, C. "A Framework for the Comparative Analysis of Organizations. *American Sociological Review,* 1967, *32,* 194–208.

Rosenshine, B. "Content, Time, and Direct Instruction." In P. L. Peterson and H. J. Walberg (eds.), *Research on Teaching.* Berkeley, Calif.: McCutchan, 1979.

Rowan, B. "Shamanistic Rituals in Effective Schools." *Issues in Education,* 1984, *2,* 76–87.

Rowan, B. *A Comparative Analysis of School Recognition Systems.*

Unpublished manuscript, College of Education, Michigan State University, 1987.

Rowan, B., Edelstein, R., and Leal, A. *Pathways to Excellence: What School Districts Are Doing to Improve Instruction.* San Francisco: Far West Laboratory for Educational Research and Development, 1983.

Scott, W. R. "Organizational Structure." *Annual Review of Sociology,* 1975, *1,* 1–20.

Simpson, R. L. "Social Control of Occupations and Work." *Annual Review of Sociology,* 1985, *11,* 415–436.

Smart, J. C., and McLaughlin, G. W. "Education Specialty Areas." *Educational Researcher,* 1982, *11,* 6–9.

Snow, R. E. "Individual Differences and Instructional Theory." *Educational Researcher,* 1977, *6,* 12.

Sykes, G. "Reckoning with the Spectre." *Educational Researcher,* 1987, *16,* 19–21.

Thompson, J. D. *Organizations in Action.* New York: McGraw-Hill, 1967.

Tyack, D. *The One Best System.* Cambridge, Mass.: Harvard University Press, 1974.

Vance, V. S., and Schlechty, P. C. "The Distribution of Academic Talent in the Teaching Force." *Phi Delta Kappan,* 1982, *64,* 22–27.

Walton, R. E. "Establishing and Maintaining High Commitment Work Systems." In J. R. Kimberly, R. H. Miles, and Associates, *The Organizational Life Cycle: Issues in the Creation, Transformation, and Decline of Organizations.* San Francisco: Jossey-Bass, 1978.

Weick, K. E. "Educational Organizations as Loosely Coupled Systems." *Administrative Science Quarterly,* 1976, *21,* 1–19.

Wise, A. E. *Legislated Learning.* Berkeley, Calif.: University of California Press, 1979.

THREE

Fostering Teacher Professionalism in Schools

Gary Sykes

This chapter takes up the question of professionalism in teaching, a theme prominent in the educational reform movement of the eighties. The rhetoric of professionalism has long been employed in the teaching field but has taken on new urgency and new meaning in recent years. Concerns about the recruitment, retention, and renewal of able, committed teachers, their initial and ongoing education, and the conditions of their work in schools have served as a focal point for a range of policy initiatives.

A series of danger signals have alerted policymakers to trouble concerning the status and health of the teaching occupation. Indications have been the following: teaching is neither recruiting nor retaining the academically talented, the education of teachers is inadequate, that salaries have declined substantially, the career structure rewards advancement out of or disengagement from teaching, and schools are not organized, managed, or provisioned to support good teaching. Certain of the remedies selected in response have been familiar: increased salaries, scholarship and loan forgiveness programs, and more stringent requirements for teacher education and state licensure. Others have introduced novelty: merit pay, career ladders, peer evaluation schemes, and induction programs for beginners.

The familiar remedies supply additional resources to a resource-starved occupation but do not attempt reform. The more novel remedies seek more fundamental change within schools, including the introduction of new roles and responsibilities for teachers, shifts in educational authority relationships and in the labor-management compact, alteration of teaching's incentive structure, and promotion of more complex conceptions of teaching. The unifying theme for all these initiatives has been "teacher professionalism." In answer to the questions, "Why professionalize teaching and to what end?" a number of responses emerged.

First is a concern with the intellectual quality of the people entering and remaining in teaching. If teaching is to compete successfully in the college labor market, then status inducements regarding financial and social status and working conditions are necessary. Likewise, if the occupation is to retain accomplished teachers, career rewards must be high. A second goal has been to create organizations that promote teaching excellence, encourage steady improvement, and inspire commitment and high morale. Pursuit of this goal involves creating new work norms, patterns of interaction, and structural supports for teachers.

The proposal to professionalize teaching also promotes a conception of teaching that emphasizes the cultivation and exercise of judgment as the essential aspect of what teachers do. According to this view, teaching is nonroutine work that requires considerable expertise in accommodating diverse learners and in pursuing a complex, ambitious agenda of learning. A knowledge base in education exists to guide and inform teachers' judgment, and this knowledge must be progressively represented and conveyed in norms and standards of educational practice. If schools are to respond to the educationally disenfranchised, the children at risk, and to pursue in earnest the call to educate children in conceptual understanding and complex reasoning, they will require teachers with superior knowledge, skill, judgment, and commitment.

The introduction of this theme into educational policy and practice has been problematic. The concern for recruitment has resulted in often dramatic salary increases, and a shortage of teachers no longer appears imminent. Likewise, standards for entry and training have been strengthened in many locales. But the more ambitious reforms that focus on teaching in schools — changing authority relationships, reforming the structure of career and work incentives, the emergence of new roles for teachers, and the promotion of new norms and standards of educational practice — have proceeded slowly and fitfully, with both successes and setbacks.

One version of the proposal to professionalize teaching implicates broad concerns: the occupational ethos of teaching, the organization of educational practices, and the expectations of the public. To understand the possible results of such a transformation of schooling requires an inquiry into the conditions of schoolteaching in light of the theory of professionalism. The central sections of this chapter pursue this inquiry, which leads in the final section of the chapter to a set of principles for school-based teacher professionalism.

Delegating control over important private and public matters to professionals is one way of organizing and regulating services. This method entails the "surrender of private judgment" to experts. Experts possess specialized knowledge and skill, acquired through years of study and practice and certified through formal credentials, that entitle them to assume grave responsibilities over others. In our society, professionals exert influence over many aspects of life, and since the turn of the century the spread of the professions has been a notable development. Practices once carried out informally by community members are now the exclusive legal province of professionals, and there has been a corresponding shift in public perception. Our society is widely regarded as having grown complex through an explosion of knowledge and technology. Specialization is necessary for everything from plumbing to surgery to personnel management. Problems that at one time we might have tried to solve ourselves with a little help from friends, we now turn over to experts. Vast systems have arisen to rationalize and finance the exchanges between professionals and their clients.

If professionals have become commonplace in our society, constituting by some accounts a "new class," we regard them with increasing ambivalence, even distrust (see Merton, 1976, and Metzger, 1987). In fact, as a distinct policy choice, professionalization is one among several options for providing services. David Kirp argues that policy questions may be settled by recourse to political bargaining, legal norms, or bureaucratic standards, rather than to professional judgment (Kirp, 1982, 137–138).

These alternative frameworks represent value judgments regarding collective problem solving that appeal variously to technical expertise, democratic procedure, fairness and uniform treatment, consumer choice, and so on. As any student of American history will recognize, each of these alternatives has been heralded at one time or another as the salvation of the schools. "Take politics out of the schools" is followed by "Let the community decide" or "Let parents choose."

Each framework influences what will be provided, by whom, and on what terms. Each has its own built-in constituency — teachers, lawyers, bureaucrats, or school boards — with a special stake in policy outcomes. Each has legitimacy. Kirp favors a dynamic tension between them, concluding that no single approach to the provision of education is desirable. Legalism can ensnarl schools in procedures, professionals can deprive parents of voice in decisions regarding their children, and bureaucratic rules can undermine the exercise of wise professional discretion. Over time and on average, the pulling and tugging between these approaches is best calculated to yield that elusive ideal, the public welfare.

In our mixed system of governance, which features public and private sources of influence and professional and bureaucratic forms of control, the tensions between these approaches are likely to persist, and the task of those who administer policy and engage in practice is to construct a balance between them. The professionalizing of teaching makes a claim for more authority (A), regard (R), resources (R), and knowledge (K), or "ARRK." This acronym forms the ark of the professional covenant, a biblical trope meant to convey the importance of trust and the nature of the compact between a profession and the public. Can teaching become a public trust? To answer this question and thereby explore the prospects for the professionalization of teaching, this chapter considers each of these elements, then takes up the implications for educational practice in the schools.

The Authority of the Teacher

A common observation about our schools is that adults in general, and teachers in particular, have lost authority in recent times. There is always reason to be suspicious about such claims and the attendant implication that in prior eras things were different. When adults speaking to youth begin a sentence with "Why in my time . . . " or "When I was growing up . . . ," we all know that a cliché will follow. Then too, anyone familiar with the two Willards — Elsbree and Waller — or with such classics as the *Hoosier Schoolmaster* is likely to scoff at a backward glance that beholds the teacher as a paragon of authority. But "loss of authority" arguments, while impeachable, are useful to review for the conditions and perceptions they reveal.

One version concentrates on teachers' relations with students, arguing that teachers have increasing difficulty gaining their respect and maintaining discipline in the classroom. Parents, particularly the increasing numbers who are well educated, are more inclined to criticize teachers, to undercut teachers' authority with their children, and to fail to exercise their own authority (see Coleman, 1987, for this argument). The social support necessary to teacher authority has eroded, forcing teachers to rely more on personal charisma than on socially conferred authority (Grant, 1981, 1983). As support for authority weakens and teachers receive less deference and esteem, several responses emerge. One is withdrawal. Teachers either leave the profession or psychologically disengage from the work, "retiring on the job," as the saying goes. Another response is burnout. The effort to establish authority with dozens of students year after year through personal appeal alone drains even the best teachers of energy and enthusiasm. By its very nature teaching is emotionally demanding work, but testimony by veteran teachers in recent years suggests that the work has become increasingly difficult (McLaughlin, Pfeifer, Swanson-Owens, and Yee, 1986).

Yet a third response is to make deals with students, to negotiate treaties, and to exchange modest academic demands for compliant student behavior. William Muir (1986) has argued that in the absence of authority, teachers must resort either to coercion or exchange to engage students with academic work. As any number of recent studies suggest, recourse to exchange has deeply influenced the curriculum and instruction in many schools (see, for example, McNeil, 1986; Powell, Farrar, and Cohen, 1985; and Sedlak, Wheeler, Pullin, and Cusick, 1986). The very emergence of the theme of exchange in multiple, independent analyses is a tip-off that exchange has become a dominant mode of control, especially in secondary schools.

A second version traces the migration of authority from the classroom teacher to a variety of agents outside the classroom, including state and federal governments, school boards and administrators, textbook publishers, social scientists in the university, and others. Contributing to this loss of authority has been the centralization, legalization, and bureaucratization of schooling (Wise, 1979; Kirp and Jensen, 1986). To an extent unimagined even twenty years ago, school days today *are* rule days, with the intensification of student and teacher testing, curriculum specifications, program and funding regulations, contract provisions, and the rest, often cascading simultaneously into the classroom from several levels of the system. If teachers are street-level bureaucrats, then the aim of much recent policy has been to reduce and direct their discretion, not to enhance or cultivate it. The process has diminished their authority.

To this point I have spoken of authority in a commonsense way. It may be useful to introduce some analytic rigor into the discussion, for the concept of authority, along with the related concept of power, is one of the indispensable building blocks of social science, with roots deep in Western philosophy. Authority has received many definitions, a sampling of which provides clues to common elements:

"The right to control, command, or determine" [Random House Dictionary, 1971, p. 100].

"The rightful exercise of power to create the means of the coordination of action" [Simon, 1948, p. 12].

"The possession of a status, quality, or claim that compels trust or obedience" [Lukes, 1978, p. 642].

"A legitimate basis for inequality" [Elmore, 1987, p. 69].

These definitions point to the importance of a moral or political order that provides the ground for claims of authority. There is a shared belief that an authority has the right to issue commands that must be obeyed because of that right. Authority is the legitimate exercise of power, but there must be a community of belief about its proper exercise. The use of force signifies the failure of authority, as does resort to persuasion, which "presupposes equality and works through a process of argumentation" (Arendt, 1961, p. 93). Authority, then, rests not only on legitimation but on dependence — on the claim that subordinates should obey, and on the possibility of dire consequences if they do not. Hence authority involves an inequality between those who issue and those who obey commands that is supported by reason and by the threat of coercion.

Pursuing this line of analysis a bit further, authority possesses a reserve of reason, underpinning legitimacy as a form of control, and a reserve of powers, underpinning dependence as a form of control. The acceptance of authority makes recourse either to reasons or to power unnecessary. Challenges to authority, then, may be met either with reasons or with power.

Why should teachers have more authority over educational matters than they have at present? On what basis can they claim authority? The ideology of professionalism supplies one answer. The legitimation of professional authority involves three distinct claims: "First, that the knowledge and competence of the professional have been validated by a community of his or her peers; second, that this consensually validated knowledge and competence rest on rational, scientific grounds; and third, that the professional's judgment and advice are oriented toward a set of substantive values" (Starr, 1982, p. 15). These claims, as Starr notes, correspond to the attributes—collegial, cognitive, and moral—usually associated with the definition of a profession. We are used to hearing that "the doctor knows best" (although we are increasingly inclined to call this into question). Professional authority, by this account, rests on the parallel assertion that "teacher knows best." "The special problem of constructing authority in schools," writes Richard Elmore, "is that it depends heavily on the teacher's role in the creation and propagation of knowledge" (1987).

Does Elmore really mean the "creation" of knowledge or, a different claim, its social appropriation in support of the teacher's status as authority? Most doctors, after all, do not participate in the creation of medical knowledge, but nevertheless derive social benefit from association with scientific knowledge produced elsewhere and often embodied in new technologies, drugs, and therapeutic regimens. The most common explanation for the rise of medical authority during the Progressive Era was the improved competence of physicians based on a quickening round of scientific discoveries; yet as Starr notes, the growth of science might rather have reduced professional autonomy by making doctors dependent upon organizations.

So there are two interacting historical dynamics. One involves the creation and legitimation of a knowledge base, the other its appropriation by an occupational group seeking advancement. Administrators, like teachers, seek to professionalize and so vie with teachers in gaining organizational control over new knowledge. In fact, the matter is likely to be yet more complicated. First, university-based social scientists may contend with teachers in controlling the definition and transmission of teaching knowledge. Second, administrators may vie with teachers over the organizational control of teaching knowledge. The knowledge terrain, then, will be doubly contested, with a number of alliances possible among these competing interests.

The prospects for asserting teacher authority on the basis of expert knowledge are further complicated by public perceptions of teaching. For a variety of reasons (which I will now review), it will be difficult to make credible the claim of specialized knowledge in teaching. Nevertheless, this claim must and will be pressed because it is so central to the meaning of professionalism. But here I want to take up a different and more novel claim: that a democratic theory of education requires a strong measure of authority to be vested in teachers.

This argument, advanced by Amy Gutmann (1987), turns on its head the traditional charge that professionalism is antidemocratic. From the Jacksonian Era onward, democrats in the populist tradition have opposed the privileges attached to office and disputed the knowledge claims of elites. We need not accept the leveling tendencies of radical populism, however, to acknowledge the democratic argument against professional privilege. Is there a more hallowed principle in education than the local control of schools, by which we have meant control by communities through school boards? Nor do we need a complex set of arguments to justify the rights of parents in determining the education of their children. On what basis, then, might one argue for a democratic professionalism?

The starting point, following Gutmann, is to recognize several limits to the exercise of legitimate democratic authority. The first such principle is *nonrepression,* which "prevents the state, and any group within it, from using education to restrict rational deliberation of competing conceptions of the good life and the good society" (p. 44). She continues, "Adults must therefore be prevented from using their present deliberative freedom to undermine the future deliberative freedom of children."

The second limit on democratic authority is the principle of *nondiscrimination,* which "prevents the state, and all groups within it, from denying anyone an education good on grounds irrelevant to the legitimate social purpose of that good" (Gutmann, 1987, p. 44). This equity principle guarantees that all children will be provided a nonrepressive education.

These two principles provide grounds to limit the rights of the state and of parents in determining the education of children. Children are members of both families and states; consequently, the authority of each must be partial to be justified. Parents cannot possess the freedom to limit the opportunities of their children or perpetuate racial and religious intolerance in their children. States cannot indoctrinate children into a particular way of life in the interests of social harmony.

There must be institutionalized challenges to political authority, and teachers represent one such challenge. Gutmann sees governments as perpetuating a common culture and teachers as cultivating the capacity for critical reflection on that culture. In short, teachers serve to shed critical light on a democratically created culture (p. 76). The principle of nonrepression, then, supplies democratic content to the concept of professionalism among teachers. Teachers must resist communal pressures and remain sufficiently detached to cultivate critical judgment in students, yet be sufficiently connected to communities to understand the commitments students bring to school.

Gutmann goes on to argue that professionals can gain too much autonomy and so succumb to "the insolence of office." In our society, doctors and lawyers may indeed have more authority than their expertise warrants. But there is an opposing problem, when professionals secure too little authority. Then, they cannot carry out their responsibilities because they lack not the perquisites of office but the necessary resources.

Although the claim of expertise carries insufficient moral weight by itself to override democratic authority, the requirements of a nonrepressive education do; such an education requires professional control by educators.

When democratic control precludes teachers' exercise of intellectual discretion, Gutmann argues, "(1) few independent-minded people are attracted to teaching, (2) those who are attracted are frustrated in their attempts to think creatively and independently, and (3) those who either willingly or reluctantly conform to the demands of democratic authority teach an undemocratic lesson to their students — of intellectual deference to democratic authority" (p. 80).

This position has philosophical appeal, but it presents difficulties in practice. Teachers in many communities across the country may find the principles of democratic professionalism small comfort in the face of powerful community norms.

Consider Alan Peshkin's (1978) ethnographic study of

Mansfield, a single rural community in the U.S. heartland. There he found a close congruence between community ethos and the school. "Mansfielders strive to hire not the best teacher, in an intellectual sense," he observes, "but the teacher who will best serve Mansfield. . . . They would reject teachers as unsuitable who were 'too intelligent for this community'" (pp. 199–200). Fitting in becomes the chief criterion for selecting schoolmen and women, an observation Waller would have found unsurprising.

Peshkin recognizes the dilemma here: "If education is perceived as best when it attempts to maximize the intellectual potential of a child, then MHS may be faulted. But if in places like Mansfield the schools contribute to a sense of personal identity and to low alienation, then something of compensating value may have been gained" (p. 200).

Much depends on what we as a people want from our schools, but we do not speak with one voice. Parents want to expand opportunities for their children but also want to maintain traditional values and ensure the stability of communities. We stand in awe of scientific, artistic, and scholarly accomplishments yet exhibit a deep strain of anti-intellectualism that often masquerades as pragmatism. We pay lip service to the notion of teachers as a class of independent intellectuals, but mark off "academic freedom" as applying only to those teachers who happen to work in colleges and universities.

"An education for freedom and for virtue part company in any society," notes Gutmann, "whose citizens are free not to act virtuously; yet it is at least as crucial to cultivate virtue in a free society as it is in one where the citizens are constrained to act virtuously" (p. 38). This is the essential tension that must be sustained within a democratic society, and according to this theory, teachers have a vital role to play in fostering a society at once free yet virtuous.

Teachers and the Effects of Regard

The proliferation of programs to recognize and award good teachers signifies a concern with how our society regards its teachers. If individuals called to service are asked to make material sacrifices, then the work itself must provide its own reward, together with a certain measure of gratitude preferred specifically from the persons served and generally from society in the form of symbols, ceremonies, and rituals. But a current worry centers on our society's low regard for teachers and its effects on their recruitment, morale, and commitment, and their capacity to teach.

As with the concern about teachers' authority, some of the arguments are historical. Teachers have often come from modest social backgrounds and often been the first family member to attend college. In recent years, the college-educated segment of the population has increased in our society, with two consequences. Teachers are no longer among the best-educated members of many communities. The minimal status they once enjoyed is slowly eroding. For many college graduates today, teaching represents downward, not upward, mobility.

These trends may contribute to teaching's recruitment problems, but they affect morale and commitment as well. As David Cohen (1987) has noted, an ironic consequence of educational success has been to quicken the round of criticism leveled at schools. An educated public is more apt to detect and express outrage at instances of poor teaching. As all teachers get tarred with the same critical brush, they begin to feel beleaguered and unappreciated. Teacher morale is a problem in many schools, and there has been a steady decline in the percentage of teachers who claim they would enter teaching if they could choose over again (National Education Association, 1987, p. 58).

By other accounts, however, teaching has always suffered an equivocal regard in our society. Lortie argues that teaching "is honored and disdained, praised as 'dedicated service' and lampooned as 'easy work.' It is permeated with the rhetoric of professionalism, yet features incomes below those earned by workers with considerably less education" (1975, p. 10). Teaching, it appears, never enjoyed a golden age; its recent troubles compound a long-standing occupational liability.

This unfortunate social fact has consequences as well for the work of teaching. Lortie points to the "disjunction between task imperatives and status constraints." In a telling section of his analysis, he compares the tasks of teaching — reaching students, managing group behavior, recognizing and responding to the individual needs of students — with other kinds of work that make similar demands. In all cases he finds that teachers have fewer resources and less control over them than theater directors; they have less discretionary power and fewer resources than managers; they have less formal recognition to support their judgments than psychotherapists. Teachers therefore can be said to be comparatively poorer in the status resources that facilitate accomplishment of tasks (p. 167).

Beginning in the late 1950s, teachers turned decisively to unionization as a collective advancement strategy, a move that led to increases in wages, benefits, and job protections. But unionism could not secure improvements in social position or regard. To the contrary, the militant assertion of teacher rights may have undercut esteem for teaching as a noble, helping profession. As the economic gains of unionism began to slow, professionalism reappeared as a promising strategy to regain the high ground and to enhance the image of teaching.

Is professionalism as traditionally conceived capable of elevating the status of teachers? Much current scholarship casts a harsh light on the self-aggrandizing tendencies of professionals and suggests that this model is not worth adopting, even if this were possible (for a review, see Metzger, 1987). Two forms of censure have appeared in the literature. One regards the historical process of professionalization as a uniquely Anglo-American attempt to reorder the basis of inequality and for the social transmission of privilege (see, for example, Larson, 1977, and Collins, 1979). In a democratic society that had no landed gentry, no nobility by birth, and no military class, professionals became the dominant elite, or rather the "professional-managerial class," for professionalism took shape alongside the rise of corporate capitalism. Of central importance to this new aristocracy was a university-based credentialing system that arose to legitimate social inequalities under the guise of meritocratic access.

"Viewed in the larger perspective of the occupational and

class structures," notes one analyst, " . . . the model of profession passes from a predominantly economic function — organizing the linkage between education and the marketplace — to
a predominantly ideological one — justifying inequality of status
and closure of access in the occupational order" (Larson, 1977,
p. xviii). The cachet associated with the professional, then, had
as much to do with his social class background as with his special
knowledge and advanced degrees. This model of the profession,
then, is the perfect antithesis of teaching as an open-access, mass
occupation associated with low status programs and déclassé institutions.

The second line of attack points to the uses of professional
status in controlling clients. Superior status is a powerful resource
because the authority exercised by professionals includes not
only their skills in performing services but their capacity to judge
the experience and define the needs of clients. Doctors and
lawyers, for example, have the power to label clients, to define
their problems, and to prescribe the acceptable range of solutions. In any number of fields, close scrutiny has revealed that
professional judgments on these matters serve the interests as
often of the professional as of the client (see, for example, Freidson, 1970a, 1970b; Barber, 1983; and Lipsky, 1980).

The cultural authority gained by professionals, their
capacity to define situations and impose judgments of meaning
and value, has two faces. Such authority is necessary to the conduct of professional work, and constitutes a valuable resource
in human service occupations. Professionals often must advise
their clients to make painful changes and decisions in their lives:
give up custody of a child; have an operation; go on a diet. Professional status lends weight and authority to their opinions,
which they render in the best interest of the client. But such
authority is also highly susceptible to abuses, for the interests
and biases of the professional come into play in interchanges
with clients. Again, the doctor-patient or the lawyer-client relationship hardly seems an appropriate model for teacher-student
relations.

If older critiques of professionalism emphasized the relation between social class and occupational status, newer work

highlights the significance of gender (see, for example, Harris, 1978, and Tyack and Strober, 1981). Teaching is a mass occupation that draws from a different social stratum than the elite professions, but equally important, it is a feminized occupation. In a patriarchal society women occupy subordinate roles, and their lack of cultural authority is associated as much with their gender as with their occupational position. The feminized occupations have always suffered subordinate status, which is in part associated with the nature of the work itself (Brumberg and Tomes, 1986, p. 287).

Professional status, note sociologists (for example, Abbott, 1981) is in part dependent on client status, and children have little status in our society. Many adults deal with children without special training, knowledge, or position, so the claims of teachers to special status are suspect. Teaching was institutionalized as "women's work" out of economic necessity. A rapidly expanding school system required a large, pliable, and inexpensive labor force. But a supporting ideology took shape as well, emphasizing woman's nature as dictating her proper sphere — hearth and home, and nurturing roles such as teacher or nurse. In the meantime, men of affairs would be in charge of schools, hospitals, and clinics; women would labor dutifully for men.

If this is the historical legacy, the contemporary women's movement, the drive to ensure equity and expand human rights, and the dramatically increased participation of women in the labor force have created a new set of conditions. Will these developments result eventually in a cultural revaluing — by men and women alike — of what has traditionally been women's work? Not, according to feminist scholars, if teaching aspires to traditional professionalism, which is predicated on male conceptions of work and career.

Feminist critics such as Sari Biklen (1986, 1987) and Sara Lightfoot (1978, 1983) point out that commitment to a professional career is only possible within a sexual division of labor that assigns women primary responsibility for childrearing and housekeeping, so that men may uninterruptedly and singlemindedly pursue their careers. When women, however, enter the professions and attempt to balance the demands of motherhood

74   Restructuring Schools

with those of work, they are faulted for showing insufficient commitment to the profession. Yet, as Biklen has argued, women elementary teachers feel that they have always worked, despite their discontinuous work histories and subordination to their husband's careers. Their deepest ambition is not to advance in a career but to improve their teaching.

Feminist scholarship, then, calls us back from the lure of professionalism — from images of wealth, status, and position — to the ideals and realities of teaching. The advancement of teaching must not come at the expense of the work itself. "Professional" reforms must not devalue teaching or ignore conceptions of the work by those who perform it. And if teaching continues to be women's work in our society, then reform must encourage compatibility not competition between parental and work roles.

How to construct a suitable regard for teaching is a most elusive goal, for regard is a diffuse, will-o'-the-wisp effect of culture and social structure that is not susceptible to social engineering. Yet regard, with its origins in social status, gender, and position, is a powerful factor in the creation of professionalism, which influences recruitment and commitment and serves as a resource in accomplishing human service work. If reforms are unlikely to exert direct effects on status, then they must at least be sensitive to indirect and slowly developing effects, while observing the physician's cardinal maxim: first, do no harm.

Teaching and the Control of Resources

Authority and regard are important, but to most teachers, the real problem is resources. Teachers argue that the underfunding and low level of support for education is the fundamental impediment to greater professionalism. They point to poor salaries and benefits, lack of quality instructional materials, rundown schools, overcrowded classes, the absence of support staff, and the presence of unqualified teachers who have not met even minimal requirements. They point to gross disparities in resources as well. Within states, some districts spend considerably more on public education than others, providing higher salaries, more in-service opportunities, better working conditions, and greater community support. So there are terrible inequities in the system as well. Some schools — those in inner city and rural areas — have never been able to attract and hold their fair share of good teachers or provide them with decent working conditions.

If the base support is inadequate, so is the support for professional growth and development. One of the hallmarks of the professional is to continue learning throughout a career, deepening knowledge, skill, and judgment, staying abreast of important developments in the field, and experimenting with innovations that promise improvements in practice. This hallmark of professionalism, however, requires more than individual commitment and a socializing orientation. It requires a supporting organization and that most precious resource of all — time. Horace must compromise his ideals, Theodore Sizer (1984) notes, because he cannot respond individually to all his students. He cannot write extensive comments on 150 compositions per week because the demand on his time is simply too great.

Teachers are so busy preparing lessons, teaching classes, providing extra help, grading homework, coaching sports, chaperoning student activities, monitoring study halls and the lunchroom, overseeing recess, and the rest, that they have little time for study and reflection. Just keeping school in the United States requires an enormous expenditure of time and energy each day.

But as countless commentators have noted, the schools are not organized to encourage inquiry, reflection, or innovation. The litany is familiar: Teachers work alone and receive little feedback. Many teachers neither observe teaching nor have their teaching observed by colleagues. Schedules preclude much collaborative planning. Funds are unavailable for work in the summers. Teachers have little access to sabbaticals, to conferences and workshops, to good university courses. Districts vary in their resource commitments to staff development, but most offer two to three days of teacher training per year and tie up most of their teacher-development budget in salary increases for desultory course taking and empty credentialism at local universities.

So professionalism conceived as commitment to reflection and inquiry into teaching, continuous growth of knowledge and skill, and innovation, receives little material or organizational support in most schools. Rather, professionalism so conceived comes out of the hide of most teachers and requires unusual dedication. Years ago, Willard Waller (1932) wrote about the narrowing effects of teaching on "the teacher personality." More recently, Seymour Sarason (1972) has described the deadening effects that years of teaching and the culture of schools have on many teachers. A vibrant professionalism has never developed in the schools.

Resource inadequacy, then, has contributed to teaching's recruitment and retention problems, undercut teachers' capacity to teach well, and limited the possibilities of commitment to professional ideals. Teachers resent "society's" hypocrisy in demanding more of them than society is willing to pay for. They often compare themselves to physicians in battlefield hospitals, under fire, lacking medical supplies, overwhelmed with the number of casualties pouring in. They resort to triage techniques simply to cope. But the difference, note teachers, is that these are the normal or typical conditions of their work, not rare or extraordinary circumstances.

Told to "act professional," teachers often respond with resentment, rightfully regarding such injunctions as patronizing attempts to keep them in their place, to squelch discontent, and to deny the legitimacy of their complaints that education is underfunded and unappreciated. Teachers abandoned the genteel rhetoric of professionalism — and disbanded the NEA as their umbrella organization — when they came to recognize that the ideology worked against their interests; that what professionalism meant to administrators, school boards, and university professors was docility and obedience. This was a conflict over the control of schools and over the allocation of resources.

Against this image of struggling, resource-starved teachers we can counterpose "the professional": a handsomely paid individual, sitting in a plush office, in command of the full resources of modern science and technology, in charge of a large support staff, and with a client load that allows for a regular golf game on Wednesday afternoons. In fact, however, this image of the professional does not correspond to the realities of professional work in our society. The free-standing, fee-for-service professional is in the small minority today. Most professionals work for large organizations that must conserve costs and ration resources.

The management of professional work has become a central challenge in our service economy today, and the primary conflict between managers and professional staff centers on resources. Professionals may retain technical control over their work, but as Eliot Freidson (1986) notes, "the management exercises direction by the use of its exclusive power to allocate the resources necessary for the work, indeed, the very existence of the jobs of the rank and file" (p. 149). Teachers enviously compare their limited circumstances with the freedom and control of university professors, and higher education does appear favored, but Freidson argues that even in the groves of academe, real power is control over the budget.

Much professional work, then, suffers from resource shortages, a condition that some commentators regard as inevitable. In exploring the work patterns of street-level bureaucrats, for example, Michael Lipsky (1980) describes the short cuts and strategies such workers must use to cope with huge client loads, uncertain knowledge, accountability pressures, and other aspects of their work situations. He points out that demand for services is likely to expand as rapidly as supply. Especially among indigent clients there is an infinitely elastic demand for better police protection, more family and individual counseling, job training, additional welfare, health care, and a variety of other services. Lipsky's analogy for this phenomenon is the Long Island Expressway. Traffic along this corridor is perpetually heavy, and when a massive construction program expanded the highway to open new lands, the traffic soon increased to maintain the jam at a higher volume.

While demand for human services expands in response to supply, expanding the supply is itself problematic. Sarason (1972) brings the point home in describing the "myth of reduced class size." Congress, he argues, might pass a law tomorrow requiring that all classes in the United States be twenty students or less, and appropriate funds to support such a decree, but our society could not produce enough qualified teachers to meet this demand.

Resource shortages, then, plague human service work of all kinds, not just the work of teachers. Most professionals claim they must compromise their ideals due to lack of resources. This problem is endemic to service work. As Freidson notes, "all choices are limited by the resources allocated differentially by management and by the absolute level of resources available to management." The consequence of these constraints, he argues, is increased impersonality of services. Professionals often "are organizationally impotent even though technically autonomous" (Freidson, 1986, p. 178).

Professionals in all fields constantly seek more resources for their work, justifying their demands with appeals to client welfare. In this sense, professionalism is likely to cost more than other reform strategies. In the name of professionalism teachers seek higher salaries, smaller classes, more time for planning and reflection, better and more plentiful materials, improved staff development, and other costly items. Public officials interested in containing educational costs are therefore likely to resist such initiatives. They observe that educational costs rose substantially during the period when test scores and other quality indicators declined. Getting tough, not throwing money at the problem, looks like the best bet and makes for good politics.

Teaching is a public profession, and teachers subsist on taxpayer support. There will always be competition for public funds and tensions between professional ideals in teaching and the publicly supported means to realize them in practice.

Knowledge in Teaching

Educators have spoken for years about "the knowledge base of teaching," a hopeful phrase usually intended to indicate the rich offerings of social science. Indeed, over the past twenty years there has been an impressive growth in knowledge about teaching, some of which has directly improved the practice itself.

Yet the notion of a codified knowledge base, a "science of instruction," draws blank stares and skeptical questions from those outside the academy, indeed from many teachers. "What knowledge?" they ask. "And where do I go to find it?"

As I have already indicated, this question of knowledge is central to the prospects for professionalism in teaching. Professional status and authority rest on a claim to knowledge. Without credibly advancing such a claim, teachers cannot secure the privileged position they desire. The issue usually is formulated in this manner, suggesting that we simply get on with discovering or inventing the knowledge base. But the matter is not so simple.

The mere existence of knowledge useful to a complex practice is insufficient to guarantee its effects on the public's imagination. To support the claim of professionalism, new knowledge must produce a demonstrative effect, a convincing display of its power. The majesty of the law, the miracle of new cures, the wonders of engineering and architectural feats, these contribute to the mythology of professionalism. The social significance of new knowledge is as important as its efficacy in practice.

Equally important is control over the knowledge, its appropriation by the group seeking professional status. It is not clear that the knowledge represented in handbooks on teaching will ever benefit the interests of teachers, even if it might improve their teaching. As I have indicated, university-based academics and school administrators also have interests to advance and defend. From one angle, then, there is the potential for conflict among these three groups for control of teaching knowledge, and the interesting question concerns the alliances that form.

Consider first the question of the knowledge itself. Can we make a convincing case that special knowledge is required to teach well, knowledge that can be transmitted through formal programs rather than simply acquired via experience on the job?

Most people in our society have spent hours watching teachers, and the work appears fairly ordinary, fairly routine. When people recall the great teachers who have touched their lives, it is the vivid human qualities they remember — personality and style, passion and caring, even their eccentricities. Good teaching, then, seems to be less a matter of technique, skill, and knowledge than of personality. "It is difficult to disentangle teacher character from teacher competence," notes Sara Lightfoot (1983, p. 250).

Philip Jackson (1986) adds another point in arguing that only modest claims to special knowledge in teaching are warranted. He observes that much teaching in our society is nonspecialized and occurs without credentials or other professional trappings. Informal teaching takes place at home, in Sunday schools and summer camps, and on television. Teachers in our most prestigious institutions — elite private academies and universities — do not possess special credentials. There seems, then, to be considerable, commonsense evidence that no special knowledge is needed to teach well. If Harvard or Hotchkiss do not require teaching credentials, why should the public schools do so?

In a recent essay, David Cohen (1988) lends historical depth to this observation. He describes a long tradition of teaching, extending at least from medieval times to the present, in which instruction is a commonplace, informal act carried on within home and community. This long-standing and widespread approach regards teaching as telling and children as empty vessels into which adults pour knowledge. More sophisticated conceptions of teaching and learning are modern inventions that have yet to gain acceptance outside academic circles. Dewey, Piaget, and other scholars may make a powerful case for learning as active construction of knowledge by the knower, but there is nothing self-evident about this view. "School instruction floats on a sea of popular practices," notes Cohen, "and these practices have an historical life of their own." "Efforts to reform schoolteaching subsist within a society in which unspecialized and largely traditional teaching and learning go on everywhere," he argues (p. 27).

Knowledge-base conceptions that build on findings from vanguard cognitive science are likely to fly in the face of powerful, commonsense notions of teaching held by children and adults. Rather than enhancing the status of the teaching profession, such notions may appear outlandish or faddish and serve ironically to discredit the profession. Public reaction to such past reforms as the new math suggests that, regarding teaching and learning, the experts had better not stray too far from familiar and trusted traditions.

There is yet another factor complicating efforts to establish a special knowledge claim in teaching. In most fields, professionals assert exclusive jurisdiction over a domain of knowledge and practice. Teachers, however, must share the domain of children's learning and development with parents (Lightfoot, 1978). They do not possess the moral authority to erect a high-walled kingdom of special knowledge. They must share responsibility with parents, and this means reducing social distance and demystifying school knowledge. In other fields, social distance and mystification enhance the claim to expertise, and possession of the knowledge contributes to social distance. This circular relation builds professional status but is impermissible in teaching.

These conditions limit the prospect that teachers will be able to associate with high status knowledge. Research on teaching goes forward, however, and the journals brim with confidence in the progress made. The results are intriguing. They include robust, albeit probabilistic, findings, instructional theories, soft technologies, new materials, and much advice and many prescriptions for teachers. Who will benefit from this gradually accumulating knowledge? How will new knowledge be represented, tested, transmitted, and employed?

New knowledge traverses several routes into practice. One path leads from policy through administrative procedure into the classroom. State and local policymakers appropriate social science knowledge in order to gain greater control over teaching. The means include testing regimens, evaluation systems, prescribed texts and instructional materials, lesson and unit planning guidelines and formats, and mandated in-service training. Knowledge is used to improve administrative monitoring and oversight of teaching. The aim is to identify measurable outcomes, to specify effective instructional processes, and to ensure that teachers comply with established routines prescribed by research.

Such uses of knowledge are not necessarily antithetical to professionalism. The growth of technical knowledge in other fields has served to enhance the status and competence of the practitioner, not to reduce his autonomy. Researchers have for some time been sensitive to the uses of research knowledge by teachers. Many now argue that such findings are valuable in directing teaching practices but must be interpreted and adapted by teachers in light of their knowledge of their locality and their intentions for particular students (for development of this argument see Gage, 1985; Fenstermacher, 1980; and Brophy, 1988). Research knowledge provides principles, not rules, in guiding teacher judgment and decision making. Lee Shulman (1983) underscores this perspective by drawing an analogy between teachers and judges. The latter draw on a large body of law, which they must interpret to resolve particular cases. So too teachers must consult a body of findings and principles in making decisions within their realm.

Schools must have means to coordinate and control instruction. Agreements among school faculty members on matters of curriculum, instruction, and assessment are necessary and can be based on findings from research as well as knowledge of local circumstances. The second-grade teacher depends on the work of the first-grade teacher and may need to plan cooperatively with other second-grade teachers. The university model featuring a collection of individual scholars who occasionally come together in committee to review the curriculum would be wholly inappropriate for most K–12 schools. In fact, recent criticism of higher education suggests that increasing specialization coupled with the extreme autonomy and individualism of university professors has not been healthy for undergraduate education.

But the emphasis in prescriptive uses of knowledge is not on the school-level coordination of instruction but on external accountability. Teachers do not participate in setting goals or planning such systematic instruction. The knowledge flows from the university into policy and administration. The knowledge is applied to teachers in an attempt to hold them accountable. Teachers themselves neither generate new knowledge nor decide when and how to use it. The result is to deprofessionalize teaching, reducing teachers to functionaries and teaching to routine. The alliance of university-based social science with policy and administration serves all interests except the teacher's (and perhaps the learner's).

Administrative uses of teaching knowledge appear as a dominant trend, dating back to the efficiency movement of the Progressive Era (Callahan, 1962; Cremin, 1961), but alternatives are evident as well. In some schools teachers actively construct the curriculum and develop new programs, drawing on the fruits of research and theory coupled with their own experiences. Less visible than the high-profile administrative and policy-initiated uses of knowledge, the tradition of local efforts centered in particular schools, sometimes in districts, and often in informal, extended networks of teachers has served as a robust, countercultural trend to bureaucratic approaches.

Teachers themselves have participated in the generation and appropriation of knowledge in their work, and as Donald Schön (1983), among others, has argued, social science is just beginning to explore the epistemological issues regarding teaching. In the post-positivist era, there is a growing recognition that social science has provided an incomplete if not misleading account of complex practices such as teaching. The findings of social science can certainly inform the work of teaching but cannot by themselves constitute the knowledge base. In fact, multiple, competing conceptions of expertise underlie professional practices (Kennedy, 1987). There is no single paradigm of professional knowledge, and all practices struggle with the formulation of theory and practice, critical inquiry and received wisdom, general principles and clinical case knowledge, the cultivation of judgment and the development of skills.

In teaching, interest has grown in new forms and kinds of knowledge that might supplement behavioral science at the same time that it empowers teachers. Terms such as expertise, craft knowledge, the "wisdom of practice," and case knowledge suggest the interests of various investigators (see, for example, Berliner, 1986 and 1988; Shulman, 1986 and 1987; and Wilson, Shulman, and Richert, 1987). The nature of such knowledge and the methods of identifying, testing, and sharing it are all problematic, but the search along these lines bespeaks dissatisfaction with a skills-oriented approach to teaching.

The School as a Professional Community

What are the implications of the foregoing analysis for the organization of schools? Professionalism as a reform theme appears as a necessary complement to other initiatives. To provide excellent teaching on a widespread basis, the schools must promote commitment to high ideals and the opportunity to become increasingly skillful in the craft of teaching. Approaches to school organization that emphasize bureaucratic regularity, legal norms, or consumer preferences will not adequately cultivate either commitment or expertise among teachers.

The professional covenant stressing authority, regard, resources, and knowledge supplies the constituent supportive elements. But professionalism in teaching must take on a distinct meaning, one that accords with the historical evolution and social circumstances of the occupation. Traditional images of professionalism that emphasize elite status, private power, social distance from clients, and single-minded pursuit of careers will not serve teaching. Taking the school as a locus for a professionalism distinctly suited to teaching, I propose seven principles to guide the formation of professional communities within schools.

1. Complement Bureaucratic Accountability with Professional Responsibility. This is the cardinal maxim because professionalism relies on trust: We entrust vital matters to professionals, and what warrants that trust is commitment to standards enforced by a community of peers. Requirements for entry to practice are one important locus for standards, and the classic bargain struck by the elite professions substitutes regulation of the worker for regulation of the work itself. An extended, rigorous professional education, coupled with stringent licensure procedures serve to warrant knowledge, skill, and norms. Professionals then enjoy discretion in the performance of their work, and they are evaluated by peers against standards developed within the profession.

In education, professional norms and standards will never replace public accountability measures but can serve as an important complement to them. School faculties can work collegially to develop norms of conduct and standards of practice to guide their work and represent their commitments to the public. Whereas external accountability tends to be input- and output-oriented, taking the form of curricular specifications, materials selection, monitoring systems, standardized testing, graduation requirements, and the like, professional norms and standards focus on the work itself and represent both ethical commitments and conceptions of "best practice" derived from research and professional consensus within the field.

What might such school-based professional standards for teachers look like? In a comprehensive high school, the parties to such standards might include the full faculty of the school for certain standards, academic departments for other standards, and ad hoc working groups for still others. For example, school faculties might formally work out a set of expectations regarding teachers' noninstructional responsibilities, their duties to parents, or their obligations for professional growth. A language-arts department might create a standards framework that sets forth guidelines for the teaching of writing. Such a framework can incorporate advances in research on the writing process, a language-arts philosophy, and procedural guidelines for teachers on such matters as feedback on student compositions.

Fashioning explicit commitments in the form of norms and standards serves several important functions in creating a professional community. First, the process provides a forum where teachers as a collegium can deliberate on matters of practice. Second, the formal statements can serve as a representation of both the knowledge and ethical bases of teaching. Third, the process and its results can communicate conceptions of practice and professional responsibility to the public, underscoring the obligations that teachers take upon themselves. And fourth, such deliberations and agreements can guide the daily practice of teaching.

The articulation of norms and standards must be school-based because the process is as important as the outcome, must involve all teachers, and must be continuous. Annual statements can set goals and targets for teachers as well as establishing universal norms. The process vests control over standards in teachers themselves, providing a forum and a format where teachers' understandings and intentions can inform the framework of standards that guides teachers' practices. The shortcomings and insufficiencies of external accountability procedures are well known. They require supplementation through locally developed standards that represent the commitments and expertise of a professional community.

2. *Promote Professional Socialization Processes Within Schools.* Universities convey necessary liberal and technical knowledge to prospective teachers, but socializing them into professionals takes place within the work setting. Conceived as a set of attitudes and dispositions, professionalism is a psychological construct requiring organizational support. Research on teaching has identified factors, such as expectations and sense of efficacy, that influence effectiveness. The disposition to hold high expectations for student learning and to believe in one's own ability to encourage learning are critical to good teaching.

Furthermore, teaching is different from other occupations in that newcomers have already experienced a lengthy "apprenticeship of observation" as students watching teachers work. Consequently, the need is to resocialize beginners, particularly if the students they teach are different from themselves and if the methods they use are nontraditional. As Lortie (1975) has noted, there is a conservative bias built into teaching based on both recruitment and socialization patterns. If professionalism is to include experimentation with new methods of teaching and commitment to teaching a socially diverse body of students, then school-based processes are necessary to inculcate values and norms as well as to impart skills.

There are three points of reference for formal induction experiences. The first is the state's interest in promoting a standard of safe practice for entry. States increasingly are mandating intern and induction programs as part of licensure requirements. A second potential source of influence is the employing organization. Most districts provide very minimal support and supervision to beginning teachers, but they do have an interest in conveying district policy and procedure. The third influence is the profession, with the focus on norms and standards that compose the obligations of teaching.

These interests differ. The state aims to establish a set of minimum, uniform criteria of competence. The district anchors its concern in the terms and conditions of employment. The profession seeks to instill a broad set of obligations that promotes trust in teacher competence, judgment, and discretion. These aims are not incompatible, but conflicts may arise between them. For example, districts might establish policies that violate professional teaching norms. A mixed system of authority within the school appears best calculated to promote student learning and welfare, but at present there is little attention to professional socialization of teachers. The arrangements taking shape through state and district policy in many locales, however, may create conditions for stronger, school-based socialization.

For example, as part of the development of state-mandated intern and induction programs, school faculties can supplement minimal standards and criteria with professional norms that help shape and direct mentor-novice exchanges. Such norms may refer to technical knowledge and ethical precepts and may be universal or particular. Their introduction can help convey and establish a dual membership: in the school community and in an extended professional community. Each community serves as a source of authority in regulating teacher conduct, and if skillfully managed, the potential tensions between these sources may be productive, for each alone is open to greater abuse than they are when acting together, as Gutmann's theory of democratic professionalism makes clear (Gutmann, 1987).

3. Strengthen Lateral Connections Between Teachers Concerning the Construction and Coordination of the Curriculum. Teacher involvement in the development of the curriculum is essential to the meaning of professionalism in teaching. Curriculum is broadly conceived to include the scope and sequence of objectives; underlying theories and models of knowledge, of the learning process, and of learners; methods and models of teaching and assessment; instruction materials; and the means for the coordination and collaborative development of these matters. The curriculum is the province of teaching, although not the sole province.

Curriculum development is critical to professionalism because it provides a concrete focus for teacher planning and decision making, a context within which to join theory to practice, create a common language of purpose and analysis, and acquire and employ the knowledge justifying teachers' claims of professionalism. The tendency in much educational policy and practice is to separate ends and means, that is, to institute a functional split between content and methods. School systems organized on bureaucratic principles tend to constrain everything but the interactive process of teaching, reducing the kernel of discretion to method alone. But the division between content and method is artificial. Content and method interpenetrate and form the natural unit for educational planning and for the exercise of professional judgment.

As Joseph Schwab (1969) has argued, curriculum development requires arts of the eclectic and deployment of multiple theories. Furthermore, continuity of curriculum is necessary, both vertically from grade to grade, and horizontally across subjects and disciplines. Both points suggest that curriculum construction and enactment are a communal, not a solitary, endeavor. Teachers must collaborate across grades and subject areas to bring a wide range of knowledge to bear on their work and to ensure coordination and continuity. These are the task-related lateral connections concerning teaching that school organization and resources must encourage. In particular, teachers must have time to work together, and they must have access to outside resources. This leads to the next principle.

4. Create Status-Equalizing Access to External Sources of Knowledge. Local development of school programs has two obvious benefits and two equally apparent defects. The benefits include responsiveness to the learners and to the community, particularly as the community becomes a rich curriculum resource, and proprietorship of the curriculum by teachers, which contributes to their sense of engagement and competence. The defects include parochialism and the potential exclusion of other legitimate interests.

To counter these weaknesses, teachers must have access to outside sources of knowledge to enrich their curriculum work and to connect it to external sources of expertise and authority. In particular this means interchange with university-based scholars on matters of teaching, learning, and curriculum. The current mode of desultory course taking in pursuit of modest salary

increases and additional credentials does not constitute the necessary connection with sources of higher-order knowledge. More
promising approaches include creation of interdisciplinary professional development schools or teacher centers, establishment
of joint positions such as adjunct faculty, and sponsorship of
collaborative research and development projects in the schools.
Such initiatives would tend to legitimize teacher knowledge and
status, strengthen connections to relevant bodies of theoretical
and empirical knowledge, and effectively foster creation and use
of relevant knowledge.

Teachers also must reckon with authoritative pronounce-
ments on curriculum issued by state and local agents of the
public. The school curriculum is a locus for professional knowledge and an instrument of teaching practice. But the school
curriculum is also a powerful source of social and cultural values
and a battleground of competing interests. Teachers alone may
not control the curriculum, but they must employ professional
knowledge and judgment in interpreting, enacting, and sometimes resisting public curriculum policy.

*5. Create Informal Leadership Opportunities for Teachers in Con-
nection with the Corporate Improvement of Teaching.* The incentive
structure for teaching is upside down: Rewards go to those who
leave teaching, not to those who progressively deepen their commitment and skill. Schemes that would introduce permanent
ranks for advancement in teaching risk bureaucratic rigidity,
procedural entanglements, and an increase of organizational and
interpersonal conflict. Yet structural support is necessary to make
viable a career in teaching. The concept of career need not imply, but neither should it preclude, advancement opportunities.
The task for management and organization is to create positions that teachers may rotate through and temporary responsibilities that provide teachers with new challenges.

The creation of new roles and tasks for teachers must be
connected to the improvement of teaching as a whole. Such new
roles and tasks would serve to legitimate teachers' work outside of direct contact with students, would contribute to the
creation of a learning community, and would underscore the
cardinal professional commitment to continuous growth. New

responsibilities might include teacher induction and evaluation, staff development, practical inquiry, and school-based policy setting. Many teachers may not seek advanced responsibilities, but options for some would be valuable, particularly if such positions were well supported with preparation and training for the new roles, administrative backing, and sufficient resources. The aim of new roles and responsibilities for teachers, however, should not be simply to create a career structure for and retain good teachers. The aim should be to increase the competence of all teachers and the effectiveness of schools by bringing the talents of teachers to bear on collective efforts to improve education.

6. *Legitimate and Provide Time for Engagement of Teachers in a Range of Responsibilities Aside from Direct Instruction.* This principle enables the others and goes to the heart of the resource question. If teaching is equated solely with student contact and consequently with isolation from other adults, teachers will have few opportunities to improve their practices or to develop professional orientations and commitments. To implement the other principles, teachers must have time to plan, to confer, to observe teaching by other teachers, to discuss practice, to read and write, to travel, and to reflect and inquire. Furthermore, these activities must be communal as well as individual, for their dual aim is improvement of both schools and individuals.

The organization and management of schools is deeply implicated in carrying out this principle, for time is at once the most flexible and the most precious resource of an organization. Finding or creating time is the central imperative in the management of teaching, and many approaches to do this are available. School administrators can do the following: create schedules that provide common planning time for teachers; construct teacher teams that plan and instruct together; secure additional funds for teacher planning and development; draw on community resources to enrich the staffing mix in schools; and focus resources on teacher-held positions within and between schools that increase opportunities for teachers to confer on matters concerning curriculum and instruction.

Two factors most seriously compromise teachers' capacity to acquire and exercise professional judgment and skill in their work: too many students to teach and too little time, while working in teaching, to work on teaching. Like other professionals, teachers require enabling conditions in order to be effective, but in too many locales these are absent. In some cases, schools are simply underprovisioned: More resources are needed, and educators must secure greater funding from the public. In other cases, however, school systems are badly organized and administered, with available resources poorly used. The responsibility of administration, then, is both to secure the necessary resources and to use them wisely. From this chapter's perspective, this means creating conditions that provide manageable "case loads" and that legitimate the time that teachers spend on professional activities.

7. *Increase Sensitivity Within the Policy System to the Impact of External Mandates on Teachers and Teaching.* This principle is similar in spirit to the requirement that environmental impact statements accompany new federal regulations. The responses of teachers to external regulation are often regarded as recalcitrance on their part, not as sensible adaptations in light of teachers' intentions and understandings. Distrust of teachers sometimes provokes policy mandates and inducements, but implementation often produces mixed results. Adverse effects include mandates that have not been adequately funded, lack of system capacity to respond, unrealistic timelines, incorrectly specified problems, and unanticipated and counterproductive consequences. When teachers, for example, note that excessive testing undercuts their capacity to engage students in meaningful learning, this is not resistance by them to accountability. There should be a flow of information between levels of the policy system, so that public officials heed teachers' professional judgments about the impact of policy as well as impose policy. The thrust of this principle is not to argue against policy-driven efforts to influence teaching but to urge a place for professional judgement by teachers in shaping policy. The voices of teachers have been absent in the debate about current reforms, a result of the marked antagonism between organized teachers and public officials. But if bureaucratic accountability measures are necessary to check the abuses of professionalism, bringing teachers' judgments to bear on the

effects of policy is equally necessary to offset the evident inadequacies of bureaucratic methods. Dialectical tensions between methods of control are useful, and "talking back" to those who impose policy from outside is a requirement within a professional community that supplies useful challenges to policy.

This chapter has explored four themes central to the meaning of professionalism. The general import has been that the classic professional model is unsuited to the circumstances of teaching but that the virtues of professionalism do apply to the occupation and practice of teaching. Thus, the task in the future is to construct a professional model that accommodates teaching's distinctive aspects. One place where such a model can be developed is the school, where a community can be organized that supports the proper authority and expertise of teachers. The construction of such local communities and their connection to external sources of authority and knowledge on teaching and learning is one important task for policy and practice in the future.

References

Abbott, A. "Status and Status Strain in the Professions." *American Journal of Sociology,* 1981, *86* (4), 819–835.

Arendt, H. "What Is Authority?" In H. Arendt (ed.), *Between Past and Future.* New York: Viking, 1961.

Barber, B. *The Logic and Limits of Trust.* New Brunswick, N.J.: Rutgers University Press, 1983.

Berliner, D. "In Pursuit of the Expert Pedagogue." *Educational Researcher,* 1986, *15* (7), 5–13.

Berliner, D. "The Development of Expertise in Pedagogy." Charles W. Hunt Memorial Lecture. Paper presented at the meeting of the American Association of Colleges for Teacher Education, New Orleans, Feb. 1988.

Biklen, S. " 'I Have Always Worked': Elementary Schoolteaching as a Career." *Phi Delta Kappan,* 1986, *67* (7), 504–508.

Biklen, S. "Schoolteaching, Professionalism, and Gender." *Teacher Education Quarterly,* 1987, *14,* 17–24.

Brophy, J. "Research on Teacher Effects: Uses and Abuses." *Elementary School Journal,* 1988, *89* (1), 3–22.

Brumberg, J., and Tomes, N. "Women in the Professions: A Research Agenda for American Historians." *Reviews in American History,* 1986, *2,* 277–296.

Callahan, R. E. *Education and the Cult of Efficiency.* Chicago: University of Chicago Press, 1962.

Cohen, D. "Schooling More and Liking It Less: Puzzles of Educational Improvement." *Harvard Educational Review,* 1987, *57* (2), 174–177.

Cohen, D. "Teaching Practice: Plus Ça Change . . . " Issue paper 88-3. East Lansing, Mich.: National Center for Research on Teacher Education, Michigan State University, 1988.

Coleman, J. "Families and Schools." *Educational Researcher, 16* (6), 32–38, 1987.

Collins, R. *The Credential Society.* New York: Academic Press, 1979.

Cremin, L. *The Transformation of the School.* New York: Vintage Books, 1961.

Elmore, R. "Reform and the Culture of Authority in Schools." *Educational Administration Quarterly,* 1987, *23* (4), 60–78.

Fenstermacher, G. "A Philosophical Consideration of Recent Research on Teacher Effectiveness." In L. Shulman (ed.), *Review of Research in Education, 6.* Itaska, Ill.: F. E. Peacock, 1979.

Fenstermacher, G. "On Learning to Teach Effectively from Research on Teacher Effectiveness." In C. Denham and A. Lieberman (eds.), *Time to Learn.* Washington, D.C.: National Institute of Education, 1980.

Freidson, E. *Profession of Medicine.* New York: Dodd, Mead, 1970a.

Freidson, E. *Professional Dominance.* New York: Atherton, 1970b.

Freidson, E. *Professional Powers.* Chicago: University of Chicago Press, 1986.

Gage, N. *Hard Gains in the Soft Sciences: The Case of Pedagogy.* Bloomington, Ind.: Phi Delta Kappa, 1985.

Grant, G. "The Character of Education and the Education of Character." *Daedalus,* 1981, *110* (3), 135–150.

Grant, G. "The Teacher's Predicament." *Teachers College Record,* 1983, *84* (3), 593–610.

Gutmann, A. *Democratic Education.* Princeton, N.J.: Princeton University Press, 1987.

Harris, B. *Beyond Her Sphere: Women and the Professions in American History.* Westport, Conn.: Greenwood Press, 1978.

Jackson, P. "On Knowing How to Teach." In P. Jackson (ed.), *The Practice of Teaching.* New York: Teachers College Press, 1986.

Kennedy, M. "Inexact Sciences: Professional Education and the Development of Expertise." Issue paper 87-2. East Lansing, Mich.: National Center for Research on Teacher Education, 1987.

Kirp, D. "Professionalization as a Policy Choice: British Special Education in a Comparative Perspective." *World Politics,* 1982, *34* (2), 137–174.

Kirp, D., and Jensen, D. *School Days, Rule Days.* London: Falmer Press, 1986.

Larson, M. *The Rise of Professionalism.* Berkeley: University of California Press, 1977.

Lightfoot, S. *Worlds Apart.* New York: Basic Books, 1978.

Lightfoot, S. "The Lives of Teachers." In L. Shulman and G. Sykes (eds.), *Handbook of Teaching and Policy.* New York: Longman, 1983.

Lipsky, M. *Street-Level Bureaucracy.* New York: Russell Sage Foundation, 1980.

Lortie, D. *Schoolteacher.* Chicago: University of Chicago Press, 1975.

Lukes, S. "Power and Authority." In R. Nisbet and T. Bottomore (eds.), *A History of Sociological Analysis.* New York: Basic Books, 1978.

McLaughlin, M., Pfeifer, S., Swanson-Owens, D., and Yee, S. "Why Teachers Won't Teach." *Phi Delta Kappan,* 1986, *67* (6), 420–425.

McNeil, L. *Contradictions of Control.* New York: Routledge & Kegan Paul, 1986.

Merton, R. "Sociological Ambivalence." In R. Merton, *Sociological Ambivalence and Other Essays.* New York: Free Press, 1976.

Metzger, W. "A Spectre Haunts American Scholars: The Spectre of 'Professionism.'" *Educational Researcher,* 1987, *16* (6), 10–19.

Muir, W. "Teachers' Regulation of the Classroom." In D. Kirp and D. Jensen (eds.), *School Days, Rule Days.* London: Falmer Press, 1986.

National Education Association. *Status of the American Public School Teacher, 1985–86.* Washington, D.C.: National Education Association, 1987.

Peshkin, A. *Growing Up American.* Chicago: University of Chicago Press, 1978.

Powell, A., Farrar, E., and Cohen, D. *The Shopping Mall High School.* Boston: Houghton Mifflin, 1985.

Sarason, S. *The Culture of the School and the Problem of Change, 2nd Edition.* Newton, Mass.: Allyn Bacon, 1972.

Schön, D. *The Reflective Practitioner.* New York: Basic Books, 1983.

Schwab, J. "The Practical: A Language for Curriculum." *School Review,* 1969, *78,* 1–23.

Sedlak, M., Wheeler, C., Pullin, D., and Cusick, P. *Selling Students Short.* New York: Teachers College Press, 1986.

Shulman, L. "Autonomy and Obligation: The Remote Control of Teaching." In L. Shulman and G. Sykes (eds.), *Handbook of Teaching and Policy.* New York: Longman, 1983.

Shulman, L. "Those Who Understand: Knowledge Growth in Teaching." *Educational Researcher,* 1986, *15* (2), 4–14.

Shulman, L. "Knowledge and Teaching: Foundations of the New Reform." *Harvard Educational Review,* 1987, *57* (1), 1–22.

Simon, Y. *Nature and Functions of Authority.* Milwaukee, Wis.: Marquette University Press, 1948.

Sizer, T. *Horace's Compromise: The Dilemma of the American High School.* Boston: Houghton Mifflin, 1984.

Starr, P. *The Social Transformation of American Medicine.* New York: Basic Books, 1982.

Tyack, D., and Strober, M. "Jobs and Gender: A History of the Structuring of Educational Employment by Sex." In P. Schmuck, W. Charters, and R. Carlson (eds.), *Educational*

Policy and Management: Sex Differentials. New York: Academic Press, 1981.

Waller, W. *The Sociology of Teaching.* New York: John Wiley, 1932.

Wilson, S., Shulman, L., and Richert, A. "'150 Different Ways' of Knowing: Representations of Knowledge in Teaching." In J. Calderhead (ed.), *Exploring Teachers' Thinking.* London: Cassell Educational Limited, 1987.

Wise, A. *Legislated Learning.* Berkeley, Calif.: University of California Press, 1979.

FOUR

Organizing Schools to Encourage Teacher Inquiry

Hendrik D. Gideonse

Teaching continues to be in crisis. Excessive demands on teachers' time and responsibilities are coupled with minuscule incentives. The system has become highly bureaucratized, and teachers and administrators often resign themselves to achieving minimal results and lose sight of fundamental aims. Efforts to apply intellect and energy to existing problems founder in the face of overt and covert opposition. Consider the following testimony from a refugee from teaching:

> I worked very hard as a teacher. Not only did I teach seven classes a day (four different preparations), but I began attending evening classes at the university in order to update and expand my content knowledge and my teaching expertise. As my workload increased, WIFM's (what's in it for me?) began to invade my thinking. The work in my university courses added to the four plus hours of preparation and paper-grading made the $200 raise on the pay

Note: An early and considerably shorter version of this chapter was published by the *Journal of Curriculum and Supervision,* 1988, *4,* (1), under the title "Practitioner-Oriented Inquiry by Teachers: Meaning, Justification, and Implications for School Structure."

scale inconsequential. At school, any requests for student information from the guidance office or for materials to be ordered through the city-wide media center meant I had to do all the record-searching or locate and fill out the order forms. The coffee-toting guidance counselor and librarian became thorns in my side. Attempts to advance a young man into a programming class commensurate with his ability met with stony resistance. Uncovering the fact that twenty-one of twenty-four seniors failing my pre-calculus class had PSAT scores in the seventeenth percentile and below even though they had three years of *A* and *B* math grades on their records, brought disdain and dislike from my principal. His answer to my question about how best to help these students was simple, "Develop twenty-four individual educational programs." His unspoken answer was, "Give them the *A*'s and *B*'s and get the parents off my back!" It did not take long for both students and parents to realize that they had a sympathetic ear in the principal's office. I wanted everyone to gain their knowledge by work-ing (I thought that was the way it was supposed to be), but the most important thing to the principal, parents, and students was the grade, whether it reflected true knowledge or not. Teaching in the "reflective practitioner" style . . . be-came an impossibility due to the lack of time, numerous impediments, and seeming lack of support. The course to follow became increasingly obvious. I had to resign.

Testimony by practitioners on the problems within schools is clearly matched, if not exceeded, by public demands for dramatically higher school performance. Those demands are sometimes couched in relative terms, in the sense that current levels of achievement are compared unfavorably with past per-formance. Sometimes public concerns reflect fears about the long-term social consequences of the system's current perfor-mance, particularly for the poor, some minority groups, and troubled adolescents. Still others reflect the fear that schools will fail to meet projected needs for a technologically sophisticated citizenry in economically demanding times.

In the last half dozen years, notably since the release of the report of the National Commission on Excellence in Education (1983), the nation and the states have been deluged by numerous and sometimes contradictory prescriptions for educational reform. These include recommendations that teachers receive higher pay on entering the profession and greater opportunities for advancement within teaching. Career ladders and merit pay should be instituted. Greater professionalism has been demanded of teachers. Higher standards for recruiting teachers and judging their performance have been demanded. Numerous calls have appeared for restructuring schools. More accountability in setting the objectives of teacher preparation has been sought from institutions of teacher education. At the same time, however, severe limitations have sometimes been imposed on those same institutions. Alternate routes to entry into teaching have been proposed, some of which virtually bypass anything approaching professional preparation whatsoever.

This chapter accepts as legitimate the call by both teachers and public for fundamental reform. The discussion here rests on the conviction that teachers' ability to achieve better performance is beyond their control as schools are presently organized and operated. In short, the organization, the very frameworks, of schools implicated by the refugee teacher's remarks must be transformed. The essence of the transformation of those frameworks lies in the creation of roles and organizational structures for teachers and schools that will guarantee consistent teacher performance because they are based on two kinds of knowledge: (a) established theoretical and clinical knowledge and (b) site- and child-specific knowledge.

Donna Kerr has recommended that "both state and local education agencies should engage sociologists of work and social psychologists to redesign school as a workplace." "Teaching," she says, "would appear to be a case of an inherently interesting activity that schools have, in effect, reduced to a numbing repetition" (Kerr, 1983, p. 143).

Teaching requires specialized knowledge (see Chapter Three). Indeed, three reports having direct bearing on teacher preparation all speak about the availability and implications of specialized knowledge for the future of teaching (National Commission on Excellence in Teacher Education, 1985; Carnegie Task Force on Teaching as a Profession, 1986; the Holmes Group, 1986). Even otherwise problematical reform initiatives rhetorically acknowledge the essential ingredient of specialized knowledge in teachers' professional preparation and performance.

Disagreements about the knowledge that undergirds professional performance in teaching do exist, however. Sometimes they arise over the different kinds of knowledge that teaching candidates should acquire. Some reformers place heavy (if not virtually exclusive) emphasis on a liberal education and a subject matter major. Other critics, while acknowledging the importance to teaching of competence in both the liberal arts and a particular subject matter, insist that teacher education institutions pay equally strong attention to professional knowledge bases (for example, the Holmes Group, 1986). Some, making their own assessment of professional knowledge bases, question whether sufficient knowledge exists to draw any inferences about restructuring teacher preparation programs (Jackson, 1987).

The recent Texas legislative decision (SB 994) to cap at eighteen semester hours, including student teaching, the number of credit hours that candidates may be required to take in their preservice preparation for teaching, demonstrates the belief that little professional knowledge exists in the educational field. Texas represents only the most recent of a handful of states whose public policy initiatives on teacher education explicitly or implicitly reject the existence or worth of specialized professional knowledge capable of informing teaching.

Most of the discussion about the knowledge needed for effective teaching has been conducted in the context of debates about the preservice preparation of teachers. This chapter focuses on the implications of knowledge-based teaching practices for the organization of schools and for the roles of teachers. (For a broader analysis of the implications of research inquiry as a basis for educational reform, see Gideonse, 1983.) The discussion rests on two assumptions. The first is that, just as the initial preparation of teachers should reflect certain knowledge bases, so should the organization of schools. The second is that the specific information and the accumulated knowledge (sometimes called the wisdom of practice) derived from the site-specific inquiry and learning of teachers is as vital to the performance of teachers as the more generic knowledge bases that are imparted during initial preparation in the domains of general education, a particular subject matter, and professional practice. This chapter's intent, therefore, is to address the kinds of clinical, evaluative, or problem-solving inquiries that would make teachers more effective in their day-to-day performance. This inquiry pertains to the specific sites where teachers work, the specific children they teach, and the planning and evaluation activities teachers must undertake to guide their teaching.

New Assumptions for Old

The present organization of schools is based on two assumptions: (1) Teaching is largely telling, and (2) children should be grouped according to age by year (see Goodlad 1984, chapter four).

These assumptions explain both the existence and the size of today's classrooms and the grades into which students are placed. They explain the specialized preparation accorded teachers of children of distinct age groups, the daily schedules of schools, schools' physical layouts, the forms of curricular pathways, and the choices (or, more accurately, the substantial absence of choices) available to parents seeking schools for their children.

They are not, however, the only assumptions that could be adopted. A rather different set could be employed, a set that arises from our knowledge of teaching and learning, which is today considerably more advanced than that available when the present organization of schools was first determined. Those alternative assumptions include:

> Children present themselves to schools with very different life experiences and readiness for the tasks of learning. They are not the same just because they are the same age.
> Children learn at different rates and in different ways.

Teaching is an intellectual activity involving the organization of tasks, materials, and time to identify and achieve learning objectives.

These assumptions state that teachers engage in intellectual work and that they should be motivated to achieve results and committed to practices that are self-correcting and problem solving. It suggests that teachers' status will rest, ultimately, on their success in grounding teaching practices upon unique forms of specialized knowledge — knowledge that is both foundational of teaching and imparted in teacher preparation and that is situational and developed in the course of teaching itself. This chapter addresses a number of questions arising from these assumptions:

What is the character and role of specialized knowledge in a profession?

What is meant by practitioner-oriented inquiry?

What are the implications of such inquiry for school organization?

What will help teaching become more reflective, that is, more characterized by systematic inquiry?

The Role of Specialized Knowledge in a Profession

Reduced to its essence, a profession has three characteristics. It serves a deep and abiding societal value, it operates according to a rich fund of specialized knowledge, and it controls entry to the profession and the conditions of its practice.

Teachers, in fact, serve a deep and abiding societal value. In our own culture, I would argue, teaching has the quintessential public responsibility of preparing succeeding generations of citizens for the many responsibilities of membership in a free society. On the other hand, it is clear that the teaching profession at present controls neither entry to nor the conditions of its own practice. If there is a way to change this, it lies in addressing the third fundamental characteristic of a profession, namely, its specialized knowledge: Practice must be transformed to permit the full acquisition and application of the specialized knowledge and skills of successful teaching.

Grounding in and utilization by professionals of specialized knowledge holds two promises. The first is improved professional effectiveness. To the extent that practitioners know the principles, theories, and emergent hypotheses as well as the full range of technical skills of their profession, and to the extent that they know the specifics of the settings and clients with whom they work, the likelihood increases that their planning, instruction, evaluation, and articulation with the work of others will have the intended outcomes.

A second promise, however, in the case of teaching, is the likelihood that teachers' performance will come to be judged, as is other professionals', not solely by results, but by responsible performance in the use of their specialized knowledge and skill. In the long run, achieving desired societal or client ends is important to a profession, but status and respect are not accorded solely on the basis of success in achieving individual client ends. Such status goes to all professionals — win or lose, success in achieving clients' aims or not — whose responsible use of their specialized knowledge, skill, and decision-making processes, at least equal to any a layperson might employ, is perceived to serve the needs of the larger society.

Professional knowledge acquires its special status in several ways. First, its status may arise from its conceptual difficulty or the extent to which it is counterintuitive. Second, knowledge may be special, not because it is difficult, but because it is privileged. That is, it arises from settings and interactions access to which is controlled by virtue of the need to respect privacy (a need, in teaching, that arises from the often delicate quality of interpersonal relationships, especially those between minors and adults). Third, some knowledge is considered special because the ability to perceive relevant data, interactions, circumstances, activities, and conditions emerges only after considerable training, cumulative experience, or socialization into a set of pertinent norms and expectations.

Specialized knowledge embraces theoretical and practical, abstract and concrete understandings. Most important, it requires practitioners to link theory with practice, the abstract with the concrete.

Teaching, of course, is an applied profession, not just an

academic one. While its sources of knowledge include the academic fields (especially the behavioral and social sciences and the humanities), it is supported also by the "how to" specializations of the educational profession: learning and motivation theory, curriculum design, small-group processes, instructional and behavioral management, evaluation, and so on.

Specialized knowledge on teaching embraces results acquired from the formal inquiries of research and scholarship as well as from the situationally specific inquiry of teachers. It also embraces the habits of mind associated with commitment to self-conscious action on the basis of knowledge — skepticism, the application of logic, the insistence upon evidence. As a concept, specialized knowledge includes processes of analysis and decision making associated with the application of knowledge. It implies a commitment to change practices as one's understanding evolves. Teachers committed to practice-based and specialized knowledge can expect to face — and, therefore, be disposed to resolve — the ambiguities that arise when the generalizations of theory are applied to the concrete complexities of the education of individual children.

Probably one of the most obvious knowns about teaching and learning is their great complexity. Furthermore, the meaning of instruction and student behavior and achievement is susceptible to interpretation from a variety of disciplinary, cultural, and professional perspectives.

Has professional preparation for teaching as it is currently practiced effectively used the instruments of knowledge and inquiry? On two counts, the record is uninspiring. First, until the last decade or so, teacher education programs have been defined more in terms of curricular logic derived from the nature of current teaching practices (as understood and interpreted by former teachers who have staffed the programs) than in terms of any store of formal scholarship or empirical research. Indeed, the American Educational Research Association's *Handbook of Research on Teaching* was first published in 1963 and is only in its third edition (Wittrock, 1986). Furthermore, neither scholars and researchers nor practitioners have been in charge of the policy frameworks — regulations for certification or program approval standards—that substantially shape teacher education. The final arbiters of such matters have been lay authorities like the state boards of education or administrative officials in state educational agencies. These policymakers have, in the main, been neither steeped nor socialized in specialized knowledge in education and could hardly be expected, therefore, to base their actions on it. For years this political reality remained unchallenged, in large measure because of public assumptions that teaching is not particularly demanding intellectually and that on-the-job experience is far more crucial to success than formal study.

A second reason teacher education programs have not incorporated professional knowledge or aimed to develop capabilities for inquiry in candidate teachers is the structure of current practice in education. As already noted, two assumptions— that teachers are tellers and that they are custodians of groups of children of the same age—actually control the conditions of education. The resulting model of schooling—children reporting to school at the same age, in the same size class groupings, at the same times every day—obstructs the application of foundational and situational knowledge to the complexities of teaching.

Vignette: A Visit to Lakeland

The following vignette illustrates some features of schools that have been organized around professional inquiry.

I had been looking forward to my forthcoming visit to Lakeland Learning Center for several weeks. When first phoned by my two former students, George and Maria, I was intrigued by their description of teaching practices marked by continuous inquiry and learning by the staff, continuous progress by the students, and full pupil participation in the learning community of the school.

As I walked into the school with the stream of youngsters that Wednesday, I watched the youngest children go off to a large room where they convened in small groups, each led by an older student or parent, the room lightly supervised by a single teacher and several aides and parents. Other children were checking a schedule board on which were tacked computer print-

outs with their names, room locations, and brief descriptions
of study assignments.

George and Maria were waiting for me. They greeted me
warmly, suggesting I just watch the students as each checked
his or her notice and took the action indicated. When I asked
Maria why the youngest children went directly to the large open
room, I was told that not all of them had mastered reading well
enough to take direction in the fashion of the older children,
so they were pregrouped with their student aide or parent of
the week for oral reading practice. A pleasant chime sounded,
and the bustle noticeably increased and then diminished as the
halls emptied. A different chime sounded. A last few children
hurried to their destinations.

George and Maria flanked me as they prepared me for
their first instructional planning meeting of the day with the five
other teachers with whom they were collectively responsibe for
the 163 six- to nine-year-old pupils. Today the teachers would
review social studies. (Yesterday they had reviewed mathematics,
the day before language arts and other humanities. Tomorrow
they would cover science. Friday was reserved for possible need
for additional planning time in one of the four core curricular
areas.) George and Maria explained to me how earlier in the
year, based on differences in training, experience, and interest,
the teachers had divided up leadership responsibilities for the
curricular areas (as well as for instruction and evaluation) and
service as coordinator/representative for the Learning Center
Professional Council.

Working with computer printouts of small-group work
progress reports recorded by the students themselves and confirmed in teacher-led instructional groups, the seven teachers
present reviewed individual and group progress against curricular aims the teachers had worked out in response to the broad
goals defined by the local board and state authorities. The
teachers' discussions made frequent reference to comprehensive
student progress records. Individual student needs and achieve-
ments were discussed and checked against continuous progress
evaluation reports, and small-group assignments were adjusted.

Spirited discussion took place over how to allocate large- and small-group assignments for the several curricular areas over the next several weeks. As I watched, a couple of the teachers keyed entries into their computer terminals. Maria explained to me that the small-group work assignments (the ones Lakeland's students were at the very moment engaged in, even as the teachers were undertaking their planning) could be adjusted according not only to task but also to membership; this opened up the prospect of forming groups that included students who had already mastered concepts with other peers who had (or had not). I learned that instructional assignments or choices were often drawn from a great variety of trade and text materials, from exercises stored in the school's computer, and from a materials bank operating in the Learning Center's resource center and library. The small-group assignments were also based, in part, on student preferences, allowing children to group who wanted to pursue curricular aims using certain materials or regarding certain topics (as contrasted to aims that might otherwise have been assigned by teachers).

Lakeland students engaged directly in peer instruction. Teachers closely monitored student progress as well as their own problem solving, which was directed toward how better to help selected individual students achieve curricular objectives. The meeting had taken fifty minutes.

The seven participants gathered their materials just as the chimes sounded. I followed Maria to her first instructional session, in mathematics, and observed a couple of students pick up and put litter in fresh cans in the halls as they passed and one drop a card in a conveniently located box labeled "What Needs Cleaning or Repair?" This is a device Lakeland uses to alert the building administrator to needed maintenance or custodial chores. I noted a display case labeled "Lakeland Monthly Citizen Awards" with polaroid pictures of students (plus some adults) with two- or three-line citations under each picture describing the basis for each individual's award. In class after the second chime, Maria first asked if any students had query or feedback cards stemming from the morning's small-group activities. She received a half dozen or so from the forty students present, sorted them as they were handed to her, and placed them in her planning folio.

Maria began with a short demonstration lesson in multiplication, and then asked students to group themselves into four-person teams to work together a set of multiplication exercises on chalkboard easels scattered around the room. As she distributed the sheets to everyone, she reminded the students that each child was to get an opportunity to try, and that the task of each student who watched was to work along mentally with the student who was "up" in order to be ready to assist should the student choose any particular spectator for help. Maria added that she would walk around the room to observe and assist, herself. She started them off by saying she was curious to see which group of students would be first to successfully complete a round in which each student had a chance to take a multiplication exercise to a successful conclusion, with or without assistance from peers. As she circulated, Maria made notes of students who made careless mistakes, who apparently hadn't mastered the basic tables yet, who seemed to be having difficulty participating, or who were particularly skilled at offering explanations and assistance to their peers. (Maria told me later that this last item was employed in forming student study groups; effort was made to provide effective student instructional leadership wherever possible.) Before any of the groups had completed their round of exercises, Maria, to meet needs she had identified on her walk around the room, broke in on the activity for a moment to reteach some of the concepts she had covered in the demonstration lesson. The groups resumed work, and in a few minutes first one, and then a second, finished with some boisterousness and enthusiasm. Maria acknowledged their leadership and directed the children to start their homework since they had finished early. In rapid succession the other groups finished, and turned their attention to their individual homework assignments.

When the chimes sounded again, Maria directed me to George's social studies class which turned out to have only fifteen students and was conducted as a group, Socratic fashion. George was covering a unit on the concept of community, using the experiences of the children (who came from different parts of the district and varying socioeconomic backgrounds) as input to the discussion. I noticed that he was careful not to correct misimpressions outright, but to encourage the use of evidence provided by students themselves in order to improve their understanding. He was equally careful to sort out subjective impressions from questions of fact, and he encouraged students to consider how they might go about finding answers to matters in which they found themselves in dispute. He skillfully used the students' collective experience with the community they constituted in school (which included accommodations for the hearing-impaired and orthopedically impaired children among them) as a way to both reinforce and illuminate the concepts of cooperation, caring, authority, government, geography, inside-of-group/outside-of-group, and so on. For example, he acknowledged approvingly the two members of the class whose pictures in the awards display spoke of their individual contributions to Lakeland.

After the session I asked George about the small size of the student group. He noted that in language arts and social studies the subject matter this week was much more flexible than usual. In addition, in these areas there were fewer opportunities to limit the tasks to things with which students could help each other. Accordingly, the teachers had taken advantage of opportunities to undertake temporary larger group instruction in mathematics and science in order to allow smaller student-teacher ratios in language arts and social studies, as we saw here.

I saw more of the same kinds of varied instructional strategies in the two class sessions. I also had a good look at one of two twenty-five-station computer labs used in science instruction. The last timeblock of the day was set aside for students to work singly or in small groups on outside-of-class assignments. Two teachers of the team, on a rotating basis, and several parents were available to assist as tutors as the need arose. The other five teachers asked me to join them for the day's debriefing session. One teacher had already received a couple of messages from tutors about matters they would like to see brought before the group. One message involved a child who seemed upset about something that had little to do with school. The other message had to do with the need to spend time assisting students in their own peer-teaching activities, indeed, with a suggestion to convene some of the older students as part of their out-of-class learning time in the days immediately ahead. The remainder of the time was devoted to a debriefing on the day's instructional activities, what worked, what didn't, where problems and opportunities arose, and things to work on before the next scheduled curricular planning session the next day. The cooperative but still challenging nature of the professional interactions were obviously stimulating to the participants.

Analysis: Lakeland as a Center for Inquiry

"Lakeland Learning Center" is clearly a place whose organization of learning and teacher roles departs substantially from that in the overwhelming majority of today's schools. What kinds of teacher inquiry are represented in this setting?

Planning and Design Responsibilities. "What should I teach?" Several levels of inquiry are suggested by this simple question. Prescriptive statements from the state, the district, and possibly the individual school, establish curricular parameters for teachers. Such statements, however, provide only the most general kinds of guidance, even when they are very detailed. For each prescribed aim in the overall curricular scheme teachers need to decide specific methods and materials to use. To make responsible choices, teachers need to ascertain how each educational objective relates to those that precede it, those that parallel it in other learning experiences, and future objectives that will follow. Teachers need to review the range of available learning materials. Is an assigned text sufficient to achieve a certain educational goal, or does it need to be supplemented? Are the extra materials readily available, in sufficient quantity or in a form that all students can gain access to or reproduce? These questions suggest the processes of inquiry in which a teacher must engage to prepare specific curricular plans and strategies.

"How should I teach?" The identification of curricular aims and content triggers the next phase of planning. What instructional approaches will be used to achieve curricular ends? These approaches will in part be determined by the methodological repertoires of individual teachers. They will depend in part on the students' familiarity with instructional strategies that require their active participation. They also will depend on the cognitive complexity of the curricular goals, and on the needs of students at discrete points in time, needs themselves ascertained through inquiry and evaluation techniques.

"Who are my students?" All teachers, in one way or another, inquire into the characteristics of their students. They ask: What characteristics and abilities does this student have that bear on the learning objectives for which teacher and student are jointly responsible? What are the student's social and familial contexts that bear on school performance?

"What do these children know now?" Teachers, of course, generally assume that children's previous instruction (whether their own or others') has been successful. When such assumptions are invalid, however, the negative implications for instructional success are clear. All effective teachers, therefore, in one way or another assess children directly to learn "where they are." Such information is invaluable in curricular planning. To the extent that learning is sequential or cumulative, unknown or inadvertent gaps can prove crippling to a child's subsequent performance.

"How shall I assess students' learning for which I am responsible?" The teacher has the duty to measure students' performance against the goals of instruction. Choosing and/or designing and developing the appropriate instruments to do this entails inquiry.

"Is failure to learn the students' responsibility or mine?" Teachers are not only obliged to assess the performance of their students. As professionals they are obliged to assess their own performance. Teachers can utilize the performance of their students to form reasonable hypotheses about the effectiveness of their own instruction. Well-designed tests, for example, can be used to identify items on which student performance is so uniformly bad as to point to shortcomings in teaching rather than in individual students. The evaluation of student performance, thus, is a type of teacher inquiry aimed at individual assessment, quality control, and continuing professional development.

Curriculum Planning and Design. "What's going on here?" Teachers may encounter disruptions in their classes or school. They may encounter conflict among themselves or among practitioners and parents, or community representatives. What is actually happening in such situations is not always apparent. In such circumstances, teachers will seek answers through strategies that draw on their perceptiveness, ability to empathize, shrewdness, political skill, or sensitivity. Such inquiries are often complicated by the need to act quickly. The ability to assess constructively what is going on and to respond rapidly and professionally is an important type of teacher inquiry.

"How can we solve this problem?" It makes little difference what kind of problem is to be solved. When the problem is approached in the fashion suggested by the question, an inquiry process has begun. The inquiry may go no further than two people agreeing on an immediate course of action. On the other hand, the inquiry may come to involve an entire instructional or curricular team or school staff (for example, finding more effective ways to communicate with pupils' parents). It may go beyond the school to the district (for example, addressing racial isolation, developing local school councils, or considering new candidates for alternative schools). In such cases, the activities undertaken in response to the problem are likely to be much more complex to manage than the ones undertaken in response to a more localized teacher concern. These activities are inquiry processes nonetheless.

For an excellent and moving account of teachers as inquirers see Eleanor Duckworth (1986), who provides an engaging illustration of how teachers need continuously to learn in order to teach. Sharon Feiman Nemser makes a similar point when she writes approvingly of a veteran teacher for whom "learning is part of the job of teaching" (Nemser, 1983, p. 150).

Implications of Teacher Inquiry for School Organization

Redefining the teaching role so that it is informed by specialized knowledge entails major departures from the ways teachers now use their time and the ways organizational structures where they work are now designed. A new set of roles for teachers and of forms of school organization is necessary if teaching is to become based on the products and processes of inquiry rather than on assumptions about teacher "performance" and custodial functions.

Teacher Role. When teaching is guided by the processes and products of inquiry, the teacher's role will come to focus relatively more on instructional and curricular problem solving and decision making. Without wholly abandoning the role of delivering instruction to students, teachers will spend more time on diagnosing learning needs and developing and prescribing suitable instructional and learning strategies. Teachers will be able to explain the reasons for their decisions as well as the derivations of those reasons from either theoretical knowledge or the requirements of specific schools and children. Being explicit about reasons is important, because they constitute, in effect, hypotheses used when applying specialized knowledge to particular, practical needs; the reexamination of failed hypotheses is the basis of future professional and institutional development.

Character of Professional Interactions. Professional inquiry is rarely an individual enterprise. Excepting the occasional late afternoon committee meetings, however, teachers currently practice their profession in virtual isolation from one another. Schools that pursue an inquiry orientation toward teaching will have to provide opportunities for extensive professional interactions where teachers can work together to identify learning problems (and common aspirations) and devise strategies to address them.

Collaborative effort has many advantages. It will bring many intellectual perspectives to bear on the tasks of teaching and learning pursued in the school. It will bring the professional expertise represented by the group to bear on such matters as instructional practices, evaluation, curriculum design, and communication with parents. It will allow teachers to share what they know about individual children with each other. It will allow them to share responsibility for defining, implementing, and achieving standards of performance, the essence of what it means to be professional (Darling-Hammond, 1987, p. 354).

Classification of Children. Through formal research, student evaluation, and the accumulated wisdom of practice, we know that young people of the same age display great differences in motivation, cultural norms, performance, ability, and other instructionally relevant variables. The existing organizational school structure fails to account for knowledge of these differences well at all. New schools and the instructional possibilities within them will need to accommodate learning differences between children more effectively. But schools cannot do this without rethinking the basis for classifying and grouping children. Neither can they do it without rethinking the parameters around which the curriculum is organized. Also, they cannot do it without providing opportunities for much greater variety of instructional arrangements.

Student Role. As the roles of teachers alter, so must those of students. For example, children of different ages can work together. Alternatively, although sociologists and practitioners alike know of the tremendous power of peers, the structure and climate of today's schools virtually oblige teachers to work against peer influence rather than through it. Peer can mean "same age" as well as "same performance level," or peer can mean any child in a given learning community.

New forms of school organization should be designed to permit and facilitate active learning by students, in contrast to passive participation where teaching is not believed to be going on unless an adult is standing in front of a group of children talking at them! If teachers no longer spend the bulk of their time "performing" for students, students' passivity in contemporary schools will have to give way to more active learning and more responsibility for their own progress. Students will almost certainly need to assume greater responsibility for following teachers' directions, for example, for locating prescribed instructional materials and using them, either individually or with other children.

Uses of Time. Schools organized around teacher inquiry will reflect new assumptions about how teachers should spend their time. Teachers will be expected to spend time planning, designing, and evaluating instructional activities and their students as learners, both in school and out. The time teachers spend in direct instruction will diminish proportionally. Greater portions of teacher time will be spent working with other adult professionals.

Students' use of time will also change. The more dramatic shift will be in students' orientation to time as a parameter of their learning. Rather than have each child spend essentially the same amounts of time on achieving objectives, with resulting variations in their levels of accomplishment, each student will expect to spend the amount of time he or she needs to acquire a common core of learning; in learning-oriented schools, differential grading should give way to the concept of mastery. Teachers and schools should dedicate themselves to continuing diagnosing, designing curriculum, creating materials and experiences, and "delivering" them to students until the students achieve success. Shifting the meaning of evaluation from the summative judgment of children to formative judgments makes evaluation a starting point for educational action rather than the end point.

Quarter-long and year-long terms would almost certainly be replaced by considerably smaller units of time to measure student accomplishment. Albert Shanker, president of the American Federation of Teachers, for example, speaks approvingly of the Boy Scout merit badge approach, an immediate-reward solution that might suggest ways of surmounting the difficulties in the current year-by-year approach to evaluation in which schools now operate. Conceptualizations for a continuous progress approach to curriculum and to student evaluation already exist. They only need to be fully developed and applied. Once the age-grade, Carnegie-unit lockstep is finally abandoned, a far more flexible and discretionary curricular system can be substituted.

Authority Relationships. Any organization requires carefully defined and widely understood authority relationships. Schools are no exception. Changing operating assumptions, however, will require changes in traditional authority relationships.

Schools organized to permit teachers to engage in and act on inquiry, in effect, would locate basic authority for the actions of teachers in specialized theoretical, clinical, and school and child-specific knowledge. Authority relationships in inquiry-based schools, therefore, would have to be much more collegial and far less hierarchical than they are now. Knowledge-based authority structures are collegial rather than bureaucratic. Teams of teachers representing diverse professional functions, specializations, experiences, and perspectives would make major decisions over education. The role of the school administrator would become much more explicitly administrative, facilitating and coordinating educational decisions made by teacher teams.

Physical Facilities. The physical environment of schools will ultimately have to change. Schools will need to provide spaces conducive to teacher deliberations. If not individual teacher offices, then work stations that fulfill the same purposes will need to be provided. The so-called (and ubiquitous) "egg-crate" structures of schools with their individual classrooms will have to yield to buildings with variegated spaces, conducive to less rigid instructional arrangements. Finally, symbolic of the importance of student's responsibility for learning, schools should probably provide permanent work stations for students, which students can, in effect, consider their "offices."

The features discussed above do not exhaust the possibilities of organizational change. For example, it is likely that change will occur in teachers' relationships to parents and the school community. Other changes will take place in the hiring, continuing professional development, and replacement of professional staff, in the technologies of teaching that become possible, and in the costs of the new schools.

Watchwords of the new education structures will in all likelihood be:

Flexibility (for example, of time, curriculum, grouping of children and teachers, instructional approach, and so on)

Individualization of instruction

Consultation (among professionals and with the learner and the learner's family)

Data-based decision making

Mastery and performance orientation

Self-correction

Teacher accountability for student performance

Continuing professional development as part of day-to-day school operations

Collegial professional management

End of age-isolation of learners

Reduction of teacher-presented material; greater utilization of print and electronic media

Differentiation of functions among teachers

These concepts are not new. What will be new is the commitment to act upon them through a systematic effort to redesign the role of teachers and their workplace.

Getting Started

In the 1950s a revolution took place in the airline industry. The purpose of the industry did not change, nor did the principles of flight. What changed was the means of propulsion. It was not a change that occurred as a consequence of gradual improvements in piston and propeller technology; the change involved its replacement by a new technology, the jet engine.

Americans do not seem to be seeking changes in the basic purposes of America's schools. They are seeking greater effectiveness, improved equity, increased sophistication, and greater responsiveness to emergent needs and the increasing complexities of social, economic, technological, and environmental realities. But the advances required cannot be achieved by tinkering with the existing "means of propulsion." Inquiry-dependent roles for teachers will not come about by gradual modification of present organizational structures of schools, any more than gradual improvements would have transformed piston engines into jets. In each case, the concept advanced, whether a new form of aircraft propulsion or the functioning of teachers according to preexisting and locally generated specialized knowledge, constitutes a radical innovation. The purposes remain the same, but the technologies to achieve them represent fundamental departures.

Designing new school organizations to accommodate inquiry-based teaching roles will entail major efforts. Fullscale development projects to this end cannot be small. Furthermore, no single approach can be mandated; the development of competing models must be pursued. The projects will require both design and development phases.

The task goes far beyond drafting more exacting and powerful versions of the modest vignette included in this chapter. Teams of teachers, scholars, and researchers will need to agree upon the specification of educational functions. Those functions will then need to be aggregated, assigned, and orchestrated into a coordinated set of roles for teachers, parents, students, aides, and administrators. The perennial problems of teaching will need to be identified and the techniques and processes of their resolution modeled in terms of the new structural arrangements. Curriculum development specialists will need to devise new systems of curricular organization that introduce much greater flexibility and possibility for internal reinforcement of aims across curricular domains and levels of student achievement. Materials and media resource requirements will need to be derived. Technical arrangements will need to be developed for storing, retrieving, and/or reproducing an optimal range of permanent and disposable educational materials. Architects and engineers will need to turn their attention to the physical space implications of these conceptions, designing new kinds of school facilities as well as retro-fitting the existing stock of school buildings. By any standards one might imagine, these will be huge though necessary tasks.

The work has already begun. Examples include the Coalition of Essential Schools, the National Network for Educational Renewal, the National Education Assocation's new initiative for Learning Laboratory Districts, the American Federation of Teachers' Center for Restructuring, the National Governors' Assocation's Restructuring Schools Project, and the Holmes Group's forthcoming report, *Tomorrow's Schools.*

Some comparisons may help suggest the scale of the effort that will be required for eventual success. First, in the heydey of the first generation of large-scale curriculum development sponsored by the National Science Foundation, each new project commanded multimillion dollar budgets. (The amount expended would be three times as much in late 1980s dollars.) With a few exceptions, each of these projects encompassed a single curricular area and a single age-grade student population.

Second, the annual cost of the operation of the ERIC system, the federal government's main source of information on education research and practices, is about six million dollars.

Resources on a much greater scale than these will ultimately be required each year for ongoing programs to develop the detailed specifications of schools suited to inquiry-based teaching, to model their characteristics and functions, and to test the models at demonstration sites. Where might such resources come from?

There are four possible sources of funds. Federal support on the scale required seems unlikely. Federal budgets are tight, and executive and legislative ambivalence and skepticism about educational research and development is long standing. The possibility of federal appropriations and grants for such activities should not be dismissed out of hand, however. The usefulness of such activities beyond the state level should be apparent. The tantalizing ubiquitousness and scale of federal investments in research and development in many other fields still make the federal government a prime candidate for substantially expanded investments in education, too.

A glimmer of hope for renewed federal attention to the scale of effort needed, as well as possible changed assumptions about the value of educational research and development, may be found in the April hearings of the House Subcommittee on Select Education (Congressman Major W. Owens, chair) and the recent release of the majority staff preliminary report, *Educational Research, Development, and Dissemination: Reclaiming a Vision of the Federal Role for the 1990's and Beyond* (Majority Staff, Subcommittee on Select Education of the Committee on Education and Labor, House of Representatives, 1988).

States have become more likely sources of funds for educational reform than in the past. Many states continue to support reform measures. Because of the growing recognition of the complexity of reform (and also because of competition between state governors), states may be willing to support experiments in school restructuring.

Another possible source of funds is foundations. Several have been willing to consider supporting—and in fact supported—the founding of the Holmes Group and the National Board for Professional Teaching Standards. They may also be responsive to proposals to design and develop schools where the newly qualified, functioning, and certified teachers could work.

The last potential source of funds is the corporate sector. The business community is understanding of the research and development requirements of educational reform. The recent reports of the Committee for Economic Development strongly advocate the need for restructuring schools (Committee for Economic Development, 1985; 1987). Perhaps such positions can be translated into support for targeted development efforts.

Concluding Reflections

As has been shown, an inquiry and decison-making orientation toward teaching entails sweeping changes in the practices of teachers, their working relationships with one another, and the manner in which schools are organized and structured. The school day will look different. The ways children present themselves to schools, how they are organized once they get there, and what they do will be altered.

These proposals will help both improve the effectiveness of teachers and professionalize teaching because they will increase the predictability and performance of teachers. If the profession can achieve the latter goal, one that would be understood and applauded by the public, then teachers will also achieve their personal aspirations. Increased public trust will increase teachers' status, make their profession more attractive to capable candidates, and increase their economic rewards.

There is, moreover, another way of viewing the proposal this chapter advances. Robert Merton introduced the idea of manifest and latent functions (Merton, 1968). The concept led, in education, to the development of a distinction between the explicit purposes and functions of schooling and the so-called hidden curriculum (Shulman, 1986). Much of the concern exhibited by those who have considered hidden curricula has been stimulated by perceived discrepancies between manifest and latent functions in education, especially the extent to which latent functions (for example, bureaucratic organization, emphasis on control of student and teacher behavior, fractionalized and imperfectly articulated curricula, and emphasis on teaching rather than learning) impede achievement of education's manifest aims.

To what extent can educators consciously strive to achieve more constructive agreement between latent and manifest functions, between the explicit and the hidden curricula? Consider the following.

As noted earlier, the case can be made that the basic purpose of schooling in our society is to educate young people in the performance of their many roles and responsibilities as members of a free society. We have created a representative democracy to embody and sustain our freedoms. Serving that democracy is the manifest purpose of schools.

Designing new school structures that operate on the authority of specialized knowledge (including essential knowledge that is generated locally) would almost certainly result in collegial institutions. Collegial institutions bear many striking similarities with small democracies. They operate by consensus. They display respect for individual expertise and need (including an unwillingness to override either summarily). These are characteristics that look much like polities that respect individual rights that might otherwise be infringed by the majority. In collegially organized schools the varied expertise and experience of the professional staff would be tapped regularly to achieve each school's purposes. The collaborative activities of teachers might be rarely seen by students, but the fact that they were taking place would influence the school in a variety of subtle ways. Insofar as a school's operation was fully collegial and collaborative, it would meet the broader democratic aims that guide schooling. The "hidden curriculum" of the school's organizational structure would meet the manifest purpose of the school's aims.

A second aspect of agreement between basic function and larger aim can also be suggested. If our schools are for our democracy, what they are about is learning. Agreement between the surface phenomena and deeper structures of schools could be achieved when the school as an institution itself manifested signs of learning.

The principal reason for gearing teaching roles and school structures to the generation and application of specialized knowledge is to adjust professional behavior to achieve the purposes of education. Indeed, the modification of professional and institutional behavior based on experience and evidence would be one way of describing what was meant by learning by an institution. To the extent that schools adjust their practices based on experience, they demonstrate agreement between their own behavior and the larger learning aims that they seek to serve.

Finally, as we consider the issues that confront free peoples today, it is readily apparent that schools must do everything in their power to develop higher-order cognitive processing skills in their students. Consider, for example, the intellectual, technical, and social demands of contemporary (to say nothing of prospective) technology. The world faces the ever-present threat of nuclear destruction or accident. The interactions between global resource utilization, environmental concerns, and a world population of more than five billion are of huge moment in our lives, our children's, and their children's. The moral, economic, social, and political demands and implications of such concerns

are indicative of the analytically and judgmentally complex matters that face our citizenry.

The credibility of a school staff seeking to instill in young
people a capacity for higher-order thinking if they do not themselves display such capacity in their day-to-day work, will, pre-
dictably, be low. Active teacher involvement in the application
and pursuit of specialized knowledge is one way for schools to
demonstrate agreement between institutional practice and curricular aims.

In concluding with these three observations on the need
for greater functional agreement between the proposed roles and
structures and the basic aims of schools, no oversimplification
is intended. The relationship of manifest to latent functions may
well be a many-leveled phenomenon; the more one examines
latent functions, the more hidden contradictions one may find.
Nevertheless, the idea of deliberately striving to achieve agreement between the overt purposes of schools and the basic roles,
processes, and structures that characterize them suggests one
more set of reasons for grounding teaching and the other practices of schooling on specialized educational knowledge, including the portion of such knowledge that must be generated at
the schools themselves.

References

Carnegie Task Force on Teaching as a Profession. *A Nation
Prepared: Teachers for the 21st Century.* New York: Carnegie
Forum on Education and the Economy, 1986.

Committee for Economic Development. Research and Policy
Committee. *Investing in Our Children: Business and the Public
Schools.* New York: Committee for Economic Development,
1985.

Committee for Economic Development. Research and Policy
Committee. *Children in Need: Investment Strategies for the Educa-
tionally Disadvantaged.* New York: Committee for Economic
Development, 1987.

Darling-Hammond, L. "Schools for Tomorrow's Teachers." In
Teachers College Record, 1987, *88* (3), 354–358.

Duckworth, E. "Teaching as Research." In *Harvard Educational Review,* 1986, *56* (4), 481–495.

Gideonse, H. D. *In Search of More Effective Service: Inquiry as a Guiding Image for Educational Reform in America.* Cincinnati: University of Cincinnati Press, 1983.

Goodlad, J. I. *A Place Called School: Prospects for the Future.* New York: McGraw-Hill, 1984.

The Holmes Group. "Tomorrow's Schools: Design Principles for Professional Development Schools, a Report of the Holmes Group," forthcoming.

The Holmes Group. *Tomorrow's Teachers: A Report from the Holmes Group.* East Lansing, Mich.: The Holmes Group, 1986.

Jackson, P. "Facing Our Ignorance." *Teachers College Record,* 1987, *88* (3), 384–389.

Kerr, D. H. "Teaching Competence and Teacher Education in the United States." In L. S. Shulman and G. Sykes (eds.), *Handbook of Teaching and Policy.* New York: Longman, 1983.

Majority Staff, Subcommittee on Select Education of the Committee on Education and Labor, House of Representatives. *Educational Research, Development, and Dissemination: Reclaiming a Vision of the Federal Role for the 1990's and Beyond.* Washington, D.C.: U.S. Government Printing Office, 1988.

Merton, R. K. *Social Theory and Social Structure.* New York: Free Press, 1968.

National Commission on Excellence in Education. *A Nation at Risk: The Imperative for Educational Reform.* Washington, D.C.: U.S. Government Printing Office, 1983.

National Commission on Excellence in Teacher Education. *A Call for Change in Teacher Education.* Washington, D.C.: American Association of Colleges of Teacher Education, 1985.

Nemser, S. F. "Learning to Teaching." In L. S. Shulman and G. Sykes, (eds.), *Handbook of Teaching and Policy.* New York: Longman, 1983.

Shulman, L. S. "Paradigms and Research Programs in the Study of Teaching: A Contemporary Perspective." In M. C. Wittrock (ed.), *Handbook of Research on Teaching, Third Edition.* New York: Macmillan, 1986.

Wittrock, M. C. (ed.). *Handbook of Research on Teaching, Third Edition.* New York: Macmillan, 1986.

FIVE

Redesigning Teachers' Work

Susan Moore Johnson

When, in 1983, merit pay became the public's remedy of choice for the problems of public education, teachers and their unions resisted doggedly (Olson, 1983). There were, they argued, no adequate measures of teaching competence that would permit administrators to determine accurately whose work deserved higher pay. Promoting competition among colleagues would reduce rather than increase the productivity of schools because teachers would conceal their best ideas and pursue their own interests rather than the general good. Moreover, performance bonuses might perversely reward teachers for success with able students while discouraging efforts with those who progress more slowly. Finally, teachers resented policymakers' efforts to entice them with the prospect of one-time bonuses for a select few when many teachers held second jobs just to meet basic living expenses. By seeking to provide recognition for exemplary teachers, potentially at the expense of many others, the reforms threatened egalitarian norms that the profession supports (Bacharach, Lipsky, and Shedd, 1984; Johnson, 1984c; Murnane and Cohen, 1986; Astuto and Clark, 1985).

This vehement opposition by teachers provoked two kinds of responses from education-watchers. Some concluded that teachers were regressive and self-protective, dodging risk and fearing opportunity (Currence, 1985). Others took from teachers' arguments a better understanding of their schools and of the

125

work of teachers, an understanding that informed subsequent reform initiatives. Policy analysts who were intent on making progress rather than assigning blame began to take seriously the lack of compatibility between early reforms and the world of teachers and schools, and to consider how they themselves might better intervene to address the challenges of schooling (Sirkin, 1986, p. 16). In 1986, the Holmes Group and the Carnegie Task Force on Teaching as a Profession sought to make teachers the allies, even the agents, of reform, and gave currency to a new set of proposals that would engage teachers in making their profession attractive and rewarding.

It is clear that, although the same label — "reform" — has been attached to both recent efforts to improve schooling, the two approaches differ fundamentally. Earlier reformers set out deliberately to transform teachers' norms and practices by imposing mechanisms for behavioral reinforcement and accountability. The blueprint for change was drawn from the tenets of competition followed by industry and rationalization used by bureaucracy (National Commission on Excellence in Education, 1983). Policymakers believed that they, by themselves, could and would reform schools.

Subsequent policy analysts reviewed the failures of this policy and concluded that educational reform must come from within schools rather than be imposed from without, and that teachers must be granted the opportunity, authority and sufficient discretion to effect changes in schools. Some advocates of teacher-driven reform believe that this approach will ultimately enable the United States to regain its competitive advantage in international trade. Other proponents argue that teachers, like any workers, are entitled to professional respect and institutional support. Whatever their logic, advocates of such reform did not presume to transform teachers. Rather, they recommended altering the context of teachers' work so that teachers might effect change. Progress in reform would be ongoing; policies would be informed by teachers' best professional judgment, practices made consistent with the schools' purposes and needs, and the effort as a whole propelled by teachers' energy and commitment.

This second approach to school reform would seem to be more sensible than the first, but it is also more complex. To say that teachers should assume responsibility for directing their schools is not to say how they should be given that responsibility. There is no specific blueprint for change offered by this reform, only general goals and beliefs that must be translated into individual sets of coherent policies and workable practices. Organizing reform through teachers will undoubtedly yield both successes and failures, and similar initiatives may work in one district but fail in another because of differences between local contexts, approaches, and personnel. In order to increase the prospects for success, it is important for those who advise and participate in such reforms to consider all that is known about schools as educational organizations and the past efforts to improve them. To proceed in ignorance or disregard of these is to ensure repeated failure.

The Character of Schools and Teachers

Because the merit-pay proposal was at such odds with who teachers are and how schools operate, it illustrated forcefully the importance of recognizing the unique character of schools. Schools are human-service organizations where techniques are varied and responsive to individual requirements, rather than factories where procedures are rationalized and predictable (March, 1978, p. 223). The clients of schools are children with varying strengths and needs and not uniform raw materials. Education is a lengthy and complicated process, requiring the interdependence and cooperation of many teachers over many years. No one individual can be assigned the full responsibility, credit, or blame for the outcome of a child's education (Johnson, 1984a). Moreover, there is only a vague consensus about what the goals of schooling should be (March, 1978, p. 223). Finally, although school districts are administered by bureaucracies where relations of dominance and subordination persist, the links between the various units are more akin to slinkies than pistons (Meyer and Rowan, 1978; Weick, 1976). Efforts by higher-level administrators to regulate the priorities of teachers and the practices of schools are likely to lose their force as they work their way through the organization to the classrooms (Berman, McLaughlin, and others, 1977; Elmore, 1983; Boyd, 1987, pp. 92–95). If a reform is to endure and to influence instruction and learning, teachers must become its advocates rather than its adversaries.

Teachers, too, are not what many outside the schools— particularly those in business and politics— have taken them to be. First, their interests are centered on teaching and its psychic payoffs; teachers teach because they like to teach. Lortie calls the classroom the "cathected forum" (1975, p. 131). Some contend that teachers have adjusted their expectations to schools' notoriously scarce supply of external rewards; others argue that the character of teaching itself, rather than its institutional context, leads teachers to be satisfied by success with their students. Whatever the explanation, teachers have repeatedly been shown to seek the gratitude of students and parents, the esteem of peers, and the respect of the community while eschewing public recognition or prizes that would single out and publicize their individual successes. Although they seek a respectable wage and the status it implies, teachers, in their teaching, are not entrepreneurs in search of opportunities for financial gain. They are rarely enticed by a bonus to be won at a colleague's expense because, ultimately, they must rely on cooperation and support from their peers, even though they teach their students isolated from one another. As a group, teachers are not afraid of being expected to measure up to certain standards, as some have charged; in fact, they perform before exacting critics every day. Rather, polls suggest that teachers would endorse merit pay if it were supported by a fair and reliable assessment system and if it would promote rather than undermine cooperation in the schools (Mac-Now, 1983; Toch, 1986). But since they believe that neither condition can be met, they subscribe to the standard salary scale (Harris, 1986, p. 18).

While in 1984 analysts soon and accurately predicted the demise of the merit-pay reform, it is less certain what the fate of current reforms will be. A closer consideration of three distinct, but related, proposals in this chapter will explore the variety of issues they raise. The first, called differentiated staffing, would

create new roles for teachers permitting them to combine classroom teaching with work in research, curriculum design, and
administration. In some instances, these roles would be incorporated into steps on a career ladder. According to a second
reform, called peer evaluation, teachers, rather than administrators, would assess their colleagues' work and decide who would
be tenured or terminated. A third set of proposals, called collectively school governance, would augment the involvement
of teachers in the governing of schools by granting them greater
participation in, and authority over, school policies and practices.

In considering the prospects of such proposals, we must
examine carefully what they imply for teaching and schools, the
interdependence of school faculties, the primary focus of teachers'
work on the classroom, the egalitarian norms of teachers, and
the importance of the principal's role. Also, we must assess
whether they acknowledge teachers' needs for support in their
work, the limits of evaluation practices, the political character
of local policymaking, and the loose coupling of educational organizations. If they do not, the answer is simple: However inspired, well-intended, and carefully designed the proposed
reforms may seem, they will not work. If they fail, policy analysts
and politicians will probably sigh knowingly over the resistance
of teachers rather than consider the limitations of their own
designs for change.

Differentiated Staffing: Career Ladders

Proponents of differentiated staffing anticipate that it will
reduce some of the stresses thought to be endemic to teaching
as it is currently organized. It is often said, particularly by those
who do not teach, that teaching is repetitive and stagnating.
One veteran teacher observed, "Our task is horizontal. We do
it over and over and over" (Regue, 1986). Researchers have
reckoned that the cost of working unremittingly with children
and being isolated from peers is high (Little, 1982; Rosenholtz,
1984). Not only are assignments said to be unvaried and numbing, but teaching is criticized for giving no opportunities for advancement. To move up, a teacher must move out. In 1975,

Lortie noted that the "unstaged careers" of teachers (p. 99) deprive them of "cycles of effort, attainment, and renewed ambition" and the prospect of "major status gains" in the classroom (p. 99). In 1986, the Holmes Group lamented education's "flat career pattern, roundly condemned as teaching's 'careerlessness'" (The Holmes Group, 1986, pp. 31–32).

Proposals for differentiated staffing have many purposes. They are intended to vary the character of teachers' work by supplementing classroom teaching with related responsibilities for research, organization of curriculum, or administration. Such proposals for job diversification resemble those for job redesign in the private sector (Hackman and Oldham, 1980), which responded to Argyris's contention that individuals are more productive when their jobs are challenging and take full advantage of their skills and potential (1957). Teaching as currently practiced, some contend, is not challenging, varied, or rewarding enough.

Some advocates also expect that differentiated staffing will extend the expertise and wisdom of teachers into other parts of the school organization, complicating a value system that is increasingly driven by norms of accountability, efficiency, and productivity. Finally, when differentiated roles are incorporated into steps on a career ladder — for example, in master teacher and career professional teacher programs — differentiated staffing promises a career with publicly acknowledged and financially rewarded advancement.

Unlike the evidence on merit pay, the historical and empirical evidence on differentiated staffing is mixed. Freiberg, who had studied differentiated staffing plans during the 1970s, recently concluded: "If continuity is the measure of a new idea's success, then this innovation registered more failure than progress" (Freiberg, 1984/1985, pp. 16–17). A career-ladder plan in Temple City, California, reputedly "the most cited program in the literature of the 70's," closely resembled those of many current proposals. It "had four steps from associate to master teacher and provided earnings up to $25,000 a year in 1969 dollars." Freiberg concluded that the plan ultimately failed because of unanticipated costs, teacher opposition, insufficient evaluations, and dissension. Notably, the program eventually defeated its own purpose by losing its potency as an incentive because it benefited only a select few.

In 1972, Edelfelt argued that differentiated staffing carried with it enormous organizational demands. He found that initiatives to differentiate staff failed to redefine the formal roles and relationships of school personnel and that local districts resorted instead to erecting a ladder of status: "The search to identify new teaching roles got shunted aside because it was much easier to identify hierarchical roles" (Edelfelt, 1972, p. 47). Similarly, in 1984, Bacharach, Lipsky, and Shedd criticized career-ladder proposals for being "job" ladders, a "hierarchical ordering of separate jobs, each with distinctly different responsibilities," rather than career ladders that rewarded growing competence in the classroom.

Recently, Malen and Hart (1987) studied the early implementation of career-ladder reforms in Utah and found considerable evidence of what Hackman and Oldham (1980) called the "vanishing effects" phenomenon, in which organizations transform "job redesign innovations into conventional activities" (Hackman and Oldham, 1980). At the district level, they found "the widespread and persistent pattern of short-term, egalitarian distribution of benefits among senior teachers for familiar or routine work" (Malen and Hart, 1987, p. 16). Teachers and principals doubted the long-term stability and educational legitimacy of the innovations. Career ladders offered teachers rotating job assignments rather than guaranteed promotions: "The agreement was that others deserved the chance to do the job." One teacher characterized the career ladder as a "step ladder; you step up and you step down" (p. 17).

One might conclude prematurely from such accounts that efforts to differentiate staff are destined to fail. However, many schools already have differentiated roles for teachers that have endured over time with the strong support of teachers. Such roles are traditional rather than externally created positions, such as department heads in junior and senior high schools and grade-level or team leaders in elementary and middle schools. The holders of these positions are simultaneously responsible for teaching and administration. They attend to both their class-

rooms and collegial concerns, and they have credibility with
teachers as few other administrators do (Johnson, in progress).
They often enjoy higher status than their classroom-bound colleagues, and they usually are paid more. In addition, where
budgets allow, aides supplement teachers' efforts, often carrying out routine tasks that do not require high levels of professional expertise.

In their study of exemplary-teacher evaluation practices
in four local districts (Wise, Darling-Hammond, McLaughlin,
and Bernstein, 1984), Rand researchers found that expert teachers
already were assisting in teacher evaluation and development.
It is important to note, however, that these roles were developed
locally in response to identified needs rather than in response
to state-level incentives or mandates.

What, then, does this mixed evidence imply for current
proposals for differentiated staffing? It suggests that teachers do
not reject by reflex the idea of combining teaching and nonteaching duties or the creation of professional levels within their
ranks. Differentiated staffing may be acceptable to teachers
because it promises to bridge the gap between teaching and
nonteaching roles, to blur the distinctions between teaching and
administration, and to promote understanding between the
classroom and the school office. The permanence of the roles
of department head and team leader may, ironically, be explained by the impermanence of the appointments, which are
often short-term or rotating. Although many department heads
hold their positions permanently, it is always understood that
they may one day return to the classroom full time and that
if they fail in their jobs, they can be relieved of them. Consequently, teachers seem to regard them as colleagues rather than
as bosses, and perhaps, in response, the department heads and
teams leaders learn to be useful and to cope creatively with the
ambiguities of their roles.

Teachers' support for career ladders is less enthusiastic
and is moderated by distrust of evaluation practices and suspi-
cions about administrative patronage. The career ladder with
its hierarchical promotions and pay is a permanent structure;
decisions are irreversible. Teachers fear that unworthy teachers

will be chosen and, in some cases, assigned responsibilities that are ever less useful and more distant from the classroom.

This is not to assert that teachers always oppose permanent rewards that would recognize excellence in teaching, for it is reasonable to introduce permanent rewards for acquired expertise. Teachers would probably support such rewards if it were not for their distrust of the assessment procedures on which they must be based. Most teachers consider current practices of evaluating their work to be inexact and ineffectual, reporting that administrators are unskilled and uncertain, or precipitously judgmental in their decisions (Toch, 1984; Johnson, in progress). Since teachers do not believe that promotional decisions would be based on explicit standards and extended observations by many observers, they can only expect that such decisions will be influenced by favoritism or poor judgment.

It seems likely that, if local districts are to develop evaluation systems that adequately support career ladders, teachers must be active in devising and administering them (Wise, Darling-Hammond, McLaughlin, and Bernstein, 1984). Peer evaluation is the second challenge of the current reforms to be considered here.

Peer Evaluation

Proposals for teacher peer evaluation would remodel the split-level hierarchy of school organizations and reinterpret the egalitarian norms of the teaching profession. Although schools are generally acknowledged to be flat organizations in which teachers and administrators are highly interdependent (Lortie, 1975, p. 200; Duckworth and Carnine, 1987, pp. 459–471), they feature distinctly dominant and subordinate roles. Administrators hire, assign, and assess teachers and reserve for themselves final decisions on transfer and tenure (Elsberg, 1987). By assuming the task of judging their peers, teachers will both abridge administrators' authority and challenge standard expectations of teachers to protect one another.

The current creation of local peer-evaluation plans is taking place against the backdrop of a national effort by the recently

established National Board for Professional Teaching Standards
to grant professional certificates to teachers who demonstrate
"high standards of professional competence" (Olson, 1987).
Under this program, teachers are to be judged by peers on the
basis of comprehensive measures now being developed by researchers at Stanford University (Shulman, 1987). Teachers,
who compose two-thirds of the Board's membership, are increasingly assuming greater responsibility for its policies and
practices.

Although this national initiative has had no direct impact
on local school districts, its well-publicized progress legitimizes
local proposals for peer assessment. Notably, local programs
receiving the greatest attention are ones initiated by teachers
and their unions rather than administrators, and drawn up in
response to local needs rather than external exhortations. Peer
appraisal plans in Toledo (Darling-Hammond, 1984), Rochester, and Cincinnati (Johnson, 1988) suggest that teachers are
willing and able to assume responsibility for policing their
ranks.

Cincinnati's experience is illustrative. Inspired by their
counterparts in Toledo and Rochester, teacher-union officials
in Cincinnati proposed a peer-evaluation plan at the bargaining table in 1985. Although the proposal generated some opposition from teachers and considerable displeasure among
principals, the school board quickly accepted the plan. Despite
many fears, the Peer Assistance Plan achieved early success.
Ten consulting teachers representing the major academic areas
were selected by the Peer Review Panel, a joint committee of
teachers and administrators overseeing the program. The consulting teachers, all of whom were reported to be outstanding
teachers, were each assigned to assist and eventually assess the
work of approximately sixteen novice teachers in each of ten
schools. During the first year of the program, the consulting
teachers recommended that 5% (approximately eight) of the
novice teachers' contracts not be renewed, twice the dismissal
rate that administrators had recommended in other subject areas.

Although many teachers and administrators initially opposed the plan, support grew steadily as its success became evident. The consulting teachers were widely praised for providing

sustained, professional help to fellow teachers in need. Once Cincinnati's teachers were convinced that novice teachers assigned to the assistance plan had received constructive assistance and been granted sufficient time to improve, they supported dismissal of those who did not measure up. Meanwhile, principals came to value the consulting teachers' efforts. A year-end survey documented widespread satisfaction among teachers and principals, and during the second year, consulting teachers were asked to address the cases of experienced teachers whom principals referred to them for help.

The Cincinnati case has several important lessons for those who would promote peer evaluation plans. First, even when such a program has been inspired by the policies of other districts or the rhetoric of state-level politicians, it may be essential to fashion it locally. When teachers embark on unconventional programs, they must be certain that such programs grow out of local needs and are adapted to the legitimate constraints of local history and practice. Second, egalitarian norms do not oblige teachers to protect their peers. Fair treatment is what matters here. Cincinnati teachers were willing to grant their colleagues the authority to make far-reaching career decisions for others once they were reassured that the consulting teachers were skilled and well-intentioned. In general, teachers are troubled by the existence of even a few incompetent peers, but they are also critical of hasty or vindictive administrative decisions to discipline or fire them. Unions, often criticized for protecting incompetent teachers, in fact focus their efforts on guaranteeing due process rather than shielding poor teachers from dismissal. There is evidence that they tacitly support the termination of poor teachers when procedures are proper (Johnson, 1984c, pp. 111–133). Therefore, contrary to conventional expectations, we can conclude that peer evaluation is acceptable to teachers, when the objectives are clear, the process is constructive, and the outcomes improve the quality and status of the teaching ranks.

Third, the experience in Cincinnati suggests that administrators' responses are very important when implementing a peer-evaluation plan. Principals there came to endorse the program and to rely on the assistance it offered them in their work. Despite early concerns that management's rights had been bargained away when school officials in Toledo accepted a peer-evaluation plan, principals there also concluded that peer evaluation was a constructive process that provided services they could not offer (Darling-Hammond, 1984, p. 128). Principals in Rochester also felt threatened initially by the institution of peer evaluation and formally objected to having their authority abridged. It seems clear that during the initial stages of peer evaluation, teachers and administrators must jointly manage the program and, through this process, negotiate the difficulties that will inevitably result in the search for a new division of labor.

Finally, central to the success of the Cincinnati program were the consulting teachers' reputations for being outstanding teachers. Short of having some evaluation system that everyone agrees is equal to the task of assessing educational performance, teachers are most likely to trust the subjective judgments of respected colleagues who remain close to the classroom. However, it is important to recognize that even exemplary teachers may not know how to effectively assist and assess those whose teaching styles, strengths, and weaknesses differ from their own (Little, 1985; Shulman and Colbert, 1987). If teachers are to assume supervisory responsibilities, they either must be trained by others or develop skills in supervision themselves. The consulting teachers in Cincinnati held weekly meetings in which they discussed common problems, conferred about cases, and offered their services as demonstrating teachers. Similar kinds of support are essential for teachers venturing into what has been professionally forbidden territory in order to come to terms with their complex new relationships and responsibilities.

Teachers participating in peer evaluation not only cope with the demands and ambiguities of differentiated roles in schools, but also manage more formal authority than they did as regular classroom teachers. The Carnegie and Holmes proposals referred to earlier in this chapter would also alter the distribution of authority in schools and patterns of school governance. These raise important challenges for those recommending reform.

School Governance

The recent reform reports express a conviction that teachers must exercise greater responsibility for school governance. The Carnegie Task Force on Teaching as a Profession (1986) argues that "school systems based on bureaucratic authority must be replaced by schools in which authority is grounded in the professional roles of teachers" (p. 55). The Holmes Group (1986) contends that educational reformers cannot continue "telling teachers what to do, rather than empowering them to do what is necessary" (p. 61). Yet how teachers will assume new powers and exercise new authority is unclear. In many ways, the challenge to give teachers more power to make decisions on education is the most fundamental and far-reaching reform of all. For, if teachers and administrators change their assumptions about who has authority and how it can be exercised, educational policies and practices will eventually reflect a set of professional values different from those held hitherto.

Although many teachers challenge the legitimacy of the traditional authority structure and some unions seek to change it, administrators continue to be teachers' superiors and have the final say on school practices. It is very important to remember, however, that teachers exercise authority within their classrooms, where they make countless decisions about curriculum, instructional technique, classroom management, and standards of discipline (Lipsky, 1980; Boyd, 1987, p. 88). In some states and school districts, the recent imposition of centralized curricula or mandated testing have compromised teachers' instructional autonomy (McNeil, 1987), but most teachers report that classroom policy—what to teach, how to teach, how to use time, and how to assess progress—remains theirs to determine (Johnson, 1987a, pp. 10–12; Duckworth and Carnine, 1987, p. 459).

Teachers also are frequently active in governing departments or grade-level teams where decisions about course content and sequence and text selections are routinely made. Teachers report that it is in such forums that they exert the greatest influence over policies that extend beyond their classrooms. Because decisions made in departments or teams relate closely teachers' work with students in the classroom, they are very important to teachers whose primary interests are instructional. Also, since such decisions are implemented by those who make them, policy is more likely to correspond to practice, thus justifying teachers' investment of time and energy in making policy and increasing their commitment to their work.

This commitment to collegial decision making is rarely to be found at a level that affects the entire school, despite the fact important decisions are made at that level about such matters as the daily schedule, the responsibilities of specialists, student assignments, discipline, the provision of clerical services, and the allocation of supplies. It is principals who make such decisions, usually with little or no systematic input from staff. Full faculty meetings tend to be empty ceremonies where discussions, if they occur, center on trivial matters and where votes are seldom taken. Faculty senates and principals' cabinets are explicitly advisory and their proceedings are usually of token significance. If teachers exercise formal authority in these school-wide forums, it is because a principal respects their expertise, welcomes their contributions, and responds to their recommendations. Their authority is the result of administrative discretion rather than formal structure. Usually only under very restrictive teacher contracts is a principal obliged to comply with teachers' collective judgments (Johnson, 1984c, pp. 43–44).

While there may be some semblance of participation by teachers in school governance, teachers report having virtually nothing to do with decisions made by the central office or school board (Johnson, in progress). In most districts, policies on curricula and testing, the school calendar, hiring, purchasing, staff assignments, and building maintenance are controlled centrally, but teachers report knowing and caring little about how such decisions are made. Although teachers profess little interest in school policies that originate outside their buildings, either because they are irrelevant or because teachers are denied influential roles in making them, they often resent the effects of those decisions when they affect their schools and classrooms.

Many districts offer teachers the opportunity to serve on

district-wide committees studying such topics as staff development, student services, or curriculum development. Given the limitations of the advisory character of such committees, teachers who have held such roles often conclude that their time has been wasted, and they recount tales of reports unread or recommendations ignored by administrators and school-board members who wanted outcomes different from the ones the teachers presented.

Teachers' roles at the bargaining table during labor negotiations differ markedly from those they assume on such advisory committees, both because the school board is legally bound to bargain in good faith and because the political power of the teachers' union can be mobilized if teachers' concerns are ignored. Moreover, the outcomes of labor negotiations can be enforced by the courts. Agreements about such matters as seniority rules, nonteaching duties, or class size prescribe and limit what administrators must and can do. Consequently, teachers exercise more influence on decision making at the bargaining table than anywhere in the district outside their own classrooms.

Teacher advocates might argue, therefore, that all policy decisions should be addressed through collective bargaining. However, while the formal process of negotiation is effective in setting specific work rules, its limitations must be acknowledged (Johnson, 1987b). First, in most districts, many matters of policy such as curriculum, hiring, and budgeting are protected as prerogatives of management and, therefore, are simply not subject to negotiation. Second, while formal bargaining is effective for specifying narrow work rules, it is impractical for resolving complex problems, defining new programs, or making ongoing programmatic decisions. Finally, although much can be accomplished by teachers through collective bargaining, it is a hierarchical, adversarial process in which management usually has the final say. In most settings, unionized teachers are not recognized as the professional equals of administrators, and the process of negotiations typically accentuates their subordinate status.

A review of decision making in the schools reveals that, despite gestures in many school districts toward including teachers in making decisions, traditional patterns of dominance and subordination persist. Administrators retain the authority to define school policy and to prescribe school practice. Schools where different norms and expectations prevail, where teachers are regarded as experts who should be consulted about educational policy, are the exception. In such schools, teachers debate and decide on such matters as whether their school should become a magnet school, how the faculty might better engage parents in their children's schooling, or how school space or instructional time might be better allocated. When decisions of consequence are truly in the hands of the faculty, it is virtually always because principals have chosen to put them there and teachers have been confident and able enough to accept them (Foster, 1984, p. 12).

Because of the complex character of most school districts and the many individuals and constituencies involved in any decision of consequence, policies are likely to result from political bartering rather than rational decision making. This unpredictable path of policymaking has left many teachers deeply cynical about the prospects for their having influence in school governance. They, themselves, often resort to politics — petitioning the principal, having a word with the assistant superintendent, calling on a sympathetic board member — if they care about an issue, and many teachers report that they can influence policy better informally than formally. But they often do their politicking as individuals rather than as organized groups, thereby leading them to conclude that teachers as a group have little political influence (Johnson, in progress).

Given the generally small and marginal role in school governance that teachers typically exercise, what changes are necessary to make them more influential? First, it appears that greater formal authority must be granted through collective bargaining or through changes in school-board policy to those who hold positions such as lead teacher or to groups such as faculty senates that have, until now, rarely had more than advisory status. As advisors, teachers are beholden to administrators. In schools where principals grant teachers decision making authority, they appear to take it on willingly. One might expect, therefore, that teachers' roles in school governance will increase if their authority to make at least some decisions is guaranteed.

Although it is essential that teachers be granted some measure of formal authority, the wholesale transfer of responsibility for school governance to them seems unwarranted and unwise. The Carnegie Task Force provoked vehement opposition by suggesting that schools might be governed by executive committees of lead teachers (Shanker, 1986; Thompson, 1986). Aside from the political costs of suggesting that school administrators are dispensable, there is considerable evidence to support the importance of their roles. Principals have been shown repeatedly to be central to school success (Cohen, 1987, p. 403), and, although there are many poor principals who interfere with good teaching or are interested only in noninstructional matters, some principals are exemplary. The problem is not that their role is vestigial, but that it is too complicated; no single individual can do all that it requires. One solution may be to draw teachers into the task of managing schools, but this must be done cautiously so that both the classroom and the school receive the attention and advocacy they deserve. It seems likely that, even where schools are restructured, most teachers will continue to focus on the classroom while principals remain attentive to the schools' larger purposes, holding a school-wide perspective that no single teacher can have.

Furthermore, teachers' experience in governance is limited, and their skills are unpracticed. It is not at all apparent that many teachers seek to run their schools (Little, 1988). However, given their concern for policies that affect their teaching, it makes sense to limit and specify initially what teachers will decide—the format of a new schedule, the assignment of classroom aides, the allocations of an instructional budget, or hiring recommendations for new staff. What seems most important is that they be granted the authority to make some important decisions.

School districts also might create joint committees of administrators and teachers to set district policy and oversee practice on such matters as staff assignment, evaluations, or curriculum. On such committees, teachers would hold equal powers with administrators rather than either serve as their advisors or make all decisions on their own. Recently, such joint committees were established by union and school officials in Cincinnati to oversee the assignment of surplus teachers to understaffed schools, to administer their peer assistance plan, and to direct an experimental program in school improvement (Johnson, 1988).

Because most teachers remain skeptical about prospects for influencing district-wide policies and because their chief care is about decisions made within their schools, decentralizing school management would probably augment the role of teachers in school governance (Guthrie, 1986, pp. 305–309). Many school districts, particularly large urban ones, are highly centralized organizations that regulate and standardize school practice. By demanding conformity, school officials limit the discretion of teachers and principals to make their schools work well (McNeil, 1987, pp. 102–103). For example, one urban superintendent recently announced that he will require a single minimal reading series to be used in all schools and grades. Another superintendent prescribed a daily timetable for elementary reading and mathematics instruction. With each such centrally mandated prescription, the scope of issues to be addressed by a school's staff shrinks. Teachers are expected to comply with regulations rather than to tailor their programs and practices to the needs of their students and the strengths of their staffs.

Decentralizing school management would probably promote more governance of schools by teachers in two ways. First, it would enable teachers to address broad issues on education within a context that is meaningful to them. Currently, teachers perceive their professional interests to lie with their colleagues at school rather than at the district office and are inclined to commit time and energy to matters close to their daily concerns. Second, a decentralized governance structure provides greater assurance to teachers that problems presented to them are real rather than contrived, and that participation by teachers will not be simply ceremonial. If binding decisions about policy and practice are made at the school level, teachers can be assured that their efforts will make a difference; that their decisions will stick. If policymaking remains centralized, teachers will probably discount promises that they will have influence on policy and will believe that central office administrators control policy decisions.

As teachers' formal powers are augmented and administrators' authority is abridged, the role of the principal will be redefined. Where teachers assume administrative authority and exercise the power to enforce decisions, principals will have to provide informal rather than formal leadership. However, increasing teachers' authority in matters of policy does not mean that principals will become functionaries executing teachers' plans. As teachers assume decision-making roles, principals to be effective will need to help teachers recognize and value their own expertise, to engage teachers in broader responsibilities, and to orchestrate their work as colleagues rather than as subordinates.

Many principals are not prepared for such roles, having been expected in recent years to be aggressive and efficient school managers (Barth, 1988). However, unless principals accept shared leadership and collegial policymaking with teachers as legitimate goals, they are likely to interpret all teacher activity as encroachment and all faculty successes as failures of their own, to clutch their formal powers more tightly, and to assert their superior positions more forcefully.

Teachers, too, as participants in decision making, must adopt new attitudes. Teachers are inclined to withdraw from policymaking in their schools; they have implicitly negotiated a treaty that protects their classroom autonomy in exchange for knowing their place and leaving school management to administrators. But if collegial decision making is to thrive, interaction between teachers and administrators must be ongoing and teachers must be willing to leave the protection of their classrooms. A solitary individual or two cannot be expected to redirect a school that is set in its ways; a certain substantial number of able teachers will have to emerge who, together with the principal, can initiate, sustain, and institutionalize new school norms and practices.

Time and Money

Reform proposals raise two additional, practical issues
that may determine the outcomes of the recent reform movement. These are time and money. In fact, because the provision of adequate funds and flexible time is so essential for the
success of educational reform, these issues probably should have
been addressed at the start of this discussion. For if local districts
expect that they can reform school organization with their current funding and time allocations, they probably will fail. It is
futile to devise sophisticated roles for teachers and new authority
structures for schools if sufficient time and money are not present to support their implementation and institutionalization.

Time presents two challenges for school reform. First, in
most schools, time is rigidly structured. Second, there simply
is not enough of it. It is no surprise that differentiated roles for
teachers are most frequently found in secondary schools, where
blocked schedules permit staff to split their assignments between
teaching and nonteaching duties. Teachers in elementary schools,
with their self-contained classrooms, usually find it hard to ensure adequate instruction when they leave their classes to work
on research, curriculum development, or administration. Instructional arrangements that accommodate job sharing, teacher-
teaming, or departmentalization at the elementary level would
permit teachers to move confidently between their classrooms
and the larger school. However, blocking the school day as in
secondary school for elementary students does not win easy support. Alternatively, teachers might assume nonteaching assignments for a year or two, returning to the classroom at their
conclusion. However, local districts are seldom eager to cope
with the staffing complications such arrangements would entail. If local districts are to implement new roles for teachers
successfully, they must be open to reorganizing instructional
time and assignment of staff.

More important than the organization of time is the shortage of time. In recent years, fiscal constraints have forced local
districts to eliminate funds from their budgets that once supported
generous staffing allocations, support personnel, or time for

teachers to pursue special assignments. Many local districts simply have no budgeted time available to support the development and maintenance of new programs. Currently, teachers' days and nights are replete with obligations. If teachers are to assume major roles in peer evaluation or school governance, they must have time to carry out these responsibilities. School officials must regard the new duties of teachers as essential components of their regular assignments rather than as voluntary extras. If the school districts value this work and expect it to continue, they must allocate paid time to have it done.

It is worth noting that schools seldom make the best use of teachers' time and expertise. Many teachers reluctantly spend as much as an hour each day completing clerical tasks or serving in custodial roles — supervising recess grounds, study halls, bathrooms, and cafeterias — when the time might be better spent observing classes, developing curriculum, or deciding school policy. It should be possible for all teachers' jobs to include some responsibility for policymaking, much as they are now expected to monitor study halls or cover the classes of absent teachers. In independent schools, which provide an alternative model on this issue, teachers routinely serve on committees that oversee admissions, curricula, or student services. Incorporating responsibilities for school governance into teachers' daily schedules would require a careful redistribution of assignments between teachers and administrators. Most teachers would probably not accept such duties if they were simply added to their current ones, but many might welcome a meaningful substitute for the tiresome, demeaning tasks of monitoring halls or playgrounds.

The provision of released time would put new demands on school budgets. The expense of staffing the assignment of one consulting teacher per school in a district of modest size would probably approach $250,000. The costs of promotional ladders would be considerably more. Although many teachers may accept released time as an even trade for classroom teaching, those who assume responsibilities once assigned to administrators may expect to be paid more for their nonteaching work, even if they do not consider that work to be more valuable than teaching.

Compensating teachers with released time or supplementary pay will be costly if local districts maintain current administrative staffing levels. However, an analysis of administrative work may reveal that teachers' contributions to administration reduce the requirements for other administrators, making such reforms financially feasible. Admittedly, redefining jobs and redistributing money would provoke discontent among administrators, but for school districts with limited resources, this may be the only way to ensure that reforms become institutionalized.

Finally, school districts must not expect to cover new program expenses with the standard salary budget. In fact, reforms are not likely to gain faculty acceptance unless teachers' wages are sufficient and competitive with those of other districts. Murnane and Cohen (1986) found that the merit-pay reform survived only in districts that already offered high wages, where bonuses were truly bonuses. If teachers resent their current wages, it seems unlikely they will be ready to commit themselves to new efforts, paid or unpaid.

Conclusion

If policymakers unilaterally impose current reform proposals on teachers and schools, they will most certainly fail. By their very nature, these programs require teachers' endorsement and accommodation. Teachers must be willing to aspire to new roles, to welcome peer evaluation, and to seize new responsibilities for governance. If the reforms are introduced in ways that threaten egalitarian norms, that discount the role of the principal, that draw teachers away from teaching, that offer participation without authority, or that undermine the cooperation of school staffs, they will probably fail. Also, if school officials do not provide the necessary time and money to support the reforms they cannot succeed.

Admittedly, the current reforms provide good ideas. If adopted in response to legitimate local needs and implemented in responsible ways, they might well make schools better organizations for teaching and learning. But they will serve no better than the status quo if they compromise collegiality, disrupt instruction, or undermine morale. If they fail, many outside the schools will undoubtedly charge that teachers have failed — that the policy is sensible, but teachers have not done it justice. However, to implement flawed policies — policies that disregard the essential aims and norms of schooling — is to jeopardize what currently works in schools.

This is not to suggest that schools should not or cannot change, but rather that change should be consistent with schools as human service organizations that depend on cooperation and interdependence among staff members. Differentiated staffing can open new opportunities to teachers and extend their expertise and values into the larger organization. Teacher-peer evaluation can offer better supervisory assistance and yield a stronger teaching staff. Expanded roles for teachers in school governance can lead to schools that emphasize instructional over managerial values. But if a local district stresses the hierarchical components of its career ladder, appoints consulting teachers who can make hard decisions but not give good help, or expects teachers to govern without authority, it will have few successes to report.

The new definitions of teachers' professional roles cannot be decided or imposed by those outside shools. They must emerge from the schools, but they will not emerge fully formed nor will they be consistent between districts. Rather, this set of school reforms can be expected to evolve over time and to adapt to local requirements as teachers and school officials explore alternative approaches, experiment with new forms of behavior, and negotiate a new order.

One of the most sobering things about staffing reforms such as these is that they require many supportive conditions to ensure their successful implementation. There must be sufficient leadership among teachers and administrators to embark on new ventures. The teachers' unions must endorse labor-management cooperation. Administrators must accept an abridgement of their authority. School staffs must be ready and able to change, with teachers and principals trusting each others' good intentions. The school board and community must support the initiatives with confidence and with funding. And everyone must have the patience for the inevitable setbacks. All of these conditions must be aligned like stars in the astrological heavens simply to make reform possible. If they are not, we cannot claim to have given the reforms or the teachers a fair chance.

References

Argyris, C. *Personality and Organization*. New York: Harper, 1957.

Astuto, T. A., and Clark, D. "Merit Pay for Teachers, An Analysis of State Policy Options." Educational Policy Series #1. Bloomington, Ind.: Indiana University School of Education, 1985.

Bacharach, S. B., Lipsky, D. B., and Shedd, J. B. *Paying for Better Teaching: Merit Pay and Its Alternatives*. Ithaca, N.Y.: Organizational Analysis and Practice, 1984.

Barth, R. S. "The School as a Community of Leaders." In A. Lieberman (ed.), *Building a Professional Culture in Schools*. New York: Teachers College Press, 1988.

Berman, P., McLaughlin, M., and others. *Federal Programs Supporting Educational Change, Vol. VII: Factors Affecting Implementation and Continuation*. Santa Monica, Calif.: Rand, 1977.

Boyd, W. L. "Public Education's Last Hurrah? Schizophrenia, Amnesia, and Ignorance in School Politics." *Educational Evaluation and Policy Analysis*, 1987, *9* (2), 85–100.

Carnegie Task Force on Teaching as a Profession. *A Nation Prepared: Teachers for the 21st Century*. New York: Carnegie Forum on Education and the Economy, 1986.

Cohen, M. "Improving School Effectiveness: Lessons from Research." In V. Richardson-Koehler (ed.), *Educators' Handbook: A Research Perspective*. New York: Longman, 1987.

Currence, C. "Politicians, Teachers in Two States Wrangle Over Incentive Plans." *Education Week*, 1985, *4* (35), 1.

Darling-Hammond, L. "The Toledo (Ohio) Public School Intern and Intervention Program." In A. E. Wise, L. Darling-Hammond, M. W. McLaughlin, and H. T. Bernstein (eds.), *Case Studies for Teacher Evaluation: A Study of Effective Practices*. Santa Monica, Calif.: Rand, 1984.

Duckworth, K., and Carnine, D. "The Quality of Teacher-Principal Relationships." In V. Richardson-Koehler (ed.), *Educators' Handbook: A Research Perspective*. New York: Longman, 1987.

Edelfelt, R. A. "Differentiated Staffing: Where Are We?" *National Elementary Principal,* 1972, *52* (4).

Elmore, R. F. "Complexity and Control: What Legislators and Administrators Can Do About Implementing Public Policy." In L. S. Shulman and G. Sykes (eds.), *Handbook of Teaching and Policy.* New York: Longman, 1983.

Elsberg, T. "Accountable Leadership Depends on Principal." *Education Week,* 1987, *6* (39), 44,32.

Foster, S. G. "Effective Principals Found to Work More Hours, Favor Cooperation." *Education Week,* 1984, *3* (29), 12.

Freiberg, H. J. "Master Teacher Programs: Lessons from the Past." *Educational Leadership,* 1984/1985, 16–17.

Guthrie, J. W. "School-Based Management: The Next Needed Education Reform." *Phi Delta Kappan,* 1986, *68,* (4), 305–309.

Hackman, J. R., and Oldham, G. R. *Work Redesign.* Reading, Mass.: Addison-Wesley, 1980.

Harris, L. *The Metropolitan Life Survey of the American Teacher.* New York: Metropolitan Life Insurance, 1986.

Hatry, H. P. and Greiner, J. M. *Issues in Teacher Incentive Plans.* Washington, D.C.: Urban Institute, 1984.

The Holmes Group. *Tomorrow's Teachers: A Report of the Holmes Group.* East Lansing, Mich.: The Holmes Group, 1986.

Johnson, S. M. "Merit Pay for Teachers: A Poor Prescription for Reform." *Harvard Educational Review,* 1984a, *54* (2).

Johnson, S. M. *The Pros and Cons of Merit Pay.* Fastback #203. Bloomington, Ind.: Phi Delta Kappa, 1984b.

Johnson, S. M. *Teacher Unions in Schools.* Philadelphia, Pa.: Temple University Press, 1984c.

Johnson, S. M. "Teachers as Decisionmakers." Discussion paper prepared for the National Education Association, 1987a.

Johnson, S. M. "Can Schools Be Reformed at the Bargaining Table?" *Teacher College Record,* 1987b, *89* (2), 269–280.

Johnson, S. M. "Pursuing Professional Reform in Cincinnati." *Phi Delta Kappan,* 1988, *69* (10), 746–751.

Johnson, S. M. "Teachers at Work" (in progress).

Johnson, S. M., and Nelson, N. C. W. "Teaching Reform in an Active Voice." *Phi Delta Kappan,* 1987 *68* (8), 591–598.

Lipsitz, J. *Successful Schools for Young Adolescents.* New Brunswick, N.J.: Transaction Press, 1983.

Lipsky, M. *Street-Level Bureaucracy.* New York: Russell Sage Foundation, 1980.

Little, J. W. "Norms of Collegiality and Experimentation: Workplace Conditions of School Success." *American Education Research Journal,* 1982, *19,* 325–340.

Little, J. W. "Teachers as Teacher Advisors: The Delicacy of Collegial Leadership." *Educational Leadership,* 1985, *43* (3), 34–36.

Little, J. W. "Assessing the Prospects for Teacher Leadership." In A. Lieberman (ed.), *Building a Professional Culture in Schools.* New York: Teachers College Press, 1988.

Lortie, D. C. *Schoolteacher: A Sociological Study.* Chicago: University of Chicago Press, 1975.

McNeil, L. M. "Exit, Voice, and Community: Magnet Teachers' Responses to Standardization." *Educational Policy,* 1987, *1* (1), 93–113.

MacNow, G. "Michigan Teachers Oppose Merit Pay, Urge Reform." *Education Week,* 1983, *3* (5) 1, 17.

Malen, B., and Hart, A. W. "Career Ladder Reform: A Multi-Level Analysis of Initial Efforts." *Educational Evaluation and Policy Analysis,* 1987, *9* (1), 9–23.

March, J. "American Public School Administration: A Short Analysis." *School Review,* 1978, *86,* 217–250.

Meyer, J. W., and Rowan, B. "The Structure of Educational Organizations." In M. W. Meyer and Associates, *Environments and Organizations.* San Francisco, Calif.: Jossey-Bass, 1978.

Murnane, R. J., and Cohen, D. K. "The Employment Relationship: Lessons from an Analysis of Merit Pay for Public School Teachers." *Harvard Educational Review,* 1986, *56* (1), 1–17.

National Commission on Excellence in Education. *A Nation at Risk: The Imperative for Educational Reform.* Washington, D.C.: U.S. Printing Office, 1983.

Olson, L. "Pioneering State Teacher-Incentive Plans in Florida, Tennessee Still Under Attack." *Education Week,* 1983, *5* (18) 1, 24.

Olson, L. "Certification Panel Head Selected." *Education Week,* 1987, *7* (5) 6.

Regue, J. "After 31 Years in the Classroom, Thoughts of Getting Out, Starting Over." *Education Week,* 1986, *5* (25), 17.

Rosenholtz, S. J. "Effective Schools: Interpreting the Evidence." *American Journal of Education,* 1984, *93* (3), 352–388.

Rosenholtz, S. J. "Political Myths About Education Reform: Lessons from Research on Teaching." *Phi Delta Kappan,* 1985, *66* (5), 349–355.

Shanker, A. "A Better Use of Human Resources." *Education Week,* 1986, *5* (39), 20.

Shulman, J. H. and Colbert, J. A. *The Mentor Teacher Casebook.* San Francisco: Far West Laboratory, 1987.

Shulman, L. S. "Knowledge and Teaching: Foundations of the New Reform." *Harvard Educational Review,* 1987, *57* (1), 1–21.

Sirkin, J. R. "Governors Appear Set to Propose School Reforms." *Education Week,* 1986, *5* (25) 1,16.

Thompson, S. D. "Strengthen, Don't Diffuse, School Leadership." *Education Week,* 1986, *5* (36), 28.

Toch, T. "Survey Indicates Teacher Support for Merit Pay." *Education Week,* 1984, *2* (42), 1, 12.

Weick, K. E. "Educational Organizations as Loosely Coupled Systems." *Administrative Science Quarterly,* 1976, *21,* 11–19.

Wise, A. E., Darling-Hammond, L., McLaughlin, M. W., and Bernstein, H. T. *Teacher Evaluation: A Study of Effective Practices.* Santa Monica, Calif.: Rand, 1984.

❋ SIX

Rethinking
School Governance

Mary Anne Raywid

A call for restructuring is a call for fundamental and pervasive change. School "restructuralists" share the belief that piecemeal supplements, or peripheral modifications that leave most school practices unaffected, are likely to prove futile. Nothing short of fundamental change affecting the practices of everyone within a school will suffice. Among those who want to restructure schools, a substantial group is convinced that ultimately what must be changed is the ways schools are governed; otherwise the modifications essential to substantial improvement simply cannot and will not occur. According to this group, the relationship of schools to both their external and internal environments is so fundamentally flawed that change in how they are governed is essential for significant school improvement of any sort — curricular, instructional, and so on.

According to this group, schools are no longer in accord with their political environments — that is, with the desires of the parents and the communities they presumably serve and with the political system whose procedural principles public institutions are obligated to reflect. Nor, say proponents of this conception of restructuring, do school conditions and practices accord with the schools' internal environment as defined by the nature and needs of the human beings who populate schools — teachers and administrators as well as students.

Calls for restructuring are not currently limited to schools, of course. They draw inspiration and support from other sources. The second half of the twentieth century has seen repeated challenges to large-scale organizations of all sorts. It has been a period of increasing public skepticism about major societal institutions and of growing lack of confidence in large organizations. Pollsters have repeatedly publicized the scope of such disaffection (Harris, 1986). The public's criticism has been based on diverse concerns. One crucial set of criticisms has explicitly addressed the matter of control and governance.

The issue of maintaining democratic authority and responsibility in a society of increasing technical expertise has been a major challenge of contemporary life. In what desirable ways may experts limit political control, and how may the experts then be controlled? How can we assure quality control and appropriate mechanisms of accountability in a large-scale enterprise, without simultaneously reducing the effectiveness of the units controlled? Another particularly thorny issue for public schools has been the desirability both of including all relevant parties in decision making and of keeping the scale of decision making manageable. The problem of scale is relatively recent, but it recurs in school discussions, as the list of negatives associated with bigness lengthens and the number of justifications for large schools diminishes.

It is not surprising that one aspect of the critique of large-scale institutions has been a broad challenge to bureaucracy, the century's dominant mode of organizing large enterprises. Over the past three decades, bureaucracy has been criticized as inefficient and ineffective (the two primary grounds for its alleged superiority specifically being efficiency and effectiveness), as inhumane, unresponsive to its clients or to the rest of the public, dominated almost entirely by technological and territorial imperatives, largely out of control, and blind and impervious to the need for change. Such criticisms have been brought to bear on virtually all bureaucratically structured organizations in recent years — corporations, the church, the army, the postal service, as well as the schools.

Many of those calling for the restructuring of school governance attribute an assortment of ills to the present arrangements within education for bureaucratic control. Such arrangements are thought to be linked to (1) an unacceptable conception of the school's mission, (2) a stultifying social order within the school, (3) a counterproductive distribution of roles and functions among the players — that is, students, teachers, specialists, administrators, parents — and (4) an inappropriate decision-making structure. We will thus be concerned, as we look at proposals for restructuring school governance, to explore the ramifications of present and proposed solutions for these four fundamental concerns.

First, however, an identification of the nature and genesis of the major strategies for restructuring schools may be helpful. Widespread demand for restructuring is relatively recent and is often characterized as a second phase of the excellence movement of the 1980s (Pipho, 1986). In the early 1980s discontent with school quality generated strong pressures for improvement, but reactions and results following state-mandated attempts to change schools, as well as research done independently, have lent strong support to the idea that successful change must originate and be implemented at the school level, not outside the schools. Thus officials have sought to stimulate school-based improvement projects, and such school improvement programs have burgeoned throughout the United States.

Many such programs have sought to cultivate the particular traits identified by the effective schools literature (Purkey, Rutter, and Newmann, 1986–1987). The programs have thus attempted to improve organizational climate, build a more coherent sense of mission, generate staff collaboration, and so on. A study of four thousand high school improvement programs confirmed that there are major difficulties with self-transformation, which is what such changes entail. The researchers concluded that a large number of current high school improvement efforts "may be largely cosmetic" — "a superficial and largely symbolic response to the prescriptions . . . on school improvement" (Purkey, Rutter, and Newmann, 1986–1987, pp. 70, 65). In over half the schools where principals report improvement programs under way, more than half the teachers are evidently not aware of their existence. Not surprisingly, then, the researchers found that schools reporting improvement programs differed little from schools without them as regards the very characteristics such programs seek to cultivate — good organizational climate, staff collaboration, goal consensus, staff participation in decision making, and so on.

There are a few very notable exceptions, however, which have received wide publicity. In Hammond, Indiana, for instance, a school improvement effort enables a team operating at each school to tackle whatever dimensions of the school's practice it finds need changing. Individual schools have rearranged the schedule for the school day, changed homework policy, established a teacher-mentor program, and set up peer evaluation of teachers. As such ventures clearly suggest, however, these schools have been exempted from much external constraint and delegated considerable power; within them, authority is now exercised by teams, not individuals. In Hammond, the school improvement process has become a school-based mangement arrangement, the crucial elements of which are the additional authority transferred to the school and the sharing of that new power among school constituents (teachers, administrators, community representatives). Hammond schools are no longer schools trying to improve themselves within externally imposed limitations and internally traditional stratifications: their governance and control arrangements have changed dramatically (Casner-Lotto, 1988; McPike, 1987). There is evidence suggesting that only when control arrangements change in this way — so that the school is less restricted in its decision making and the additional authority is shared — is substantial improvement likely (Chubb, 1988).

To date, restructuralists have elaborated just two broad strategies for accomplishing changes in authority and governance patterns. One is to return authority to the school and democratize its exercise. The other strategy looks instead to more direct individual empowerment by giving teachers the right to choose or develop the programs with which they are associated, and families the right to select the school that best suits them and their children. To date, these are the only proposals for implementing the widely voiced demand to "restructure" public schools in the interests of modifying present governance patterns that have achieved much credibility. The first is known as *school-based* or *site management,* the second is the *schools of choice* concept. The two ideas are not incompatible, and indeed share a number of features. They do, however, rest on somewhat different diagnoses of current school ills and hence recommend some differences in treatment.

Site management is a proposal to decentralize and, at least to this extent, debureaucratize school control (Guthrie, 1986; Lindelow, 1981). For some but not all of its advocates, it is also a proposal for shared decision making within the school (Cairns, Molberg, and Zander, 1983). And for some, but again not all, advocates, it is a proposal for increasing the power and/or influence of parents and other citizens in school decision making (Marburger, 1985; Zander, n.d.).

Site management recommends that curriculum, personnel, and budget decisions be made within, for, and by individual schools (Lindelow, 1981)—although there is considerable variation in practice as to which of these decisions are actually decentralized, and to what extent. In theory, the authority to act, and the resources to implement the decisions, are assigned to the schools by states and districts, with each school receiving its budgetary share (the amount being determined by its enrollment) in a lump sum for its own allocation. Each school is expected to operate within policy guidelines set by the state and district—but in general, school accountability shifts from the present input and monitoring controls to responsibility for outcomes such as attendance and student achievement on state and district examinations. The preparation of annual reports on these and other matters becomes a major school responsibility, as does careful long-range planning.

All school-site management proposals call for the establishment of one or more committees—typically designated "school advisory councils"—for obtaining systematic input on school decisions from teachers, parents, and sometimes from other citizens and students as well. Site-management proposals differ, however, on the crucial feature of whether the councils are to be decision-making bodies, actually setting policy for the school, or whether they should merely be advisory to the principal, who is the decision maker. A related feature on which proposals differ is whether the principal is appointed and continued in that post by the advisory council or by the district superintendent. Obviously, these two structural arrangements are key matters in setting up a site-management system.

The schools of choice concept calls first for a commitment to the deliberate diversificaton of schools, so that each school (sometimes each mini-school and/or school-within-a-school) develops its own program that is distinctive in some way (for example, as to its orientation, curriculum, instructional approach, ethos). Families are then invited to select a school from among the available array, depending on the individual student's particular needs and interests or on family preference as to general school orientation.

The schools of choice concept has originated under more varied auspices and as an answer to a broader variety of problems than has the concept of site management, which was developed largely by scholars and policy analysts explicitly to modify school governance. Some school of choice arrangements have been adopted to accommodate students not otherwise well served within the system, others as a response to strong parent and/or teacher preferences, others in the interests of dropout prevention, others to provide pilot sites for innovation and experiment, and still others as an alternative to forced busing. The multiple roots tend to make for more varied renderings of the "choice" proposal, reflecting different features as the idea has been developed in different places. (Hence the differences between, for example, magnet schools and alternative schools — with magnet schools typically designed to attract large numbers across racial and geographic lines to programs featuring a particular curriculum or instructional style, and alternative schools more often intended to accommodate a small group with particular interests or needs.) Opportunities for choice under "choice" arrangements usually include staff, who also select their own programs in schools rather than simply being assigned to them (Raywid,

1982). Under such circumstances, teachers often collectively design the program within their school, an arrangement calling in turn for a considerable degree of independence from curricular and other mandates originating at state and district levels. In other locales, however, the "choice" arrangement has not substantially altered top-down program design and control or the way in which teachers are assigned. "Choice" programs of the first sort have much in common with site-management arrangements, while programs of the second sort do not. Even in those schools of choice which enjoy considerable autonomy, however, that autonomy has probably occurred more often informally as a natural consequence of the "choice" arrangement than by formal delegation of power over curriculum, budget, and/or personnel decisions, which is the hallmark of site management. Few communities have done what Baton Rouge has announced: a combination of the choice and site-management proposals (Snider, 1988).

As this suggests, the schools of choice proposal is a reform focusing most immediately on student needs and interests, with internal school governance changes occurring only incidentally and in the course of responding to student diversity. The site-management proposal, on the other hand, makes staff focal and is concerned primarily with enlarging the prerogatives and responsibilities of principals and teachers, and sometimes of other adults. The site-management proposal assumes that today's major problems in education stem from the highly centralized control to which schools have become subject, and the consequent distancing of decision making from the level of application. Control properly belongs in the hands of those most directly associated with a school, say advocates: its staff, its students and their families, and its community. Many site-management proponents give no hint of intent to redress present power imbalances or to establish a new balance between school, district, and state levels of control. Rather the interest is in lodging control for the operation of education primarily at the school level.

The "choice" proposal asserts that in order to respond to the diverse educational needs, interests, and preferences of a diverse population and a pluralist society, schools need to be

differentiated. It assumes that the development and sustaining
of an array of programs necessitates considerable decentralization and the collaboration of teachers in program design.

It may be well to reemphasize that both the schools of
choice proposal and the site-management proposal call for a fundamental reordering of school organization to enable the individual school to define itself to a far greater extent than is now
the case. Just such a reordering has been recommended by a
substantial number of reform reports, including the National
Governors' Association's *Time for Results* (1986), the Committee for Economic Development's *Investing in Our Children* (1985),
and the Carnegie Task Force on Teaching as a Profession's *A
Nation Prepared* (1986).

The recommendation that the school be recognized and
treated as the primary unit of education is further buttressed
by a broad array of contemporary research. John Goodlad has
urged it on the basis of his extensive study of schools (Goodlad,
1984). Effective Schools research has underscored it (Cohen,
1983). Organizational specialists are proposing it (Kanter, 1983;
Louis, forthcoming). And most recently, some have attributed
an innate superiority to private and parochial schools precisely
on grounds of the independence of each and the resulting opportunity of each to create its own identity (Chubb, 1988).

We turn now to examining how each of the two major
reorganization proposals for public schools, site mangement and
choice, would respond to the fundamental challenges earlier
identified: the conception of the school's mission, its role allocations, its social order, and its decision making. We shall also look
at the way in which contemporary school organization responds
to those issues.

The Conception of the School's Mission

A substantial part of the demand for restructuring schools
stems from the charge that schools are not doing well by the
youth entrusted to them. The particular object of this complaint
differs — including, for example, that the schools are not educating students well enough, or that they are not educating substan-

tial numbers of them, that they are failing to teach the right things, or failing to motivate or inspire, or invading what should remain the family's province, or violating individual students with unfair treatment or indifference. Each of these complaints, as well as many others, challenges the way in which the school construes its mission.

The mission of schooling—and especially of public schooling—has long been multifaceted. Perhaps the Massachusetts colonists of 1620 had the singlemindedness often attributed to them when seeking in their schools only to enable the young to read the Bible and come to know the word of God. But if so, they may be the last group with so clear and uncomplicated a vision of just what schools should accomplish. Later colonists clearly sought public and secular purposes, as well as individual and religious ones, in urging the spread of education. And many disagreements over school practice can be traced to disagreements over whether the school is primarily a public good or a private benefit. Is the raison d'être and major function of the school to prepare the young to maintain and perpetuate intact our society, government, economy? Or is the school an institution whose major function is to enable the young to realize their unique potential by developing their individual interests and talents? This is a relevant question for all institutions, and for public schools surely the answer must be *both:* They must provide both for the public good and for private benefits. Yet the varying emphasis assigned the two concerns goes a long way toward determining a school's orientation. If, for example, the school's mission is primarily to serve public interests, then such functions as sorting, slotting, and certifying students for their subsequent careers seems reasonable. Letting students succeed or fail in one program and then placing them in another one if they do not succeed is understandable. But if the school ought instead to provide a private benefit, such practices are hard to justify—and it is difficult to argue that any advantages can ever accrue to any individual by having so much as a single failing grade entered on his or her academic record!

The issue regarding the mission of the school also includes the question of just what sort of enterprise schooling is. Is the task of schooling the delivery of particular goods, such as the multiplication tables, Shakespeare, the alphabet, the Civil War, or other items appearing on cultural literacy lists? Or is it rather a matter of the dispensing of particular services, such as custodial, instructional, and developmental services? Or is it something else?

Some of the schools' present difficulties stem from particular positions on these matters, and part of the demand to restructure schools is that we reconstitute their mission. In some cases, what is sought is a shift to a stronger orientation to the public good. That certainly seems to be the message in the demand for better school performance to improve the nation's economic competitiveness. A public-good orientation has seemed to inspire much of the current excellence movement. It would recommend strengthening external control and rendering it more effective — exactly the tendencies that marked school improvement efforts of the early 1980s.

The school's general mission appears similar to that of most large-scale contemporary institutions, which is to make available a set of services to people seeking those services. That seems straightforward and reasonable enough. But in the case of the school, its mission is complicated by several features not shared by other institutions. In the first place, those to be served are not there voluntarily but are legally compelled to present themselves. In the second place, the school's mission is one of steering young, developing persons in positive directions, rather than of responding to the wishes of fully formed adults. In the third place, the youthfulness of the service recipients recommends measures designed to see that they avail themselves fully of the services. In the fourth place, our national commitments to equity and equal opportunity recommend measures that go beyond the simple laying out of services: There may also be an obligation to render them meaningful and genuinely accessible to their recipients. These differences make school service delivery unique. They also leave us feeling somewhat ambivalent about schools. On the one hand, we believe they open doors, even worlds, to the young. On the other, school functions can also be perceived as "services masquerading as gifts," the institution can be seen as both obtrusive and intrusive, and teaching can be viewed as a practice ultimately based on condescension (Komisar, 1969).

The cynicism of such perspectives underscores just how a number of people have come to perceive large schools in particular. Those who staff them have been tagged members of "the helping professions" (Ignatieff, 1985) but also as "street-level bureaucrats" (Lipsky, 1980). As they have pursued the path of other professionals and other bureaucrats, they have become targets of the kinds of resentments addressed to other such figures. Schools have adopted the bureaucratic model in identifying more and more functions for special treatment and in proliferating offices of new experts to practice them — planners, evaluators, special reading teaching, speech therapists, counselors, curriculum developers, school social workers, remedial specialists, and so on. One result has been a depersonalizing trend in schools along with the fragmentation of school services.

It has been suggested that one of the reasons for the widespread current hostility against doctors is that specialization within their profession has led to "thingification." The patient is dehumanized by the doctor who is concerned with a particular organ, wound, or disease, rather than with the individual. The doctor-patient encounter is thus not a human one but, as Erving Goffman put it, simply a transaction between a service provider and a client's malfunctioning part (Goffman, 1961). Many suggest that the school's relationship with its students has become analogous: that school is a set of transactions between a service deliverer and a client's particular area of deficiency, be that a matter of poor mathematical skills, socially unacceptable behavior, or a lack of knowledge of history (Pekarsky, 1982).

One of the major consequences of an orientation that leads to the creation of large schools has been an increasing focus on effective service delivery rather than on successful learning. In other words, the task has become provision of instruction rather than the effective educating of students. Moreover, this organizational tendency is now being buttressed by a burgeoning professional literature that focuses on the norms of good practice rather than on success with individual students. The sights have shifted. True, sound practice is not unrelated to what has been found successful — but *statistically* successful, not necessarily successful for all groups, let alone for all individuals. The sound practice approach has permitted us to judge schools and teachers not on the basis of their success but on the less demanding basis of whether they were doing what sound practice recommends. It has also suggested that professionals in education define successful teaching, because it demands specialized knowledge to do so.

There have been good reasons for such developments. As more youngsters have presented difficult challenges, and as changing circumstances have added obstacles to education, it has seemed that all we can reasonably expect is sound practice. But it appears that the limits of public tolerance and understanding have been exceeded (perhaps, for instance by such extremes as Benjamin Franklin High School in New York, which, before it was closed down by then-Chancellor Anthony Alvarado, was graduating only 7% of its students). Neither individuals nor the public at large seem willing any longer to accept the sound practice defense nor to let the definition of success remain with the professionals. This is an important part of the present preoccupation with accountability. Critics are insisting that schools shift their mission to that of engaging in practices that *succeed* in virtually all cases, and that succeed in ways students, parents, and the larger public identify with schools.

Accountability to the educational hierarchy — to one's superordinates within the school's organization (for they, after all, are better judges than the public of what constitutes sound practice) will probably also be abandoned with the shift away from the "sound practice" orientation. Complaints from outside have tended to be passed up the school's hierarchical ladder, and accountability has been diffused and obfuscated in their treatment. A focus on success demands a more direct form of accounting to the public and a clearer view of just where responsibility lies. It is likely to change the bureaucratic practice of associating ultimate responsibility with a single figure at the top of the hierarchy to one addressing much more responsibility to the individuals most immediately concerned.

Many of the current calls for restructuring address this shift of the mission of schools from correct to successful practice. The ramifications of such a shift are hard to overestimate. The difference between a call for restructuring and a call for reform hinges on an assumption about how fundamental and pervasive the needed change will prove. The assumption in this case is that we urgently need a fundamental reconstruing of what schools are for. Beyond that, however, proposers differ as to just how they would restructure. The dominant trend of the last five to ten years has been a sharp increase in the state role in education. This began to occur in the late 1970s, largely through the imposition of state competency tests to determine students' eligibility to graduate, and in some cases even to be promoted to the next grade. The effort has been stepped up during the 1980s, with curricular mandates and course-content specification, in addition to more tests. There are those who maintain that the right combinations and proportions of state and local inputs can eventually correct today's imbalances in the control of schools, and that such correctives will suffice. Others, however, are convinced that nothing short of real restructuring will do.

How would our major proposals for restructuring educational governance respond to the question of the mission of schools? Some site-management proposals seek to involve people outside the school in its governance, whereas others do not. To the extent that a site-management arrangement fails to assign major roles to community figures other than parents, it would appear to be reflecting a private benefits view of education, construing what schools offer primarily as an entitlement and advantage for the individual rather than as a matter of public interest. Although the monitoring of particular outcomes can help assure the fulfillment of larger purposes (those of the local and national communities), the emphasis seems to be on the purposes of the school's immediate constituents. Whether particular site-management arrangements reflect the democratic aspects associated with shared decision making, or whether authority remains essentially in the hands of the principal, the "subsidiarity" principle is presupposed — that is, the conviction that decisions are best reached at the level closest to their implementation. The interests most strongly voiced at that level are likely to be the immediate and personal concerns of the participants.

It seems reasonable to suppose, then, that the upshot of site-management arrangements with respect to the mission of schools would be schools more attuned to the particular characteristics of their students — to their educational needs and aspirations, and perhaps to their interests. Such schools ought to display a good deal of flexibility as compared with schools where districtwide regulations and procedures affect large numbers of students, many of whom may differ in important ways from the population of any particular school. Depending on the match between the principal and the parent community — and how the principal is appointed — site management could also mean closer alignment between the particular ethnic orientation of parents and the values reflected in the school. This would mean an increase of what is often called school "responsiveness," because the institution would be free to adapt to the orientations of particular groups. The result could be a distinctive ethnic flavor for the mission and general style that many schools reflect.

Irrespective of the extent to which a particular site-management arrangement divides authority among professional educators and between educators and parents, the increased contact implicit in the arrangement may alter their relationships. The social distance may narrow between educators as professionals and employees of the bureaucracy, and parents as "laypersons." The partnership aspects of the parent-educator connection and the home-school link may well loom larger. The arrangement should make both parents and educators more prone to see themselves as engaged in a shared enterprise directed toward common purposes. Thus, a greater sense of mutuality seems possible. Under such circumstances, the bureaucratic tendency to depersonalize service delivery should recede and the personal dimensions of education's mission should expand. The school might well become more flexible in its willingness to respond differently to individuals and their differing needs.

But although site management can conduce to all the tendencies we have just named, it need not do so. It is also plausible that the adoption of site management would change very little in any of these regards. If the school advisory council remains advisory only, and its discussions trivial or perfunctory, it is possible that the impact of site management would not extend much further than the internal shift of authority within the district's hierarchy. If the school advisory council has decision-making power, the likelihood of such tendencies as a sense of partnership and mutuality and of increased personalizing and flexibility on the part of the school would certainly be strengthened. If the council does not have such power, however, such tendencies are far less assured. It is even possible that a strong, decision-making school advisory council with a bureaucratic orientation might keep its powers strictly within the council and that the empowerment given the school would extend no further than these representatives.

It is conceivable that depending upon the extent and the adequacy of the monitoring of outcomes, site-management arrangements could neglect the interests of the public—the wider community. Our century-long tendencies toward standardization and program uniformity could give way to a problematic range of program diversity, bringing difficulties of coordination. What would assure that students moving from junior to senior high school were prepared to do so? Or that senior high school would not prove largely redundant? Or that a student could move from one school to another without considerable loss or repetition? Such challenges address the possibility that a system we now perceive as overly centralized and homogenized could become so much less so that it posed opposite problems of fragmentation and disarray. That is possible, although the many other factors also functioning to assure educational uniformity might well suffice to maintain strong likenesses between schools. These factors include such things as the wide use of particular textbooks and other materials, the similarity of teacher preparation nationwide, and the common elements in collective bargaining agreements.

There is an additional challenge, posed early in the history of the site-management idea by one of its formulators: "The key question in community responsiveness is whether the tyranny of the majority at a single school site would produce better public

policy than the tyranny of the majority in an entire district"
(Pierce, 1977, p. 17). There are two noteworthy features of the
way in which the author, Lawrence Pierce, frames the challenge:
The first is the assumption of the tyranny of the majority,
whether its jurisdiction be the school or the district. Any collective enterprise may prove unavoidably tyrannical in relation to
dissidents. But the right of a minority to register effective dis-
agreement, or to pursue its own course, is far more restricted
under the arrangements by which we organize school than is
the case in many other pursuits — for example, religion, leisure
activities, the selection of assorted professional expertise (medical, legal, and so on). Most Americans are not currently free
to pursue their own school preferences.

A second feature of Pierce's challenge is the attention it
calls to our political tradition's assumption that a larger decision base — a state instead of a district, the nation instead of a
state — may yield wiser decisions, or at least decisions where the
interests of minorities have a better chance at representation
and inclusion. Civil rights protests of the 1960s denied this
assumption and demanded community control of schools, and
the public school's continuing failure to meet the needs of particular groups continues to fuel the idea that if the disadvantaged could control their own programs, the programs would
adapt better and more successfully to what is needed.

Professor Pierce's response to the "tyranny" challenge was
to combine the idea of site management with the opportunity
to choose one's school. Thus, if a family did not share or approve of the orientation of the neighborhood school, they could
select another. Such a solution makes sense: Schools permitted
to develop their own vision of education would surely differ more
than schools can now, when they are subject to constant pressures
toward uniformity. When differences between schools, and a
particular school's resulting orientation, become so plainly logically arbitrary — the consequence of schools' choosing between
several strains of professional opinion regarding educational
means and ends — then it seems only fair that a student needing,
or a family preferring, a particular strain be free to seek it.

This does not mean that schools free enough to differ

would necessarily prove any more arbitrary than centrally controlled schools: The extent to which educational science supports
an array of different and even contradictory practice — and the
extent to which education is permanently value-based — means
that *any* school's practice must be to a large degree logically arbitrary.

Does this mean that the schools emerging from the site-
management arrangement will be idiosyncratic? Possibly, to
some extent. Experience to date suggests that they would certainly differ as to their organization and structure, and quite
probably in their programs as well (McPike, 1987). It is certainly conceivable, for example, that a neighborhood where a
number of thespians live might want the school's mission to
feature the performing arts, or that a community of professors
might want the mission to emphasize the cultivation of intellectual prowess, or that a disadvantaged community might want
a mission offering an emphasis on careers and assurances of
employability. But, proponents of site management assert, such
schools will be no less logically arbitrary than are present school
orientations and practices, a great many of which enjoy no
more — and sometimes less — community support than the alternatives they exclude.

This leads to the second major proposal for restructuring schools, the schools of choice concept. As the paragraphs
immediately above have suggested, some see the idea of choice
as a necessary concomitant of the site-management arrangement.
For others, it is the choice feature itself that is the more significant one, with school governance of lesser import.

What might be the effects of choice on the conception of
the school's mission? It seems reasonable to anticipate tendencies similar to those we attributed to site management, but
perhaps more assured and pronounced. One major difference
between these two strategies is that site management is developed
within schools whose teachers are assigned to them. It involves
no shifts in personnel and thus no new constellations of individuals. It is therefore fair to expect a range of educational
persuasions and orientations among the staff of site-managed
schools. Schools of choice, on the other hand, more typically

involve teachers who have chosen to be there (Raywid, 1982). They are likely by virtue of this to be a considerably more like-minded and coherent group. When a school's constituents have explicitly chosen to be associated with it, agreement can be expected on at least one aspect of the school that all have found of major significance. Depending on the kind of distinctiveness and identity it has built for itself, a school of choice may enjoy extensive "mission coherence," or agreement on values among the groups associated with it, staff as well as parents and students. That means there may be substantially more unanimity with respect to mission than is common in public education. This could create more differences from school to school. It would also be more conducive to producing the benefits that effective schools research and inquiries into private schools have linked to high levels of mission coherence.

Another probability related to a school's mission is that a school of choice will be even more likely than a site-management school to respond to individual students and parents. The fact that the school is chosen alters the relationship between chooser and chosen in ways that school governance changes may not accomplish. It stands to reason that a balancing of statuses and power differences and a resulting mutuality are more likely to arise in a relation to which neither of the parties involved is simply assigned or remains captive. A likely consequence is added emphasis on responding adequately to *all* individuals, rather than focusing on the average or the majority. (It must be recognized, however, that such a benefit can be anticipated only in a system providing enough attractive schools of choice to go around. In those locales where magnet schools have hundreds or even thousands of applicants for each opening, reports suggest that indifference and lack of responsiveness can be even higher in magnet schools than in the schools the magnets replaced!)

In sum, the "choice" arrangement is likely to bring an intensification of a school's private benefits orientation. Interests associated with the public good would need to be maintained either by input controls and monitoring, as under present arrangements, or by accountability for outcomes as in site management.

Since input controls inevitably restrict freedom and undermine program distinctiveness, accountability for outcomes is also the more compatible arrangement for schools of choice.

Rules and Procedures That Define
the School's Social Order

According to some, a great many of education's difficulties are traceable fairly directly to matters rarely discussed and often unrecognized. They pertain to fundamental beliefs and commitments and basic understandings of the way things work, which are so deeply ingrained as to be taken for granted, rarely discussed, and virtually never questioned. They give rise to rules and standard operating procedures that constitute the culture of a school and yield its social order. School culture is, of course, far broader than rules and procedures. It consists of norms and beliefs about students, about the world, and about life and its purpose. I refer here only to that part of this broad ideological system that gives rise to those rules of behavior, both written and unwritten, that control the interactions of school participants. In most contemporary schools, bureaucracy is believed to be the only plausible, viable form of social organization. At levels of belief too fundamental to be challenged, many of those in schools have accepted the idea that there must be differential status and authority assignments, fixed roles, clearly divided responsibilities, clearly demarcated measures of accountability, and written rules. Irrespective of how they may complain, and even of the explicit attacks on bureaucracy of the past several decades, large numbers of people who work in schools apparently continue to assume its superiority to other ways of organizing large-scale enterprises. Many accept the inevitability of bureaucratic dominance in any modern society (Clark, 1987).

Such beliefs, and the patterns of interaction between people that they produce, help yield a school's social order. This social order determines the way in which its participants behave in school, and this, in turn, generates the school's climate. There is good reason to be concerned with such matters. A widening range of research suggests that these beliefs determine how those associated with a school react to and feel about it, and that this in turn determines the importance they will assign school in their lives and the kind and amount of effort they will devote to it. This seems to be true of staff as well as of students, and it seems to go a long way toward defining the difference between a good and a poor school (Goodlad, 1984).

Within the school, bureaucratic assumptions have led to a strong tendency to generate formal rules, to the point in many schools where students at the beginning of the year receive long lists of rules to be followed in each of their classes and extracurricular activities. The need for and appropriateness of such rules as the best way to have things run smoothly and avoid chaos, is simply assumed. The need to have bosses who command, oversee, and enforce the work of teachers is similarly assumed. The separation of workers, which is fostered by bureaucratic organization, is not only accepted but reinforced in the school: The work is so organized and apportioned among the staff as to discourage if not entirely preclude collaboration. It is pursued in isolation from colleagues, "behind the classroom door" (Goodlad and others, 1974; Lortie, 1975).

In what ways would the two major restructuring proposals for schools revise this social order? Would the site-management arrangement alter it in any substantial way? Would the choice arrangement modify it? The answer in each case probably turns in significant measure on one key question regarding governance. In site-management arrangements where the authority that was shifted to the principal remained with the principal and was not shared with the school advisory council, there may be only minimal change in other regards as well. In schools of choice where the top-down control pattern remained undisturbed, other changes might also prove minimal. But assuming site-management and choice arrangements which actually dispersed authority, what changes in a school's social order might be anticipated?

Site management is a less sure source of such change than the choice arrangement. One reason for this is that even if the school advisory council members are empowered as decision makers under site management, changes for other members of the staff and other parents may prove minimal. Site management is a plan that directly affects only the representatives of teacher and parent groups, and then only in their policymaking roles; even the teacher representative's role may remain unchanged in the classroom. And other teachers may not be empowered at all. Site management is primarily a governance arrangement. It is not clear that changes in formal governance alone would serve as a sufficient catalyst for broader changes — although of course they would if teacher influence in the decision making council yielded policies specifying functions or changing key procedures (for example, establishing team teaching).

But there is little reason to believe that the switch to a representative government in schools will be accompanied by extensive changes in the school's social order. It would, of course, change the relationship to the school of the parent members of the decision-making body. But as school boards have proven, that arrangement certainly need not disturb the bureaucratic orientation of schools. Thus, we conclude that site management may, but need not, lead to broader changes in the social order of a school. Its institution may set the stage for further changes, but there is nothing in the machinery it establishes or the dynamics it sets in motion that makes it a probable catalyst of broad change of the social order within a school.

The choice arrangement, by contrast, is likely to assure broader social-order changes and to affect and empower a wider group. The new authority transferred to a school of choice is made necessary by the charge given the school to establish a distinctive program with a unique identity. This entails giving program planners responsibility and authority to create and carry out their own vision of schooling. The full teaching staff must be involved in such planning if novelty or uniqueness is to be pervasive and manifested throughout the school, and not just in supplementary classes and activities. It is this kind of involvement in planning that is thought to account for reports by teachers in schools of choice that their work is more professional in nature than was the case in their previous assignments. The program-planning obligation places a premium on reflection — and on collective reflection — as teachers seek to evolve a mission for their school, work out curriculum decisions, and devise learning activities. Because their charge is to mount a distinctive program, they cannot simply pursue existing course syllabi or follow the leadership of authors of textbooks. The situation places teachers in new and novel roles in relation to their work: Instead of being cast as consumers of curriculum designs and materials, they must function as developers of them. This means that creativity is expected of teachers rather than conformity.

In the course of the sorts of experiences just suggested, the isolation typical of teachers in most schools will probably be altered substantially. Teachers will have to be involved with colleagues in such tasks as the design of the schools mission, and collaboration may become as necessary a part of a teacher's role as independence and self-sufficiency have proved to date.

There is another fundamental regard in which choice is likely to transform teaching and simultaneously alter the social order of the school. Today's public schools are, in Tönnies's classic term, *Gesellschaft* institutions (1957). They exist, that is, by formal agreement to perform certain specified functions. Governments, post offices, department stores represent such institutions. By no stretch of the imagination do they and their clientele constitute real communities. *Gemeinschaft* institutions, on the other hand, are communities. They consist of people bound together by sentiments, shared beliefs and commitments, and feelings of kinship to one another. *Gesellschaft* institutions are marked by secondary associations (Cooley, 1962), that is, relationships restricted to the single purpose and function that has brought two human beings together. A customer and a supermarket cashier share a secondary association, as ordinarily do a lawyer and client, and in most high schools, a teacher and a student. A teacher is a mathematics or an English teacher and has no concern or responsibility for a student's performance in other classes or share in the individual's personal life. Primary associations, on the other hand, are typical of *Gemeinschaft* institutions. These are relationships marked by a range of interest and concern, such that the whole lives of participants, past, present, and future, are prospectively relevant and germane to the relationship.

It seems that the choice arrangement tends to make schools

into *Gemeinschaft* institutions and to make relationships there into primary associations. Such a tendency has been noted by a number of observers (Erickson and others, 1982). It seems to arise from several sources. First, the commonality reflected in the choice provides the foundation upon which a *Gemeinschaft* can rise — and sometimes it reflects one that is already present (Coleman and Hoffer, 1987; Salganik and Karweit, 1982).

Second, there seems to be a strong tendency in schools of choice to pursue broad educational aims that address the full intellectual and character development of students. Such schools are concerned with intellectual growth as well as with academic achievement. They tend also to be concerned with the sort of human being that is evolving — with personality as well as with character, and with tastes and proclivities as well as with knowledge and ideas (Grant, 1981). Such concerns require primary associations between students and teachers, and these in turn generate *Gemeinschaft*.

Third, there is a tendency in schools of choice to change the bureaucratic pattern of formally defined and specified roles. Role definitions in many such schools tend to be much more flexible. In a bureaucratic social order, role stability is a fundamental value. Roles may proliferate as new expertise and specialization warrants. Otherwise, however, the stability and endurance of role definitions contribute substantially to the dependability and stability of the organization. Their resistance to change is seen as a major virtue of bureaucratic organizations. Role maintenance is thus a primary value. The parallel value in schools of choice, however, is typically just the opposite: Role flexibility is a positive value, because of its capacity to increase adaptation and hence responsiveness (Raywid, 1980).

It appears then that choice has considerable potential for changing a number of aspects of a school's social order (Raywid, 1982). At least under some conditions, it leads to extensive change in the kinds of relationships that characterize a school and in the norms governing school behavior. A brief word may be helpful about the machinery for increasing the likelihood of such changes in schools of choice. First there must be the opportunity to choose a school, which in turn presumes a broad enough array of schools so that choosers can find one that appeals. The opportunity for teachers to choose seems to be at least as important as for students and their families (Raywid, 1982). If teachers are charged with designing a unique and distinctive program, they must be given the authority necessary to do so, that is, the specific authorization to set aside curricular and other mandates received from outside the school, and to devise alternative accountability measures. Arrangements conducing to teacher collaboration are needed, including shared instead of individual responsibilities and common time periods regularly set aside for collaborative work. (Such arrangements sometimes include team teaching, out-of-classroom assignments for students to free teacher time for work with colleagues, periodic staff retreats, shared summer workshops and work schedules, and so on.)

Obviously, the kind of social order ensuing from these arrangements would depart significantly from that of most schools. This is not guaranteed, however, because the progression just sketched is not inexorable: School districts sometimes adopt a choice plan and fail to initiate the conditions necessary to its successful realization. Unfortunately, the history of educational reform is full of such partial implementations, leading to what John Goodlad has called "non-events" in lieu of the improvements sought (1983). Nevertheless, for those interested in changing the social order of schools, there is a distinct advantage in an arrangement whose natural unfolding might accomplish that if not blocked.

Choice may call for different kinds of teachers, differently prepared. It will obviously place a greater premium on different personal attributes than do present school roles. Different qualities would be needed and different competencies would have to be developed. Training in cooperative work would be important, for instance, along with negotiating skills and other strategies of group endeavor. Additionally, teachers need more knowledge of their teaching fields to be curriculum designers, than if required only to carry out a curriculum assembled by someone else (Raywid, 1986b; Tanveer and Nawaz, 1979).

The Roles of the Players

One of the major criticisms often directed at schools is that they have divided up tasks and functions in ways that are counterproductive. As the previous section sought to suggest, most contemporary large-scale organizations organize and parcel out functions in predictable ways. The direction and coordination of the enterprise are masterminded from the top, and the lower one's position in the pyramid-shaped hierarchy, the narrower the range of function and the fewer the discretionary decisions to be made. Tasks, and the roles of those who perform them, are well defined and delineated, and one worker is likely to be stepping on another's toes by assuming other functions and responsibilities, or even by understanding or knowing how to perform them!

Ultimately, the principle employed to divide up the entire task and to assign responsibility for the separate parts is the logical divisibility of the total product or service. How to divide up a complex task is fairy clear in product manufacture where the parts of the product are the ultimate components. Thus, the production of each part assigned to a particular set of workers — for example, production of an automobile divides workers into groups by major components: chassis, body, and interior. Each specialist adds just one element in a precise sequence — for example, engine, door, or seatcover. The analogy is a bit harder to identify, however, in organizations established to provide a service rather than manufacture a product. Service organizations typically divide up tasks in terms of the knowledge base that undergirds each funtion — and so we get history teachers as distinct from music teachers, and counselors and administrators as distinct from teachers. Professional knowledge keeps expanding, and with it the tendency to further divide and thereby delimit the tasks and functions of individuals.

The results of these role-defining tendencies of large-scale organizations in schools have been the object of much criticism. They are also what prompts a number of critics who demand the restructuring of school organizations. Some people are convinced that the ceaseless multiplying of specialties and experts

is serving steadily to de-skill classroom teachers, leaving them
in shrinking and diminishing roles, with less and less knowledge
of the total enterprise of schooling (Cronin, 1988). Others stress
that narrow role definitions serve to alienate workers in the
school—the staff as well as the students for whom they are
responsible (Cox and Wood, 1980). Some are convinced that
today's further tightening of the top-down control arrangements
always present in large organizations is impeding the teacher's
task and alienating teachers from their work (Darling-Hammond
and Wise, 1983). Others focus on the financial consequences,
charging that a disproportionate amount of school funds is going to the "superstructure"—particularly to the administrators
necessary to coordinate school organizations—and that correspondingly few resources remain to be concentrated on instruction (Nathan, 1983). It is also alleged that the way we have
divided up the services to be performed in schools is fundamentally ill-suited to the clients to be served—that the division of
instructional areas into disciplines taught by different teachers
makes for a situation in which students remain unknown by their
teachers, just as the subjects taught by their colleagues remain
unknown to teachers (Sizer, 1984). The division between counseling and teaching, for example, in effect deprives youngsters
of contextual adult counsel and guidance. The division between
disciplinary and teaching functions undermines the teacher's
ability to maintain control in the classroom. And programs
designed to have specialists deal with particular groups narrows
still further the range of students the classroom teacher handles,
and eventually the skills and general competence of that teacher.

Several of these cases are worth examining in more detail
for what they seem to recommend for redividing tasks and functions in a school, and hence for redesigning roles. Consider first
the alleged impacts of current role divisions on students. It is
charged that the division of instruction into separate disciplines
taught by different teachers creates a situation in which the daily
experience of students is so fragmented that it denies a sense
of meaningfulness to what is taught and at the same time makes
it impossible for students to be known as individuals to teachers
(Sizer, 1984). Thus, the allocation of tasks according to expertise

in different subjects is thought to undermine the effectiveness of instruction as well as to deny youngsters the psychological support they need.

Also, negative effects on teachers are attributed to the role definitions typical of public schools. The sociology of work identifies the narrowing of worker function with a loss of meaningfulness and attendant loss of psychic reward for employment. As Peter Drucker put it, "The quickest way to quench motivation is not to allow people to do what they have been trained to do" (Hall, 1982, p. 64). According to some analysts, this particular feature of school organization is largely responsible for the "burnout" phenomenon that received so much attention several years ago. As tasks are more narrowly and rigidly defined, workers became less able to influence their own working conditions, to perceive the outcomes or impacts of their efforts, or to engage in tasks they can find meaningful. Thus, at least for some, current role definitions in schools tend to decrease teacher task engagement and job satisfaction (Louis and others, 1988).

It is thus not surprising that some find present role allocations to contribute to school ineffectiveness. By producing debilitating psychological effects on both sets of key figures, teachers and students, present task divisons are said to undermine school productivity. But the toll is alleged to be particularly heavy with respect to education's ultimate goals, which are broad or general in nature. As tasks are defined in increasingly narrow and explicit terms, it becomes more difficult to assign responsibility for the development of such traits as good character, civic responsibility, sound judgment, and critical intelligence. And estranged workers are not likely to assert themselves (which might be seen as overstepping their bounds) by assuming unassigned responsibilities.

Such charges lend added force to the suggestion that the way in which tasks are distributed in schools needs reexamination. At present the distribution is epistemologically rooted. Organizational practice in schools predicates assignments on knowledge bases, with an expanded knowledge base yielding (or justifying) new specializations. But if the consequence of this is fragmentation and ineffectiveness, what might be done instead? How ought we to apportion tasks?

One possibility is to weaken the connection now linking knowledge bases to organizational specialization, acknowledging that the requisites of effective delivery of education differ sufficiently from the requisites of scholarly expertise that the latter should not dictate the former no matter how extensive a knowledge base becomes. Heretical as this appears, there is much to be said for it. For example, despite present demands for increasing teacher expertise in the subjects they teach, it is well known that particularly in the disciplines representing cumulative knowledge (mathematics and the sciences), teachers simply cannot use their advanced knowledge in their classooms. It is also well known that the individual best versed in a subject may not be its best teacher, and that the administrator best versed in the sociology of organizations may not be the school's most effective leader.

Without arguing whether teaching or administering is an art or a science, we might at least ask whether those who organize roles in schools have identified the proper knowledge base for role allocations. It could be, for instance, that the proper base might be new combinations amalgamating knowledge, for instance, about a particular student age group (for example, young adolescents) plus a broad teaching area (for example, U.S. history and literature) plus relevant school organization and structure (for example, middle schools and junior highs). Whether or not this particular combination seems felicitous, it may well be advantageous to reexplore, without continuing just to make assumptions about, the nature of what really constitutes specialized knowledge for educators. Particularly as discussion proceeds on how to strengthen the preparation of teachers, it may be important to challenge the traditional notion that they need extensive work within a discipline, plus some acquaintance with pedagogy. Perhaps a more fundamental restructuring is in order.

It is clear that addressing extant criticisms would entail fundamental and far-reaching reorganization of schools. It could yield very different substructures and alignments of responsibilities. It might prove beneficial to redecide how best to divide

up educational tasks. Perhaps we would not base student groupings on age and ability levels but would divide students into
different sorts of groups. Perhaps we would not use the Carnegie
unit system — or if retained for students, it might not be so for
teachers, or vice versa. Possibly one, two, or three teachers would
remain with a student group all day.

In any event, it appears that the way functions need to
be distributed may not accord with the logical divisions of product manufacture or service delivery at all, and therefore that
schools are, indeed, now allocating tasks in ways that impede
instead of assuring the realization of their own goals. But short
of such fundamental rebuilding of the school as an organization, what role changes for teachers might be anticipated in the
wake of the two restructuring proposals now being urged? Would
site management or choice bring substantial related changes?

Site management would expand the roles of those teachers
involved in the school advisory council to include policymaking
(or policy advisement) functions. The roles of other teachers need
not be modified by the arrangement but could be in two kinds
of ways. First, school advisory councils often seek to involve
others by establishing task forces and other groups to study and
recommend action to the council and/or react to council questions and proposals (McPike, 1987). Teacher roles in a site-
managed school might be expanded to the extent of teacher involvement in such groups. It is also possible, of course, that
school advisory councils might adopt specific policies changing
teacher responsibilities and functions. As Clune and White concluded from their survey of site-management schools and districts
(1987, p. 32), the arrangement introduced greater flexibility and
more opportunity, but the particular use made of these varied considerably. Some school advisory councils embarked on
changes sufficiently pervasive in their effects to transform the
work of all of the teachers within the school; in other cases, the
school advisory council undertook ventures that made the council
a specific supplementary project in the school rather than an
ongoing force for change in the way the school operates (Hill,
n.d.). Thus, it is possible that the school advisory council might
not change the classroom operation even of its teacher members,
depending on the ventures it undertakes.

It is certainly plausible to believe that the added influence of parents might lead to policies modifying current role allocations within the school, particularly role allocations between parents and school staff—but then again, it might not. As suggested throughout, a great deal of the potential for change because of site management hinges upon the extent to which the school advisory council is actually given power. If it remains advisory only and without power, little may change, and in fact disappointments may generate negative feelings on the part of parents. But, as we have also tried to suggest, even if the advisory council has power, there is little in site management that provides an automatic catalyst for change in elements other than the council itself.

By contrast, choice does seem to be conducive to change in the several parts of a school's organizational structure. The need to jointly construct a school mission changes teacher work patterns from solitary to collaborative. The likelihood that unsuccessful students will leave the school by choice provides an incentive to construe a school mission that effectively serves all those enrolled. The choice feature helps generate *Gemeinschaft*. With respect to the effects of choice on teachers' roles, the evidence suggests that staff in schools of choice are likely to assume more extended roles than those assigned them in other schools (Anglin, 1979; Raywid, 1980). This often occurs by necessity, since many schools of choice are so small they lack the specialized personnel to offer particular services. But sometimes it happens for other reasons, as youngsters come to know and trust teachers as individuals and teachers become more aware of the traits and backgrounds of their students. It appears that choice is likely to usher in conditions and establish dynamics that change teachers' roles considerably. The result is staff roles far broader than in other schools. Teachers come to function less as subject-matter experts and more as experts in students.

It might also be noted that the heightened job satisfaction of teachers in schools of choice, and the stronger identification by teachers with their schools as a result, also produces a willingness to take on added functions and to assume responsibilities well beyond those of teachers in other schools (Raywid, 1982; 1986a). This yields another impetus to the role extension commonly seen in schools of choice. It may be that site management will generate comparable benefits to morale. Surely the early reports from Hammond, Indiana, and Dade County, Florida, might so suggest. To date, however, the evidence on this score is mixed and includes reports of teacher concern about increased time demands and effort (Chapman and Boyd, 1986; Clune and White, 1987; Hill, n.d.; Obermeyer, 1987).

It might also be noted that student roles, too, are likely to be expanded in schools of choice. It is not uncommon for students to teach courses, or units within courses, and in other ways to reflect a strong sense of responsibility in relation to the school. Parents and other community members also assume broader and more varied roles in schools of choice (Blank and others, 1983). In many schools they have assumed instructional functions, serving as teachers, mentors, coaches, and aides.

Governance

Current criticism of schools has come increasingly to be directed at the way schools are governed. Indeed, as stated by many, the demand for restructuring is precisely a demand for new governance arrangements and machinery. The dissatisfaction seems to attach largely to several features, of which the most frequent target is perhaps centralization.

For almost a century, a steady trend has shifted educational control farther and farther from the classroom, its final point of application. With the adoption by schools of large-scale bureaucratic organizational practices came the rationale for controlling the teacher's work and, to the extent possible, for placing the most important decisions for the classroom in the hands of administrators (Vallance, 1973–1974). That same organizational structure also served as a steady drain on the prerogatives of building administrators such as principals, as central administrators in district offices exercised more and more control.

In some states, there has long been a tendency to centralize school governance still further, assigning the county or the state a dominant role. The excellence movement has intensified this tendency and significantly increased the school control ex-

erted at the state level. State control is now exercised through
a combination of such measures as curricular mandates with
specified course syllabi and standardized state-administered
testing programs. In this way, legislatures and state education
departments have sought to control and monitor classroom inputs, processes, and outcomes. It is not surprising, then, that
the sharply tightened controls of the past five to eight years are
now yielding complaints that schools are overregulated and
burdened with stultifying homogenization. The results, some
charge, have been to impede the success of teachers and to drive
the best ones out of classrooms altogether. Many hold that present school governance does not sufficiently allow for the discretionary power that teachers need to teach effectively. Thus, some
claim, school governance arrangements block the use and application of the teacher's expertise and preclude conditions req-
uisite for professional performance.

Another effect of current governance arrangements has
been the increasing insulation of the school from public control, with more and more decisions made by those operating
the system. As one pair of analysts put it, school control was
"wrested from the people" (Zeigler, Tucker, and Wilson, 1977).
Their explanation, and that of others, for this is that direct parent
influence has been effectively blocked and walled out. Even the
indirect influence parents might exert through boards of education has allegedly been blunted by a shift in board functions.
Such boards, it is charged, often deal extensively with matters
of much less import than those they ignore. And many board
members construe their function as representing the schools to
the public, rather than as representing the public to school
authorities in the formulation of school policy (Zeigler, Tucker,
and Wilson, 1977). Accountability to the public has thus been
deflected as school employees—that is, teachers—have been held
accountable primarily to their superordinates—that is, department chairs and principals—rather than to the parents or public
that have complaints to voice or expectations to express.

In concert with these tendencies, there has been another:
a trend toward confusing value issues with matters of technical
knowledge, such that the public's prerogatives have been usurped

by educational professionals with respect to the values to be
served in schools and the priorities to be observed among them.
This tendency, identified as the "hyperrationalization" (Wise,
1979) of school practice, has placed professionals in charge of
many decisions that would earlier have been identified as clearly
issues for public resolution. It has been marked as well by a
temptation to overextend evidence and to mandate practices that
are logically arbitrary in that they enjoy no more empirical support than do alternative practices.

A final challenge of a different sort has been raised by
those who maintain that the incentive structure built into the
present organization of school governance is fundamentally
flawed. It is claimed that teachers have nowhere to go in their
careers and that the only means to increased responsibilities or
to status enhancement for them take them out of the classroom.
Moreover, collective bargaining agreements effectively deprive
them of rewards for extraordinary effort or salutary performance,
and the assignment of students to their classes by others leaves
them not only with a "captive audience" but with a group to
which they, also, are captive.

How, and to what extent, do current influential restructuring proposals address such problems? It is the site-management proposal, of course, that makes the most explicit reply to
school governance objections. Site management is immediately responsive to the challenge of overcentralized school control. It accomplishes this through decentralization, that is, by
making the school the primary unit of education and, to a
considerable extent, a self-determining unit. Authorities at
district and state levels could continue to set policy parameters
and broad guidelines — presumably, for example, with respect
to equity and standards — but individual schools would have extensive autonomy in terms of their goals, priorities, curricular
organization, learning activities, and general orientation.

The extent to which site management would affect the
autonomy of the school and the distribution of power in the
school and between school and parents would depend heavily
upon (1) the way the school advisory council is constituted and
named, (2) the functions assigned it, and (3) the way in which

the principal is named and maintained in office. A site-management plan with minimal lay representation on the school advisory council, or one in which council members are named by and strictly advisory to the principal, has not redistributed authority between school and community at all, although the principal may choose to delegate some of his or her power.

Even with such minimal change, however, one highly significant shift occurs if site management is more than merely nominal: More authority comes to reside at the school level and thus the principal potentially becomes a much more powerful figure. One must stress "potentially," however, because as long as principals are named and continue in office at the pleasure of district authorities, those authorities will be in a position to make policy at the school level. Nevertheless, the principal's position under site management will be more prominent, and the principal will doubtless be looked upon by parents and public as more responsible and accountable for school operation than the sophisticated believe principals to be now. Thus, from the standpoint of incumbents, the price of this prospective enhancement of the principalship will be increased vulnerability. There will quite probably be an increase in status for the principal — as well as in pay, according to many site-management proposals — to match the apparently expanded responsibilities (Ingram, 1979). But whether there is also an increase in power must depend upon the superintendent who chooses the principal, unless the principal is chosen another way.

By contrast, a site-management arrangement in which the principal was named by and responsible to an elected school advisory council would have substantially modified existing power and authority distributions. It would provide the foundation for a genuine reapportioning of professional and community control, as well as a return of substantial effective power to the school. But it would not be all that is necessary to accomplish these major purposes of site management. Recall that site management is ordinarily defined to mean the control of curriculum, budget, and personnel at the school level. This does not mean total control, of course; varying degrees of control are possible with respect to each. But so central are these three elements to school governance that unless at least some authority regarding them is transferred to the school, it is questionable whether site management is occurring. Yet using such a criterion, it is hard to find many instances of site-managed schools. There is evidence that of the three, budgetary authority is most likely to be transferred (Zander, n.d.), and curricular authority least likely (Clune and White, 1987). The most detailed relevant study to date concluded that over a three-year period the programs examined had progressively "shied away from involvement in decisions on budgeting, curriculum, and staffing." By the end of the study period, Claire Hill states: "Involvement in these decisions was no longer seen as desirable in the majority of the projects' school districts. Most of the projects and their central office superiors stressed school *improvement,* rather than using the term *management*" (Hill, n.d., p. 3).

To meet the minimal definition of site-management it would seem that a school must receive a lump sum budget to allocate as it sees fit, even though there may be some exclusions and limitations. Initially, for example, salaries might be excluded from this sum and regulated at the district level. The freedom to purchase services and supplies directly from private suppliers is also a budgetary prerogative reasonably excluded initially, despite the express right to allocate sums as the school sees fit. As the site-management arrangement matured, however, instructional cost decisions might reasonably also be made at the site level, and individual schools might be free to decide to purchase technical assistance services, for example, from the district or outside it.

With respect to personnel, it seems reasonable to expect that a site-managed school would be able to control hiring at least to the extent that a teacher who seemed a poor prospect for its program could not be assigned to the school by the district. As site management developed more fully, control over personnel decisions might also include the right to adopt differentiated staffing and, for example, employ one teacher and three aides rather than two teachers.

With respect to curricular control, site management might require at a minimum the school's freedom to arrange and package its curriculum as it wants—for example, to teach subjects as separate disciplines or as interdisciplinary offerings. Within courses, there should be freedom to permit the school to decide, for instance, whether history should be taught by theme or offered as a chronology of events, as a set of recurring issues, or as a number of different strands of development. In order to claim curricular control, a school should also have the freedom to supplement an externally specified set of offerings (for example, a set dictated by required tests) with offerings important to its immediate constituents even though not to others.

But it must be emphasized that in none of these three crucial regards, budget, staffing, and curriculum, do studies show site-management schools to have gained much actual authority. Recent descriptions of some programs—for example, in Rochester, New York, and Dade County, Florida—appear considerably more positive. Meanwhile, researchers note a reluctance to modify hierarchical patterns. Yet a three-year study of eight site-management ventures concluded that despite the lack of change in authority patterns, the school advisory councils in all eight districts had "significant impact" on curriculum (Hill, n.d., p. 5). Yet another study—a telephone survey of thirty site-management programs found district officials more willing to decentralize budgetary and staffing decisions than decisions on curriculum. It also concluded that although site management does not seem to create "a system of teacher governance, . . . teachers experience a greater sense of being listened to and have a greater opportunity to bring about educational improvement" (Clune and White, 1987, p. 28). If site management seems, then, to fall short of changing school control, it does appear in some instances to have accomplished some positive effects with respect to school improvement and reform.

The way the schools of choice idea responds to current complaints about school governance shows both similarities with and contrasts to that of site management. Of course choice entails decentralization also, because choice requires the deliberate diversifying of schools, which is incompatible with controlling them centrally. Autonomy and relief from standardization are necessary to create the unique and distinctive programs required by the choice concept. Similarly, differentiated programs tend to make it difficult to set standard school curriculum and other practices in motion because such programs are incompatible with the generation of standard operating procedures for everyone. Thus, although they do not call explicitly for site management, advocates of choice envision programs that depend on a considerable amount of autonomy for and control by schools.

They also envision some degree of control for schools over their own personnel. By extending the opportunity for choice to staff as well as students, they seek to ensure that prospective teachers will be sympathetic to the school's mission and identity. But advocates of choice also urge the participation of school staff in interviews and hiring decisions, with the power to conclude that a prospect is not a good candidate and should not be offered a position in the school.

The literature on choice contains little discussion of budgetary control. Although there have been discussions of relative costs, such costs have not reflected expenditures incurred by individual schools but largely expenditures taken at the district level for schools. Thus, it has been ascertained that magnet schools customarily require start-up funds, that magnet elementary schools often cost less to operate thereafter than other elementary schools in the district, and that magnet secondary schools average higher per pupil costs than other district secondary schools (Blank and others, 1983). In other types of schools of choice, per pupil costs are typically at or below district averages (Raywid, 1982). But in none of these cases is budgetary control reported to be exerted at the site level. Short of explicit provision to that effect, such budgetary control should not be anticipated to follow from the choice arrangement.

As far as matters of hierarchy and superordinate control are concerned, the choice arrangement strikes essentially the same bargain on regulation and accountability as site management: It obtains increased autonomy for schools in the form of freedom from mandates and process monitoring in exchange for accountability for outcomes. This is precisely the bargain Governor Perpich offered Minnesota schools in his Access to Excellence plan, which proposed ultimately to transform all of

the state's schools into schools of choice. It is the idea that underlies the open enrollment plan adopted by Minnesota in 1988.
It must be noted, however, that this autonomy-for-accountability
bargain faces schools of choice with a difficulty that site-management schools do not necessarily confront. Distinctive programs may differ as to educational goals or ends, as well as with
respect to means. This suggests that they need to be appraised
in relation to what they are trying to accomplish, rather than
in relation to what other schools are trying to accomplish and
what test-designers are trying to test. Their major strengths may,
indeed, lie elsewhere than in what the tests examine, which leaves
them at a marked disadvantage in test-score comparisons.

Schools of choice offer a different, and novel, response to
the charge that schools are insulated from public and parent control. Rather than emphasizing majority or consensual decision
making at the school level, choice simply offers individuals the
opportunity to find and choose the school orientation each prefers.
The arrangement in effect acknowledges that school must inevitably represent an interweaving of values, preferences, and personal orientations with technical knowledge about teaching and
learning. It also presupposes that local majority decisions may
not accord any more closely with the legitimate preferences of
individuals than do remote majority and bureaucratic decisions.
Thus, schools of choice typically leave educational decisions largely in professional hands but enable families to leave a school situation they do not like in favor of another they find more compatible
and more promising for their child. It is for this reason that advocates find that choice alters the accountability structure of school
governance quite significantly: When the individual is free to
leave a school, a powerful and immediate form of accountability has been added. Its very existence — the right to go elsewhere —
is believed to color relationships and practices within schools of
choice even short of its exercise (deCharms, 1977).

If the values of an educational program are largely inex-
tricable from its technical aspects, then choice may be a more
effective way to empower parents than power shifts within the
system. It recognizes the necessary entanglement of technical
and public questions in the design of educational programs. It

protects the professional integrity of those programs—that is, the extent to which they can be based on technical knowledge and the professional judgments of teachers. And it also protects the interests of parents by empowering them to choose among programs. Note that the choice arrangement does not promise decision-making power or prerogatives within the school. (In some schools of choice such power is extensive—indeed, some even feature joint decision making as a major theme. But it is not an element of the choice concept, and many schools of choice do not offer it.) Yet in different terms, choice offers individual families more power than even direct participation in decisions would offer: Participation does not always assure influence, but the right to place one's child in a school one has chosen—and to remove that child if sufficiently motivated to do so—carries a guarantee of personal efficacy.

Choice would not completely change the incentive structure for educators, which some governance critics are demanding, but it would tend to modify it in important ways. From the start, the opportunity to choose and be affiliated with a school reflecting one's own professional orientation—or better yet, the opportunity to develop such a schoool—is the sort of vision that brought many people into teaching in the first place. It accords with the incentives research has shown to be prominent for teachers (Rosenholtz, 1987). But at the same time, another sort of incentive, provided by choice, should serve to heighten the responsiveness of teachers to the public: The opportunity to maintain a school according to one's own vision of education is contingent upon parental acceptance and sharing of that vision. Thus, a school of choice can remain open only as long as it continues to attract a constituency. Should it become insufficiently attuned to local families, or unsuccessful in its efforts with students, the school must be redesigned or its staff relocated elsewhere. Thus, choice would appear to introduce new and fairly effective sorts of incentives.

Issues and Challenges

We can be sure that neither site management nor choice would prove a panacea for the problems of our schools and that both would introduce challenges and risks. We turn now to an examination of what might prove to be the policy issues these two school systems would need to confront.

Perhaps the first challenge is protecting the larger public interest in schools governed primarily by the educators and parents immediately involved (as in site management) or devised by educators for selection by families (as in schools of choice). Both arrangements presume that state and district guidelines would continue to reflect the public interest and keep schools operating within parameters outlined by public policy. But site management explicitly seeks, and choice entails, a considerably enlarged role in decision making for individual schools. The critics of bureaucracy believe these decisions can be made regarding currently bureaucratically imposed requirements that do not substantially affect the public interest. Nevertheless, this would bear watching under both site-management and choice arrangements and needs to remain a concern of officials at both state and district levels. Whether the public accountability arrangements evolved to date—the testing programs and data collection—would serve to sufficiently protect the public's stake in public education remains to be seen.

A second challenge is whether the interests of students are sufficiently protected under site management and choice. Although there is no reason children would not continue formally to enjoy whatever legislative and judicial protections they now possess, it is conceivable that they would not receive as much protection in all site management and choice programs as they do under current circumstances. One reason is that, particularly under site management, what is sought in principle is not checks and balances but the lodging of a preponderance of authority with the school. Thus, the overlapping responsibilities—the checks and balances—which currently afford some protections, might tend to diminish. One can also envision circumstances and programs in which children's rights, as defined by parents and teachers, could be systematically abrogated in a program tending toward rigid control. One can also envision circumstances under which what should be educational entitlements might be insufficiently acknowledged. Imagine, for example, a school in which little groundwork is laid for the later develop-

ment of higher intellectual skills — that is, in this example, processes that are crucial but detectable only at some later date,
such as the ability to compose an essay, state a hypothesis, or
translate a mathematics problem into an equation. Both particular schools of choice, as well as site-managed schools, could
be subject to this sort of ill. By and large, however, the right
of students to withdraw from a school and enroll elsewhere might
be expected to function as a strong deterrent to the tendency
of organizations to overlook the rights and desires of their clients.
Current school governance restructuralists are inclined to assume
that individuals are likely to be better guardians of their own
best interests than organizational arrangements can be.

A third area of prospective challenge pertains to whether
the integrity of technical knowledge and professional judgment
can be protected under site management and choice. Would the
participation of parents in a site-managed school, or the power
of parents in a school of choice, jeopardize whether a teacher's
established knowledge or professional discretion were permitted
to govern the situations calling for them? Or might teachers be
forced or intimidated into decisions at odds with their best judgment of what is good for children? This is a matter of considerable and understandable concern to educators. Although there
is little systematic evidence on the question, what does exist is
reassuring in relation to such professional interests as far as
schools of choice are concerned. One of the conclusions reached
with respect to the much-studied Alum Rock choice demonstration was that power enhancement seemed to favor teachers more
than parents (Cohen and Farrar, 1977). The evidence suggests
that in schools of choice the ability of teachers to protect their
professional prerogatives might be strengthened in relation to
parents, as well as in absolute terms. At the same time, increased
parent prerogatives and satisfaction rates indicate that parent
interests are not jeopardized by the plan (Blank and others, 1983;
Raywid, 1988).

But professional educators must be concerned about other
matters as well, and a separate question must be raised about
how they might fare as wage earners under site management
and choice. Certainly under each of these arrangements, pro-

tections now usually assured by contractual agreement would need to be modified or otherwise handled. For example, the contractual principle that less senior teachers should be replaced by more senior teachers during periods of retrenchment is incompatible with the autonomy of site-managed schools and the programmatic integrity of schools of choice. It is not impossible to retain such wage-earner guarantees under site management and choice, but doing so in a fashion consistent with the new organizational structures of these schools is a challenge that will need attention (Yrchik, 1987).

Still another challenge lies in the risk already mentioned that site-managed and choice schools may become marked by the tyranny of the majority. The sorts of protections maintained outside the school — the protections extended by state and district policy, for example, and by the courts — should suffice in some regards. In another respect, however, they cannot, and either of these structural reforms would introduce a real antinomy. On the one hand, research suggests with increasing force and clarity that strong agreement on values and mission contribute much to a school's effectiveness. The capacity to generate such agreement is a substantial benefit provided by choice, and site management may also be conducive to coherence. But at the same time, genuine deference and responsiveness to all of a school's constituents at any particular time could considerably dilute that strong agreement. Is there a solution that can redeem both the educational benefits and the individual rights, that can stand at such loggerheads? Some find the solution in the choice opportunity: a dissatisfied individual or group has the privilege and chance to leave one school for another. But there may be other, less extreme solutions to this problem, and it should be viewed as a question for consideration.

A final challenge to both restructuring proposals also deserves mention. Both the site-management and choice proposals entail changes in the roles of formal leadership within these schools. As earlier noted, a number of fresh responsibilities are added for the principal of a site-managed school (Ingram, 1979). Such individuals need preparation more like that of prospective district officials in addition to preparation for the instruc-

tional leadership that principals in other schools are expected
to provide (Allard, 1983). The principals or directors of schools
of choice also need to be prepared for somewhat different functions. They may be called upon to perform more often as instructional and as symbolic leaders than most principals seem
to do, with leadership generally becoming at least as important
as the management functions more typical of principalship in
other schools (Blank, 1986; Wolf, Walker, and Mackin, 1974).
It is possible, too, that this preparation challenge will not be
restricted to a school's leaders. Teachers in site-managed schools
and in schools of choice may need different sorts of preparation
than teachers typically receive. At a minimum, this is a question that needs to be examined carefully.

Beyond these challenges that both site-managed schools
and schools of choice would have to confront, each of these
reforms must deal with unique challenges. The relatively scant
evidence to date suggests that site management faces particularly
severe implementation difficulties, since districts have proved
extremely reluctant to delegate authority for the decisions that
define school management — that is, staffing, budgetary, and curricular decisions (Clune and White, 1987; Hill, n.d.). Ironically,
of the three, districts are apparently least willing to delegate curricular authority (Clune and White, 1987). Short of such a
transferral, however, and newly infused authority, the term "site
management" appears to be a misnomer. This is no minor flaw:
For a restructuralist even more than for other reformers, non-
implementation risks are a major liability. It is the nonimple-
mentation of more modest reforms that makes restructuring
necessary in the first place. If neither small changes nor large
ones can be implemented, there is simply little hope to be had
for public schools.

There is a second characteristic challenge associated with
the site management proposal: that of partial or semi-implemen-
tation. Recall that the proposal has two aspects: the transfer of
increased authority to the school level and the sharing of that
authority with teachers and parents. There are pitfalls associated
with the adoption of either of these ideas without the other. Some
have questioned the importance of simply shifting authority

within the system. As long as superintendents name and remove principals, it is charged, effective power has not shifted; how significant can it be if a superintendent merely delegates particular decisions to an appointee? There are others who insist that even such a modest change is important because it locates decisions at the level of their application. On the other hand, some find such a shifting of authority of potential risk to teachers. As some have expressed it, the transfer of decentralized authority to principals could make them dictators. Some teacher groups have recognized the ensuring risks and speculated about whether they are not better off with strong authority emanating from downtown than from down the hall. Parallel concerns have been expressed about the reduction of the site-management reform to an exclusive focus on shared authority and decision making within the school. Some observers are concerned that district officials may promote such a conception of site management, thus bypassing decentralization and failing to address the critical governance problems that recommend this reform (Kolderie, 1988).

A third challenge is that of engaging teachers in the site-management effort. To the extent that they are skeptical of how genuine administrators are in their desire to change the structure of schools, teachers may be skeptical about whether the time investment is worthwhile. According to all accounts, a significant time investment is necessary. Moreover, even for the nonskeptical, the tasks of site management do not always appear immediately germane to their function as teachers (Hill, n.d., p. 7).

Time gives rise to another challenge with which the site-management approach to restructuring must contend. There is widespread agreement that site management must be given time to develop within a school, and that the changes it brings will come slowly (McPike, 1987; Zander, n.d.). This is quite reasonable an expectation, given what we have learned about change and the need to transform the culture of a school before much else can occur (Sarason, 1982). But for those who hold that school reform is needed immediately, a strategy that takes time to bear fruit has serious drawbacks.

Finally, early research suggests that it is difficult to instill the shared authority of site management firmly in the organizational structure of a school. One of the greatest challenges to the eight site-management programs sponsored and studied by the Northwest Area Foundation was getting them to be seen in their schools as a process integral to the school's total operation, rather than as a separate project. Those associated with the school continued to see site management as just one venture parallel to other ventures under way within the school and not as a process that had been adopted to change school governance in general (Hill, n.d.). As an early report put it, "The biggest barrier of all may be largely a conceptual one. Few of the projects have . . . succeeded in seeing school-based management as a system by which the school is managed. Instead, it is seen as a 'project,' something that is added on to all the other structures and activities within the school" (Olson, 1985). This challenge is not insignificant, for restructuring is intended as a fundamental and pervasive transformation, not as a discrete program. To succeed as restructuring it must modify the way in which "business as usual" is transacted by most school participants most of the time. If they refuse to accept a restructuring proposal in this fashion, it cannot fulfill its purpose.

Three major challenges are unique to the proposal that we restructure schools by making them schools of choice. First, the choice arrangement too can face implementation problems. Simply converting schools of assignment into open enrollment schools does not guarantee that a great deal will happen. Some feel that the best way to assure the transformation that restructuring seeks is to invite and stimulate interested teachers to establish such programs. Teacher choice is important, and administrative support is also necessary, in the form of freeing schools from external constraints and directives, encouraging them to innovate broadly with respect to school organization as well as curriculum and instruction, and giving them the time to plan the program. Short of such conditions, it is possible that declaring schools to be schools of choice will change very little about them.

A second major challenge involves assuring certain sorts of equity within schools of choice. Although such schools have proved to be highly effective instruments for furthering equity, they have also posed two kinds of equity challenges. The first is how to avoid intensifying ethnic and socioeconomic segregation in schools that are chosen, in light of known correlations between such groupings and child-rearing tendencies. Although there are exceptions, it is well known that middle class and affluent parents often select open schools for their youngsters, while working class parents gravitate toward back-to-basics and fundamental schools. Care must be taken to avoid themes for schools of choice that could increase racial or socioeconomic isolation (Moore and Davenport, 1988). Experience of several sorts suggests ways to avoid this kind of segregation by choice: experience with respect to the way school themes are selected and articulated (Raywid, 1985), the way schools of choice are located (Waldrip and Lotspeich, 1978), and the way they are marketed (Hale and Maynard, 1987). But this kind of equity concern is a challenge that needs addressing in a choice arrangement.

There can be equity problems of another sort in districts where some of the schools are schools of choice and others are not. Since the schools of choice sometimes receive more favorable funding, some have cried foul, even in districts where the differential is plainly marked as start-up funds only. Even more fundamental are the equity problems raised by the departure for schools of choice of youngsters whose families are active choosers, leaving neighborhood schools to the nonchoosers. Staff in these schools have protested that the consequence is an unfair, two-tiered system. The reply of choice advocates is that the arrangement should and does bring benefits in the form of improvements not just to the schools of choice but to all local schools (Raywid, 1988). Nevertheless, there remains a challenge to help assure the realization of this kind of benefit.

Another such challenge is that of the inactive chooser (Hirschman, 1969). First, how can each family be apprised of the opportunity to choose in such a way that all are able and disposed to use it, and to use it wisely? The families most prone to take rapid advantage of the choice option are the more educated and well-to-do. Thus the interests of the less fortunate may need protecting in a choice system. What happens in such a system to children whose families fail to exercise the choice option? This becomes a challenge because the temptation is to use these nonchoosers to solve the system's problems (for example, by placing such youngsters in underenrolled programs). An all-choice system that ended up with some schools filled with choosers and others populated solely by nonchoosers would face real equity problems.

Conclusion

We began by asserting that one major impetus to restructuring schools has been the conviction that they are out of synch with both their external and internal environments. it is a conviction of growing prominence. A recent analyst has asserted that the current wave of school reform will fail because it does not address the way schools are organized and controlled (Chubb, 1988). Increasing numbers appear convinced that it is going to prove impossible to change anything very important about schools, short of extensively redesigning them (Evans, 1983; David, 1987). Restructuralists who focus on school governance share such concerns.

To date, only two proposals have been elaborated for restructuring governance of and within public schools. We have examined them, seen their implications for such fundamental questions of school organization as school mission, roles, and social order, and we have reviewed challenges specific to each. We conclude with a summary of the major advantages of site management and choice as models for the restructuring of school governance.

Site management enjoys an important advantage in the currency of the concerns it addresses. It promises decentralization and debureaucratization, which have been major demands made by school critics in the interest of ending a variety of ills. Site management is also directly and centrally concerned with "teacher empowerment," which is an item of considerable current prominence. Several of the most respected excellence reports have called for such empowerment (Carnegie Task Force on Teaching as a Profession, 1986; National Governors' Association, 1986), and a number of researchers have argued its centrality to school improvement (Darling-Hammond and Wise, 1983). These are substantial advantages because they put pressure on otherwise lukewarm school officials to adopt site management. Moreover, the proposal is enjoying a highly receptive press, and reports of relevant developments in Dade County, Hammond, and Rochester are not only promising but exciting. According to at least some commentators, even when site-management arrangements fall short of genuine management of schools by teachers, teachers feel they are being consulted and enjoying some input into decisions, which has been a morale booster (Clune and White, 1987). All these points speak for the site-management strategy.

The choice proposal also has distinct advantages. It is a package combining curricular, instructional, organizational, and governance change in one proposal. Thus, to introduce choice is to launch an effective catalyst for a number of changes in school organization and program. For teachers, it combines the need to function as a professional with the opportunity to do so. It empowers and engages teachers directly in modifying educational practice. Teachers become involved in decisions and management, but only in the context of pursuing what is most germane to them, rather than in a separate connection that suggests they as teachers are assuming new and separable functions. The choice arrangement also has the considerable advantage of starting from a clean slate with a new school — a newly assembled group — which makes change easier and more assured. And the fact that both staff and students select a school suggests that it will very probably achieve a firmer sense of mission, based on a stronger consensus and greater coherence than can schools of assignment. Choice also offers full and immediate empowerment to all associated with a school — by bringing them there in the first place and by enabling them to leave if they wish to do so.

There is reason, then, to find promise in both of these proposals to restructure the way schools are governed and controlled. Either might help bring schools into better — that is, more appropriate and more productive — adjustment with their environments.

References

Allard, W. "The Reorganization of a School System." *Catalyst for Change,* Fall, 1983, pp. 26–30.

Anglin, L. "Teacher Roles and Alternative School Organizations." *Educational Forum,* 1979, *43,* 438–452.

Blank, R. "Principal Leadership in Urban High Schools: Analysis of Variation in Leadership Characteristics." American Education Research Association, San Francisco, April 1986.

Blank, R., and others. *Survey of Magnet Schools - Final Report: Analyzing a Model for Quality Integrated Education.* Washington, D.C.: James H. Lowry & Associates, 1983.

Cairns, J., Molberg, L., and Zander, B. J. *Decentralization of Decision Making in Public Education: An Overview of School Based Management.* St. Paul, Minn.: Public School Incentives, 1983.

Carnegie Task Force on Teaching as a Profession. *A Nation Prepared: Teachers for the 21st Century.* New York: Carnegie Forum on Education and the Economy, 1986.

Casner-Lotto, J. "Expanding the Teacher's Role: Hammond's School Improvement Process." *Phi Delta Kappan,* 1988, *69* (5), 349–353.

Chapman, J., and Boyd, W. L. "Decentralization, Devolution, and the School Principal: Australian Lessons on Statewide Educational Reform." *Educational Administration Quarterly,* 1986, *22,* 28–58.

Chubb, J. E., and Moe, T. M. "Politics, Markets, and the Organization of Schools." *American Political Science Review, 1988, 82* (4), 1065–1087.

Clark, D. "Thinking About Leaders and Followers: Restructuring the Roles of Principals and Teachers." Paper given at Conference on Restructuring Schooling for Quality Education, Trinity University, San Antonio, Tex., Aug. 20, 1987.

Clune, W. H., and White, P. A. *School Based Management: Institutional Variation, Implementation, and Issues for Further Research.* Madison, Wis.: Center for Policy Research in Education, 1987.

Cohen, D. K., and Farrar, E. "Power to the Parents? — The Story of Education Vouchers." *The Public Interest,* 1977, *48,* 72–97.

Cohen, M. "Instructional, Management, and Social Conditions in Effective Schools." In A. Odden and L. D. Webb (eds.), *School Finance and School Improvement: Linkages for the 1980s.* Cambridge, Mass.: Ballinger, 1983.

Coleman, J. S., and Hoffer, T. *Public and Private High Schools: The Impact of Communities.* New York: Basic Books, 1987.

Committee for Economic Development. *Investing in Our Children: Business and the Public Schools.* New York, 1985.

Cooley, C. H. *Social Organization.* New York: Schocken, 1962.

Cox, H., and Wood, J. R. "Organizational Structure and Professional Alienation: The Case of Public School Teachers." *Peabody Journal of Education,* Oct., 1980, *58* (1), 1–6.

Cronin, B. L. *Elementary School Teachers' Reactions to Pull-Out Programs.* Unpublished doctoral dissertation, School of Education, Hofstra University, Hempstead, N.Y., 1988.

Darling-Hammond, L., and Wise, A. "Teaching Standards, or Standarized Teaching?" *Educational Leadership,* 1983, *41* (2), 66–69.

David, J. L. "The Puzzle of Structural Change." Paper given at Symposium on Structural Change in Secondary Education, National Center on Effective Secondary Schools, University of Wisconsin, Madison, July 1987.

deCharms, R. "Pawn or Origin? Enhancing Motivation in Disaffected Youth." *Educational Leadership,* 1977, *34* (6), 444–448.

Erickson, D. A., and others. "The British Colombia Story: A Final Report to the National Institute of Education." Unpublished manuscript. Los Angeles: Institute for the Study of Private Schools, 1982.

Evans, H. D. "We Must Begin Education Reform 'Every Place At Once.'" *Phi Delta Kappan,* 1983, *65* (3), 173–177.

Goffman, E. *Asylums.* New York: Anchor, 1961.

Goodlad, J. I. "Improving Schooling in the 1980s: Toward the Non-Replication of Non-Events." *Educational Leadership,* 1983, *40* (7), 4–7.

Goodlad, J. I. *A Place Called School: Prospects for the Future.* New York: McGraw-Hill, 1984.

Goodlad, J. I., and others. *Looking Behind the Classroom Door.* Worthington, Ohio: Charles A. Jones, 1974.

Grant, G. "The Character of Education and the Education of Character." *Daedalus,* 1981, *110* (3), 135–149.

Guthrie, J. W. "School-Based Management: The Next Needed Education Reform." *Phi Delta Kappan,* 1986, *68* (4), 305–309.

Hale, P. D., and Maynard, L. O. "Magnet Schools: Information Dissemination and Recruitment." Magnet Schools Assistance Program Directors Conference, Silver Spring, Md.: Mar. 10, 1987.

Hall, E. "A Conversation with Peter F. Drucker." *Psychology Today,* 1982, 60–67.

Harris, L. "Confidence in White House Drops Sharply; Other Key Institutions Show Only Slight Changes." *The Harris Survey,* Dec. 15, 1986, p. 1.

Hill, C. "School Based Management: An Assessment of the Foundation's Completed Program." Unpublished manuscript. Northwest Area Foundation, Minneapolis, Minn.: n.d.

Hirschman, A. *Exit, Voice, and Loyalty: Responses to Decline in Firms and Organizations.* Cambridge, Mass.: Harvard University Press, 1969.

Ignatieff, M. *The Needs of Strangers.* New York: Viking Press, 1985.

Ingram, R. L. "The Principal: Instructional Leader, Site Manager, Educational Executive." *Thrust for Educational Leadership,* 1979, *8* (5), 23–25.

Institute for Educational Leadership. *School Boards: Strengthening Grass Roots Leadership.* Washington, D.C.: Institute for Educational Leadership, 1986.

Kanter, R. M. *The Change Masters.* New York: Simon & Schuster, 1983.

Kolderie, T. "School-Site Management: Rhetoric and Reality." Minneapolis: Humphrey Institute, University of Minnesota, 1988.

Komisar, B. P. "Is Teaching Phoney?" *Teachers College Record,* 1969, *70* (5), 407–411.

Lindelow, J. *School-Based Management.* Burlingame, Calif.: Foundation for Educational Administration, 1981.

Lipsky, M. *Street-Level Bureaucracy.* New York: Russell Sage, 1980.

Lortie, D. *School Teacher: A Sociological Study*. Chicago: University of Chicago Press, 1975.

Louis, K. S. "The Role of the School District in School Improvement." In M. Holmes, K. Leithwood, and D. Musella (eds.), *Policy Development for Effective School Administration*. Toronto: Ontario Institute for the Study of Education, forthcoming.

Louis, K. S., and others. "Alternative Structures and the Quality of Teacher Work Life." Unpublished manuscript. University of Minnesota, 1988.

McPike, L. "Shared Decision Making at the School Site: Moving Toward a Professional Model—An Interview with Patrick O'Rourke." *American Educator*, 1987, *11* (1), 10–17, 46.

Marburger, C. L. *One School at a Time: School Based Management, A Process for Change*. Columbia, Md.: National Committee for Citizens in Education, 1985.

Moore, D. R. and Davenport, S. "The New Improved Sorting Machine." Paper presented at the Education Writers Association, New Orleans, Apr. 15, 1988.

Nathan, J. *Free to Teach: Achieving Equity and Excellence in Schools*. New York: Pilgrim Press, 1983.

National Governors' Association. *Time for Results: The Governors' 1991 Report on Education*. Washington, D.C.: 1986.

Obermeyer, G. *A Report on the Status of School-Based Decision-Making*. Washington, D.C.: National Education Association, 1987.

Olson, R. A. *School-Based Management: An Interim Report, 1985*. Minneapolis, Minn.: Northwest Area Foundation, 1985.

Pekarsky, D. "Dehumanization and Education." *Teachers College Record*, 1982, *84* (2), 339–353.

Pierce, L. C. *School Site Management*. Cambridge, Mass.: Aspen Institute Program in Education for a Changing Society, 1977.

Pipho, C. "Restructuring the Schools: States Take on the Challenge." *Education Week*, Nov. 26, 1986, 19.

Purkey, S. C., Rutter, R. A., and Newmann, F. M. "U.S. High School Improvement Programs: A Profile from the High School and Beyond Supplemental Survey." *Metropolitan Education*, Winter 1986–1987, (3), pp. 59–91.

Raywid, M. A. "The Alternative in Alternatives." Unpublished manuscript, Hofstra University, 1980.

Raywid, M. A. *The Current Status of Schools of Choice in Public Secondary Education.* Hempstead, N.Y.: Project on Alternatives in Education, Hofstra University, 1982.

Raywid, M. A. "Family Choice Arrangements in Public Schools: A Review of the Literature." *Review of Educational Research,* 1985, *55* (4), 435–467.

Raywid, M. A. "Preparing Teachers for Schools of Choice." In *Issues in Teacher Education,* vol. II, T. J. Lasley (ed.). Washington, D.C.: American Association of Colleges for Teacher Education, 1986a.

Raywid, M. A. "Success Dynamics of Public Schools of Choice." In *Content, Character, and Choice in Schooling: Public Policy and Research Implications.* Washington, D.C.: National Council on Educational Research, 1986b.

Raywid, M. A. "Public Choice, Yes; Vouchers, No!" *Phi Delta Kappan,* 1987, *68* (10), 762–769.

Raywid, M. A. "The Mounting Case for Schools of Choice." Unpublished manuscript, Hofstra University, 1988.

Rosenholtz, S. J. "School Success and the Organizational Conditions of Teaching." In J. J. Lane and H. J. Walberg (eds.), *Effective School Leadership: Policy and Process.* Berkeley, Calif.: McCutchan, 1987.

Salganik, L. and Karweit, N. "Voluntarism and Governance in Education." *Sociology of Education,* 1982, *55* (2,3), 152–161.

Sarason, S. *The Culture of the School and the Problem of Change.* (2nd ed.) Newton, Mass.: Allyn & Bacon, 1982.

Sizer, T. R. *Horace's Compromise: The Dilemma of the American High School.* Boston: Houghton Mifflin, 1984.

Snider, W. " 'Package' in Baton Rouge: Choice and School-Based Management." *Education Week,* June 15, 1988.

Swidler, A. *Organization Without Authority: Dilemmas of Social Control in Free Schools.* Cambridge, Mass.: Harvard University Press, 1979.

Tanveer, S. and Nawaz, M. "Alternative Schools and Responsive Patterns of Action in Teacher Education." *Kappa Delta Pi Record,* Dec., 1979, pp. 37–40.

Tönnies, F. *Community and Society*. (Charles P. Loomis, trans.) East Lansing, Mich.: Michigan State University Press, 1957.

Vallance, E. "Hiding the Hidden Curriculum: An Interpretation of the Language of Justification in Nineteenth-Century Educational Reform." *Curriculum Theory Network*, 1973–1974 (1), 5–21.

Waldrip, D. R., and Lotspeich, E. J. "Alternative Schools: Program Marketing and Student Recruitment." In N. Estes and D. R. Waldrip (eds.), *Magnet Schools: Legal and Practical Implications*. Piscataway, N.J.: New Century Education, 1978.

White, P. A. *Resource Materials on School Based Management*. Madison, Wis.: Center for Policy Research in Education, University of Wisconsin, 1987.

Wise, A. *Legislated Learning: The Bureaucratization of the American Classroom*. Berkeley, Calif.: University of California, 1979.

Wolf, T. E., Walker, M., and Mackin, R. "Summary of the NASP Survey, 1974." Unpublished manuscript. National Alternative Schools Program, University of Massachusetts, Amherst, 1974.

Yrchik, J. "Employee Participation Programs: Considerations for the School Site." Washington, D.C.: National Education Association, 1987.

Zander, B. J. "School Based Management." Unpublished manuscript, n.d.

Zeigler, L. H., Tucker, H. J., and Wilson, L. A. "How School Control Was Wrested from the People." *Phi Delta Kappan*, 1977, *58* (7), 534–539.

✳ Part Two

New Roles and Responsibilities for the District and State

The chapters in the first part dealt with a variety of proposals to change the structure and operations of schools. The first two chapters in this part examine school restructuring as a problem of policy and organization at the school-district and state levels. Jane David's chapter (Chapter Seven) describes existing district-level restructuring efforts and draws preliminary conclusions about the problems and strategies of restructuring as seen from the district level. Michael Cohen's chapter (Chapter Eight) analyzes the rationale for state involvement in restructuring and the possible role that state government can play. Taken together, these chapters define the local and state policy contexts for future restructuring initiatives. The concluding chapter (Chapter Nine) ties together the major themes of the book and presents three possible scenarios for school restructuring.

SEVEN

Restructuring in Progress: Lessons from Pioneering Districts

Jane L. David

Pressure on school districts to restructure is mounting, as more and more people — from corporate leaders and policymakers to educators and parents — acknowledge that the current system is not working. The very phrase "structural change" signals a conception of education reform that is very different from reforms of the past. Unlike either top-down, externally defined and imposed reforms or bottom-up, school-based improvement efforts, restructuring connotes systemic change. It grows out of a combination of (1) research findings on how people and organizations change and (2) the increasing gap between what schools look like now and what they must look like in the future to meet society's needs.

Ultimately, a school system designed to engage the minds of twenty-first century students will look quite different from present school systems, created during the industrial era. The explosion of information and mechanization of routine tasks will force schools to teach ways of learning and reasoning instead of rules and facts. Time and space will be allocated in very different ways. Roles and relationships among staff members and between staff and students will change; teacher accountability will rest on informed professional judgment and measures far more sophisticated and relevant to educational goals than current multiple-choice standardized tests. As in business and industry, flexibility to respond to a rapidly changing world will be built into the system.

But the current organization of school districts is a far cry from this vision. The core of education — interactions between teachers and students — lies buried inside classrooms within schools embedded in highly centralized, tightly regulated bureaucratic structures — school districts (for example, see Timar and Kirp, 1988; Cuban, 1988). Such structures are effective for certain goals, such as standardization, but not for the goal of stimulating innovation and change (for example, see Kanter, 1983).

Imagine a circular jigsaw puzzle with students and teachers in the center, surrounded by rings of interlocking pieces representing the demands of local, state, and federal agencies; for example, age and ability grouping of students, testing programs, textbooks, curriculum, graduation requirements, staff certification, and so on (David, 1987). Trying to change one piece of an interlocking set of pieces is not possible unless the other pieces are flexible enough to yield when the shape of a neighboring piece is changed.

Continuing the jigsaw puzzle metaphor, previous reform efforts have either added another piece to the puzzle or have tried to change one piece without recognizing the need to change neighboring pieces. Centrally defined and imposed reforms typically have added new pieces with little effect on interactions between students and teachers (Kirst and Meister, 1985). School-based reforms have tried to affect the pieces in the center without changing any surrounding pieces (David and Peterson, 1984; Berman and Gjelten, 1984).

The goal of structural change is to change the puzzle itself — to change the rigid, interlocking nature of the system to a more flexible, responsive structure. Can school districts do this? There are not many examples of bureaucratic structures transforming themselves. Kanter (1983) cites a few in the corporate world and Wissler and Ortiz (1986) cite a few examples of school district decentralization. Moreover, school districts are not independent systems; they too are constrained, often severely, by state and even federal requirements. Yet many of the constraints that lock teachers and students into old ways of operating are dictated by districts. In principle, districts can request relief from certain external demands by states and the federal government.

Research on organizational change and leadership (for example: Fullan, 1982; Kanter, 1983), provides some guidance to districts ready to take on the process of restructuring, as do reports that offer new visions of what schools and districts might look like (for example, Sizer, 1984; Goodlad, 1984; Carnegie Task Force on Teaching as a Profession, 1986). All point to the need to decentralize authority, create more professional workplaces, and focus resources on teaching and learning.

Three Restructuring Districts

To learn more about the extent to which school districts can transform themselves and what it takes to do so, we studied three districts that have undertaken restructuring efforts. We began with a telephone survey of over a hundred districts to locate those that best represented districts whose actions have led to new roles and relationships and organizational arrangements. We selected three districts for more intensive study: the Dade County Public Schools (Miami, Florida), the Jefferson County Public Schools (Louisville, Kentucky), and the Poway Unified School District (Poway, California).

These districts are by no means the only ones undergoing significant change. Those described elsewhere include the ABC Unified School District in Cerritos, California (Sickler, 1988); the Cincinnati Public Schools in Cincinnati, Ohio (Johnson, 1988); District four in Manhattan's East Harlem in New York City (Meier, 1987); the Hammond Public Schools in Hammond, Indiana (Casner-Lotto, 1988); and the Rochester Public Schools in Rochester, New York (Rodman, 1987). Based on these published accounts, our findings are consistent with their experiences.

A team of two interviewers spent two to three days in each district we covered interviewing central office and school staff. We also asked to visit schools that best exemplified new roles and arrangements. Hence, the study is purposely biased toward the positive, as the following descriptions of each district reflect. Our goal was to extract lessons from the experiences of these pioneering districts that could inform others. Following a brief description of each district is a discussion of their goals, visions, and strategies for restructuring.

Dade County Public Schools (Miami, Florida). The Dade County Public Schools are changing fundamentally their governance structure — a major undertaking in an urban district of 276 schools. Moving beyond the state's mandates and incentives for faculty participation in school governance, Dade has launched its own approach to the professionalization of its teachers through school-based management and shared decision making. Their approach evolved from a strong partnership between district and union leaders and is based on the premise that student learning requires good teachers, which in turn demands working environments that will attract the best and the brightest to teaching.

Attractive workplaces for teachers are described as those that provide opportunities for exercising discretion in the classroom as well as authority and leadership in school decision making. With the goal of creating such working environments, the superintendent launched a pilot program, directed by a newly created office of school-based management, to devolve more authority and discretion to the schools.

The district acquainted schools with the concepts of school-based management and shared decision making and provided each school with a copy of the report of the Carnegie Forum's Task Force on Teaching as a Profession. Schools were then invited to submit proposals to participate in the first wave of school-based management. Of the fifty-five schools whose faculties voted to participate and that submitted proposals, thirty-three were selected by a joint management-labor team to be part of the pilot program. These schools receive the same level of funds as all other schools, based on their enrollment and the district average per pupil expenditure of roughly $3,400 (excluding special-program budgets). However, the pilot schools receive their funds as a lump sum, allowing them significantly greater flexibility in deciding how to allocate some 90 percent of their budgets. The rest of the schools in Dade County have discretion over only the materials and supplies portion of the budget, roughly 10 percent.

Within the constraints of state rules, schools can allocate their budget however they wish; they can spend more or less on staff or equipment or utilities. If school staff are hindered by barriers posed by school-board rules, teacher-labor contract provisions, or state department of education regulations, they can request a waiver from a committee established expressly for that purpose. Schools are also free to set up whatever governing structure they wish, provided that teachers are given a significant role in school planning and decision making.

In addition to a three-day school improvement conference for teams of principals and teachers, each pilot school receives $6,250 for staff development. The teacher-director of the Teacher Education Center, which runs all district staff-development programs, encourages teachers in the pilot schools to determine their specific in-service needs. She has seen teachers in the pilot schools take more initiative for requesting the kind of training they need. Thus, one school asked for training in effective leadership, another in bilingual education, and another a writing course.

The partnership between top district officials and the teachers' union is evident at all levels of the school-based management program. In addition to the union's committee to review waiver requests, there is an understanding between the district and the union that problems between teachers and their principal will be resolved by a joint committee composed of two union and two central office representatives.

The School Based Management/Shared Decision-Making Program, a four-year pilot, is still in its early stages, so it is premature to assess its full impact. For example, much of the schools' new authority over personnel will not be realized until staff begin to turn over. Although a few schools have replaced teachers with hourly instructors or assistant principals with teachers, class-size limitations and reluctance to lay off fellow teachers restrict schools' immediate options. When teachers retire or resign for other reasons, and when school staff have had the time to create new ideas regarding organizational structures, opportunities to significantly change school structures will increase.

Nevertheless, many immediate effects can already be observed. Participating schools have set up new governance structures, instead of relying on existing committees or councils. These structures look quite different from one school to the next. For example, one school has a thirty-two-member council representing all the schools' constituencies; a subset of nine forms the basic working group for creating plans for school organizations and curriculum. Another school has a ten-member elected committee of teachers and administrators.

Schools have requested and been granted dozens of waivers. Schools can hire noncertified teachers with special talents to teach classes in their area of expertise; gifted and talented students can take an elective instead of physical education.

School staff have exercised their new authority in a variety of ways. One school added a seventh period to give all teachers a full period in which to engage in school-based management. Another school replaced its pull-out Spanish program, which required students to leave their regular classrooms for Spanish instruction, with a schoolwide program that met twice a week. One junior high council replaced an assistant principal with two teachers who devote part of their time to counseling and discipline. Another management group chose to expand their computer program and used funds to purchase computers.

No one argues that school-based management is easy. Teachers spend much more time on top of an already time-consuming job. But at the same time they are more enthusiastic and feel more in control. Principals also spend more time on the job but understand that sharing their authority with teachers (and in some schools, with parents, students, and community members) is a priority of the district leadership and leads to creative strategies that best meet the needs of their students and school community. Central administrators are encouraging schools to take risks and experiment; they are committed to bottom-up restructuring and will not pass judgment until the completion of the four-year pilot program.

Other schools have already asked to become part of this program. From the district's standpoint, this is the ideal way for the program to expand; they will initiate a second pilot program this year. District leaders are leery of spreading school-based management too quickly in their districts; they are anxious to continue to learn from the experiences of the pilot schools.

In addition to school-based management, Dade's reforms include several other major initiatives, such as: satellite learning centers (schools at the workplace); Saturday morning classes at schools throughout the district, a nine-week mini-sabbatical program of seminars, professional clinics, and research for teachers; and a program that enables teachers who voluntarily transfer to a school where they represent a racial minority to complete advanced degrees at a local university tuition-free.

All Dade County schools, including the pilot schools, will have their efforts boosted by the new teachers' contract. In addition to substantial salary increases (averaging 28 percent over the next three years), the new contract contains an entire article entitled "Professionalization of Teaching and Education" that includes the creation of

- A pilot peer intervention and assistance program to assist teachers
- A pilot career-ladder program for teachers
- A professional leave-credit bank so that teachers can attend meetings, conferences, and institutes
- A grant proposal program to fund educational issues forums planned by school faculties
- Continued teacher involvement in planning and designing new educational facilities and in selecting and assessing principals and assistant principals

Jefferson County Public Schools (Louisville, Kentucky). The leadership of the Jefferson County Public Schools (JCPS) has made a long-term commitment to restructure their system of 153 schools. JCPS leaders have articulated a philosophy of restructuring, reflecting the premise that long-term fundamental change begins with many small steps guided by a shared set of goals and values. But their philosophy goes beyond providing a common vision and vocabulary; it is observable in a series of actions that have brought together ongoing activities and resulted in new structures, players, and roles. Throughout the system, school staff are increasing their skills and knowledge in order to create more effective learning environments.

Following many years of turmoil in the district, the new superintendent in 1981 laid the groundwork for redesigning Jefferson County's schools. At the vanguard is a structure that is physically and functionally unique for a school district — the JCPS/Gheens Academy. Funded predominantly by the local Gheens Foundation, the Academy enjoys the political, moral, and financial support of the district and the community. It is both a resource for the continuing professional development of JCPS staff and a center for leading the district's efforts to restructure its schools and the teaching profession.

The Academy has grown from an abstract idea just a few years ago to an entire building with a staff of sixty under the guidance of the superintendent and the academy's executive director, who was selected for his commitment to empower teachers and restructure schools. The Academy's staff come from various district offices (staff development, in-service, library) and schools, and some are assigned part time from the University of Louisville. Looking more like an executive training center than a school district building, the Academy stands as a physical symbol of the importance of teachers and their professional development.

The Academy has an ongoing array of professional development activities for teachers and administrators and curriculum resource and production centers. Designed to promote and model collegial interaction and intellectual stimulation, it is a place where JCPS staff have access to each other and to new ideas. One principal commented that he spends one day a week at the Academy to pick up new ideas and skills.

Academy staff have introduced JCPS teachers and administrators to recent reports on educational reform and to research on structural change and effective schools as well as related literature from the corporate world. One teacher noted that: "We have gained a lot from Gheens . . . we have things here we'd never heard of before."

The superintendent and the Academy have also created a climate for their district that encourages teachers and administrators to take risks — to experiment with new instructional approaches and methods of organization. They have communicated throughout the district a vision of schools as environments for satisfying work and productive learning. At the same time they have communicated that each school's staff needs to translate this message into images and actions appropriate to the school's particular needs and circumstances, and to assess what they do in terms of their own long range goals and vision. Through this messsage, the Academy also serves as a unifying force for the variety of existing programs, projects, and innovations throughout the district.

In addition to its role as a resource for professional development, the Academy has developed the concept of professional development schools — somewhat akin to teaching hospitals in the medical profession — to translate the rhetoric of restructuring into action. Working with representatives of the teachers' union, administrators, and university staff, the Academy developed a concept paper that included "guiding images" of workplaces satisfying for teachers and environments productive of learning for students. Academy staff invested considerable effort communicating and explaining these concepts to all school staff.

Schools were then invited to become part of the process of defining and becoming professional development schools; the criterion for acceptance was commitment from teachers and administrators to reorganize their school in ways to become more productive. Representatives from the twenty-four schools selected to participate then worked with Academy staff to elaborate the guiding images into a set of visions, beliefs, and standards for the professional development schools, which was then endorsed by the school board.

The leadership of the JCPS superintendent and the actions of the Gheens Academy have created an environment for change which teachers and principals have capitalized on. Restructuring has led to the Academy, the professional development schools, and a variety of new structures and practices. It has also provided a framework and direction that helps teachers judge and experiment with many ongoing activities and view them as part of the restructuring process. For example:

• Middle schools are organized into mini-schools of roughly 150 students each run by a team of five teachers, one of whom plays the role of "team leader." Each team makes its own decisions about instructional methods, curriculum, scheduling, and materials; as one teacher described: "The schedule is entirely up to the team; we don't ring any bells. There was a time when we believed only counselors could do that." This structure has led, for teachers, to more active involvement in making decisions, more professional exchange, more willingness to experiment, and, as a result, more professional satisfaction. The reduced isolation of teachers makes them more visible and hence more accountable to each other. Because different teams create different learning environments, students who "just don't fit" one team's mini-school can move to another — an option that did not exist before.

• Teachers are more actively involved in defining and developing measures of educational success, because accountability becomes a shared responsibility. Each school writes a school improvement plan based on school descriptions provided by the district. Middle schools use self-assessment procedures developed by the Center for Early Adolescence. Teachers and administrators are learning a variety of ways to improve their understanding of classroom practice, including the use of clinical supervision.

• Two elementary professional development schools are initiating an experiment in grouping students by more than one age in which the same teacher will remain with a group of students for several years.

• Under a federal grant, staff from JCPS and the University of Louisville have created "job descriptions" for student teachers that reflect the roles and responsibilities they will be expected to fulfill in different teaching assignments. In this way both the supervising teacher and student teacher share expectations, which increases the likelihood that both will benefit from the experience. This is one of many in a growing number of cooperative ventures between JCPS and the University of Louisville.

JCPS staff are proud of their efforts. Teachers express a growing sense of professionalism; administrators are taking advantage of new opportunities for growth in leadership and management. In contrast to most "reform" efforts, which put pressures on staff to conform quickly to new standards, the approach in JCPS is to develop their human resources, which is prerequisite to the improvement of teaching and learning. The Academy is a resource for staff development, the professional development schools are, for school staffs, an "invitation to invention," and inventing new methods of educational accountability is a shared and evolving responsibility. As the Academy's motto quoted above implies, when teachers and students are successful, the Academy has succeeded.

Poway Unified School District (Poway, California). The Poway Unified School District, which is spread over the hills just northeast of San Diego, exemplifies a balance between centralized and decentralized authority. Under the twelve-year leadership of a superintendent committed to decentralized decision making, Poway combines school-site budgeting and management with shared decision making. The superintendent's philosophy is that educational decisions should be made by the professionals closest to the students. Poway's size (20,000 students), continuous growth, and predominantly homogeneous, advantaged population have provided a hospitable environment for testing the limits of decentralization.

In Poway, school-based management is not a program added to the existing structure — it is the way the school system already operates. It is the result of a lengthy decentralization and professional development process begun by the superintendent on his arrival twelve years ago. Each school receives directly virtually all the funds it will use to operate during the year, including money for staffing and supplies. Funds allocated for building maintenance, food and transportation services, and the bulk of staff development are retained by the district. At each level of decision making, staff are encouraged if not required to participate. (The union contract requires that teachers participate in decisions about the staffing budget.)

School-based management and shared decision making in Poway are embedded in a school-district culture that: (a) maintains a focus on student learning, (b) promotes continuous professional development for all staff members, and (c) values and rewards hard work. The culture and tone of the district have been set by the superintendent and are modeled by him and his small central office staff. Everyone's job, from clerks to associate superintendents, is described in terms of support for student learning. The district invests heavily in staff development that supports instructional improvement; last year's budget for staff development was $250,000.

Teachers are offered an array of staff-development programs: for example, clinical teaching, cooperative learning, and hands-on mathematics and science. Most teachers are active participants in these programs, in spite of the absence of financial incentives, because this is expected of professionals. This expectation is communicated by the quality of the training, the comfortable setting in which it is conducted, and the fact that teachers are treated to dinner in a posh country club restaurant after their training. Principals are encouraged to attend teachers' workshops, which they do (which is another incentive for teachers), and are required to attend a series of workshops on clinical supervision and on leadership and management techniques.

Planning and decision making at the district level are open to school staff and in fact could not function otherwise since the superintendent has reduced the district staff to a small number. Thus, for example, all curriculum development is done by committees of teachers, not by central office staff. The assistant superintendents for elementary and secondary schools act as organizers and facilitators for teachers; there is no district office of curriculum or curriculum coordinator. Principals participate in the superintendent's annual budget process. Teachers from each school attend monthly forums with the superintendent.

Each school receives a lump-sum budget for staff and for materials and supplies based on school enrollment. The staffing budget is allocated in terms of personnel staffing units (PSUs), each of which equals the average teacher salary plus benefits. (The principal, assistant principal, and school secretary are not included in this budget.) A combination of state and union contract rules (such as class-size limits) predetermines that most of the staffing budget will go to classroom teachers. However, every school has one or more PSUs over which they have complete discretion. One school might choose to hire several aides, another part-time specialists (for example, a music teacher), or a counselor, and another school, anticipating an enrollment increase that might not be enough to justify another PSU, might choose to hold on to the funds.

In addition to the staffing budget, each school receives an annual materials and supplies budget as well as its share of funds from the state-funded School Improvement Program and lottery. An elementary school with 800 students handles a budget of $75,000. Each school has determined its own process for deciding how these funds will be spent. In some schools part or all of the budget is divided among the teachers to be spent however each teacher wants. In other schools all expenditures are decided by a schoolwide committee and agreed on by the entire staff. The degree to which teachers are involved in school-level decisions is largely a function of the style of the principal, although all teachers are strongly encouraged by the district to maximize teacher participation and are evaluated on that basis.

Poway staff and community are exceedingly proud of their schools. They cite numerous honors and awards from the state and the U.S. Department of Education. Teachers describe themselves as professionals who are treated as such. The only blemish, acknowledged by all, is the tension between the teachers' union and management, which reflects in large part the anti-union stance of the community and district leadership. Yet even this tension interferes little with the business of education, primarily because salary increases are limited by the total funds available, which in California is determined by the state. Also, Poway has begun experimenting with "trust agreements" as a less formal mechanism for reaching agreement between the union and management on specific issues and concerns. Poway's current peer evaluation activities fall under this new kind of agreement.

Three Themes

These three districts illustrate the complexity of the restructuring process. Each is taking steps to change the many
organizational structures imbedded in a single school district.
They are changing management procedures by increasing school-
site autonomy and shared decision making, and are making
corresponding changes in the size and roles of central office staff.
They are changing how schools are organized — redesigning
schedules and curricula, creating schools within schools. They
are changing their accountability procedures — shifting responsibility to teaching staffs and providing parents with choices
among alternatives. They are changing the methods of staff
development — offering an array of professional development opportunities to teachers and principals in training centers and
at their schools.

Restructuring involves all of these pieces, but there are
too many to change at once. Having each a unique history and
circumstances, restructuring districts differ in the sequence of
their changes. Each district we describe has made some of the
changes mentioned and has plans for others. For example, Dade
County began with school-based management in pilot schools
and is now offering increased opportunities for professional
development. In contrast, Jefferson County began with an emphasis on professional development for all school staff and is
moving toward increased school autonomy. Poway began by
delegating some budgetary authority to its schools and has added
new responsibilities to its schools each year.

It is too soon to pass judgment about the ultimate success of any of these programs. Each district continues to face
difficult challenges. Will Dade County's experiment persist
beyond the pilot stage? Can Poway maintain its highly decentralized operation in the face of rapid increases in enrollment
over the next decade? How dependent are the Jefferson County
Public Schools on the Gheens Foundation, and what will the
professional development schools look like? Yet in each district,
there are positive signs, reflected especially in the excitement

and enthusiasm of the teachers. As laboratories for restructuring, the mistakes and successes of these districts offer a wealth of valuable guidance. The next section looks more closely at the steps these districts have taken to restructure their systems.

Each district has its own unique set of circumstances, and, accordingly, its own path to restructuring. Yet, comparing their very different experiences, there are common themes that distinguish in significant ways the approaches of these districts from other types of reforms. Their approaches incorporate much of what has been learned in the last two decades about the process of organizational change and educational improvement.

The following three themes are evident in the directions and actions of each of the three districts.

1. The goal of school restructuring is long-term, comprehensive change guided by a conception of schools as stimulating workplaces and learning environments. Restructuring schools is not simply a new program or approach designed to add to or change part of a school system. Its eventual goal is to change fundamentally how a school functions in order to create a productive learning environment. There are many possible routes to this goal and many possible productive learning environments. Districts are not only choosing between alternatives, they are inventing them. Therefore, *risk taking and experimentation are important components of the process of structural change.*

2. School staff members need the skills, authority, and time to create new roles and environments appropriate for them. To create and support new ways of thinking and new roles, teachers and administrators need more and better opportunities for professional development than they now have. In addition to expanding the skills of school staff, districts can stimulate the creation of new roles and learning environments by increasing school autonomy (through school-based management plus waivers) and by giving teachers a significant voice in decision making (through shared decision making), as well as giving them the time needed to take on new responsibilities.

3. Restructuring schools requires building new coalitions of support and creating new conceptions of accountability. To ensure broad-based and lasting support for school restructuring, districts begin by actively participating in the creation of new coalitions, often forging cooperative partnerships between historical adversaries. These new coalitions can be achieved by focusing on the educational goals of restructuring and by developing a shared set of expectations (including new ways of judging results) among superintendents, school boards, teachers' unions, and their communities.

These themes are elaborated below, incorporating how school-district leaders conceptualize what they are doing and the strategic choices they make, and illustrated by examples from the three districts.

The Purpose: New Goals, Visions, and Attitudes

The goal of school restructuring is long-term, comprehensive change guided by a conception of schools as stimulating workplaces and learning environments.

What Is New About School Restructuring? School restructuring is much more than "just another program." Current restructuring efforts set in motion and institutionalize new educational practices and processes that are guided by the overriding goal of creating satisfying workplaces for teachers and staff and productive learning environments for students. These efforts are not characterized by the usual prescriptions associated with reforms. They are not designed to add to or change just one part of a school system, they are not targeted to particular students or content areas, and they do not specify learning objectives or outcomes.

School restructuring is systemic and comprehensive; it is intended to change how districts and schools are organized and how individual roles are defined. Districts have chosen different approaches to change, but they share the goal of a systemwide change that will result ultimately in significantly different and improved learning environments for students. Thus it is not a matter of implementing peer evaluation or clinical supervision or school-based management for its own sake, but because each contributes to the larger goal of creating more effective teaching and learning.

Recognizing that school restructuring is a very complex undertaking, district leaders do not expect immediate results; they realize that changing an organization means changing people's attitudes, roles, and relationships. Jefferson County views the creation of professional development schools as a ten-year process. Decentralization in Poway evolved over a period of a decade or longer. In an educational system that has changed little since its current staff were themselves school children, changing how school staff members think and act is indeed a long-term proposition.

How Districts Mobilize Schools. To initiate and sustain this new kind of broad-based reform, school-district leaders have consciously created new imagery and a new language. They work to communicate the need for and goals of restructuring to staff at all levels of the system, including professional and support staff. Leaders keep district and school staff informed of the latest research in both education and related fields such as business management.

In Dade County, every school received a copy of the report of the Carnegie Forum's Task Force on Teaching as a Profession; in Jefferson County and Poway, staff cite corporate and management books and articles, including the work of Drucker and Peters. In addition to communicating new ideas, this flow of information and imagery has resulted in a common language throughout each district. In Jefferson County, the slogan "every teacher a leader and every student a success" is heard from one end of the district to the other.

The process of restructuring does not start from scratch; it starts with the practices and activities currently in place. By reinforcing the goals of restructuring, the language and imagery of effective learning environments also provide teachers and principals with a way to judge their own ongoing practices — to decide which fit their long-range goals and which need to be adjusted or phased out. Jefferson County explicitly promotes the notion that teachers can participate in restructuring in a variety of ways, as long as their actions are consistent with a set of common values. The three district's restructuring provides an overriding framework that incorporates a variety of preexisting and new activities from professional development schools to teaming in middle schools to high schools in Theodore Sizer's Coalition of Essential Schools, a reform group dedicated to focusing and deepening the high school curriculum.

District leaders have also avoided two major pitfalls of past reforms imposed from outside schools by initiating restructuring efforts in a small number of volunteering schools. In addition to expressing a willingness to participate, schools are asked to demonstrate significant staff support for change. To become a professional development school in Jefferson County or a pilot school in Dade County, school staff members were required to vote and write reform proposals.

Districts also encourage teacher participation in restructuring their schools by providing salaries commensurate with their responsibilities. Dade County plans substantial salary increases for all teachers, and a much higher ceiling — over $60,000 — for those who qualify.

How Districts Encourage Risk Taking. Restructuring schools is not for the fainthearted. District leaders know they are taking risks, and they encourage their staffs — both central office and school-based — to take risks too. Teachers and principals are asked to experiment and to continuously assess the effects of their experiments. Jefferson County's leaders argue that systematic little tries eventually lead to large changes. In Dade County district leaders encourage school staff to learn from their successes and their mistakes. School staffs are urged to experiment without fear of punishment for failures.

These districts are moving from the known to the unknown, so risks are an essential part of progress. All the districts face the challenge of getting teachers and principals to imagine new ways of organizing their roles and their work. They recognize that risk taking requires knowledge of what to do and how to judge it as well as support and flexibility. Taking risks requires more than removing external constraints in organizations where it has been systematically discouraged for so long for it to be practiced.

The top leaders in restructuring districts — superintendents, school board members, and union heads — encourage risk taking by demonstrating their own willingness to take risks in a variety of ways. For example, hiring a radical reformer in Jefferson County communicated a new attitude of top management to district and school staff. Support for risk taking is signaled by allowing waivers from restrictive rules and regulations. Without relaxing the multitude of constraints on what schools can do (for example, constraints regarding class size, teachers' hours, class schedules, and textbook selection), current practices will remain, locked into place.

District leaders encourage and reinforce risk taking through the language they use and the activities they foster and reward. Jefferson and Dade County leaders communicate to school staff that the way to be recognized is to be innovative. When districts ask schools to volunteer to restructure, as in Dade's school-based management pilot schools and Jefferson County's professional development schools, they are inviting school-staff members to take risks. District leaders are asking principals to risk sharing their authority with teachers. And teachers are being asked to take risks — for example, to work with a team where their actions are much more visible to their colleagues than heretofore, as in Jefferson County.

The People: New Roles and Relationships

School staff members need the authority, skills, and time to create new roles and environments appropriate for them.

Why Districts Increase School Autonomy. All the restructuring districts discussed here view the school — the locus of teaching and learning — as the appropriate organizational level for mobilizing change. Schools differ in the make-up of their staff and students, as well as in their resources and facilities, and

therefore need flexibility to adapt to those differences. But real
flexibility is attained only through control over resources and
relief from rules that predetermine how those resources are to
be spent. This translates into a need for some type of school-
based management that includes budgetary control and relief
from instrusive rules and regulations.

In contrast to past reforms centered on school-site budgeting or school-based management, current restructuring reforms are not driven by notions of administrative and economic
efficiency. They are driven by the understanding that innovation and hence change are stifled by strong central control and
direction, and therefore that those closest to the students should
be free, within limits, to create environments appropriate to their
students and circumstances. Thus teacher participation in school
decision making — shared decision making — is an integral component of these school-based management approaches, as is a
focus on the goal of improved learning.

Central control is not really diminished thereby, it is
redirected: It becomes a means to create innovation (by building
in mechanisms that stimulate creativity and diversity), to maintain flexibility, and to correct itself. There is no fixed amount
of authority that properly resides in schools rather than districts.
Instead there is an ebb and flow of authority, a movement away
from and toward equilibrium, in response to external changes,
new priorities, or internal imbalances. Because districts retain
the authority to inspect results and take actions accordingly, and
because the increased authority for school staff is coupled with
increased professional responsibility, these approaches are quite
distinct from the "let a thousand flowers bloom / do your own
thing" approach of the sixties.

Stimulating diversity is a top priority now because a main
barrier to improving education is the absence of good workable
models of stimulating workplaces and learning environments.
The results of experiments provide policymakers with concrete
options. As options are created, districts might exert more control and shift the balance in order to spread the best of the new
ideas to other schools.

School-based budgeting, management, and shared decision making in restructuring districts differ from similar past

reforms in other important ways. Such mechanisms are not viewed now as ends in themselves. Simply increasing autonomy, teacher participation, and flexibility is unlikely to result in different learning environments. They must be coupled with access to new knowledge and skills as well as with encouragement and support for change, such as resources to provide time for teachers to develop and experiment with new approaches. Without these complementary items, school-level planning can easily become an empty yet time-consuming process of detailing objectives and revamping policies without touching on issues of learning.

How School Districts Devolve Authority. Each school district in our sample makes different decisions about which funds and functions to decentralize and how much oversight to provide. Often, these decisions are constrained by union or state requirements such as class-size limits. In Poway and Dade County the superintendent, with school board approval and union agreement, has given schools major control of their budgets. Both districts provide each school with a budget for staffing and for materials and supplies. Dade County goes even further in giving schools an allocation for building maintenance.

Even in these districts, however, school staffs have little control over their staffing because (a) most staffing is predetermined by state and contract rules, and (b) the district has final say over who gets hired and fired. Yet the opportunity to make even small staffing decisons sends a strong signal to school staff members. In contrast to having no control over staffing, school staff highly value having the option, in Poway, to hire several part-time specialists instead of a teacher, and, in Dade County, to replace an assistant principal with two part-time teachers.

The districts also delegate responsibilities previously held by members of the district staff. For example, teachers participate in curriculum development, and district staff play a coordinating, instead of directing, role in curriculum development across schools. School staff may also create or select professional development activities in addition to what is provided by the district.

In general, the three districts delegate to the schools those functions that most directly affect teaching and learning and re-

tain systemwide functions such as transportation and food services.

Shared decision making requires principal and teachers
to assume new roles. Districts follow different strategies to ensure that this occurs. Neither the Dade County nor Poway school
districts specifies how shared decision making should operate;
each school is free to devise its own mechanism. As a result,
there is variety of forms of school governance, ranging from huge
school-wide councils that do most of their work in small committees to schools that vote simply to divide the nonstaff budget
among teachers and have representatives make staffing decisions.

Leaders in both districts take steps to guarantee that
teachers have the opportunity to participate. In Poway, the union
contract requires that teachers participate in decisions about the
staffing budget; even stronger messages to share decision making come from central office staff, who pressure principals,
through evaluation and hiring criteria, to involve their staffs
in all school-site budgetary decisions. In Dade County, although
no formal procedures have been established, district leaders
clearly signal principals that their sharing of authority with
teachers is highly valued by the superintendent and, implicitly,
plays a major role in judging their performance. Thus principals are not only asked but feel some pressure to change their
roles.

Districts grant flexibility to school staff in different ways,
usually based on agreements negotiated with teacher unions.
In Dade County, a formal process exists for teachers and principals to request waivers from the union contract, district rules,
or state statutes. Waivers are usually granted; for example, one
elementary school has gotten permission to have a common
dismissal time instead of following the district policy of stag-
gered dismissals and another school permission for shifting its
Spanish program from a pull-out program to a mini-immersion
program.

In addition to providing professional development opportunities, which will be described below, district leaders take other
steps to facilitate and support school-site decision making. Maintaining open lines of communication with school staff is one such

step visible in Poway, where there is no middle management, and in Dade County where pilot schools report directly to the central office instead of to area offices. In Jefferson County, there is direct communication between school staff and the Gheens Academy.

Districts also support school-based management by responding quickly to requests. Poway's efficient purchasing and distribution system gets materials and supplies to school staff within three days if in stock and within two weeks if they have to go to an outside vendor.

The Emergence of New Roles. Restructuring provides opportunities for a variety of new roles and relationships throughout a school district. Coupling school-based management with shared decision making promotes the idea that the responsibility of each person — district or school administrator or teacher — is to create productive learning environments. Although one might presume that this always has been what school systems are about, in fact restructuring signals a major change in how people in school systems think about their roles and relationships. The change is from an orientation characterized by controlling and directing what goes on at the next lower level of a bureaucratic hierarchy to guiding and facilitating educational professionals in their quest for more productive learning opportunities for students.

This shift is a difficult one for district staff because administrators are accustomed to telling others what to do, and teachers have been conditioned to expect to be told what to do. Both Dade County and Jefferson County administrators struggle to communicate the goals of restructuring to teachers who are looking for "another program" that prescribes what they are to do differently.

Top district leaders guide their school systems by communicating a vision of effective learning, both to the community and to their school staffs, and help provide their immediate staff with the leadership and management skills needed to transmit the same message to the next district level. Middle managers become more focused on providing services directly to schools in a variety of ways: by improving the management and instructional skills of principals and teachers, by responding to requests from them for assistance, by relocating to the school site, or even, as in Poway, being removed, in which case the funds that paid for their positions are used as additional funds for materials and supplies.

In Poway, the superintendent shifted the district to a small, flat organization over a period of years. This resulted in (a) new kinds of responsibilities for the remaining district staff, and (b) more resources for the schools. For example, central office staff in Poway spend much of their time working directly with school staff, such as coaching principals, and delegate responsibilities to them that formerly were district activities, such as curriculum development. The reduction of the size of the district office in Poway also freed up funds, which now go directly to the schools and are evident in the additional materials and supplies as well as staff positions now available; for example, in Poway each high school academic department has a fulltime clerk to assist teachers in preparing lessons.

District leaders in Poway have taken actions beyond school-site management and shared decision making that have changed the roles and responsibilities of principals. Principals are now required to participate in professional development, instructional practices, and clinical supervision, as well as leadership and management skills (see below). The annual district planning and budgeting process has also been opened to principals.

But the greatest variety of new roles being created are those being assumed by teachers in these districts, either as a direct or indirect result of district actions. Teachers are helping to create the conditions that allow them to be facilitators of learning in the classroom. Teachers are taking on new leadership roles outside the classroom. In addition to their new roles in school decision making, teachers are assuming the roles of manager, program designer, and lead or mentor teacher, among others. Table 7.1 illustrates some of these roles.

How Districts Cultivate New Roles for Their Personnel.
Inadequate time, information, and skills severely constrain the

**Table 7.1. Examples of New Teacher
Roles in Restructuring Districts.**

- Staff members of Jefferson County's Gheens Professional Development Academy, who help respond to the professional development needs of school staff members

- Team leaders, who manage mini-schools within the middle schools in Jefferson County

- Personnel managers, who create job descriptions and interview student teacher applicants in Jefferson County

- Coaches, who observe and give feedback to teachers in the classroom in Poway

- Developers, who design and provide professional development in Dade County, Jefferson County, and Poway

- Curriculum developers, who have full responsibility for designing and adapting the curriculum in Poway

- Mentors and lead teachers in Dade County and Poway who work with new and experienced teachers in a variety of ways, for example:

  Providing teachers with assistance in specific areas such as teaching critical thinking, incorporating literature into subject areas, or integrating computers in their instruction

  Establishing networks in and among schools to exchange ideas and coordinate improvement efforts

  Directing districtwide teacher education centers and mini-sabbatical professional development programs

- Lead teachers in Dade County, who manage satellite learning centers located at parents' workplaces

creation and evolution of new roles, especially for teachers. In every district, teachers are already stretched to their limits, working a full day preparing for and teaching large classes. Without district support, willingness, and encouragement, few school staff members would have the opportunity to take on new roles and additional responsibilities.

To increase available time, district leaders provide planning time, release time, and paid time in the summer for planning and curriculum development. Principals and teachers are also careful to run meetings efficiently; in Poway, principals limit faculty meetings to items requiring group discussion and provide all necessary background information in writing in advance so that meeting time is not wasted.

The other limiting factors — information and skills — are addressed through professional development. Professional development plays a very important role in school districts engaged in structural change. Whether or not such development is the centerpiece of reform, as in Jefferson County, the ability of principals and teachers to create better learning environments is a function of their knowledge and skills. The more principals know about good instruction and how to provide useful feedback to teachers, the more effective they can be as a valuable resource for teachers and the better they can support and strengthen the learning environments of their schools. The more teachers are exposed to new knowledge through formal development activities, informal exchanges with colleagues, and visits to other schools, the more they have to draw on in creating their own effective learning environments.

The failure of many past reforms can be traced to the absence of ongoing, high-quality, instructionally related professional development programs for school staffs. For teachers and principals to change the way they do things, they need formal and informal development opportunities. Each principal and teacher can benefit from different mixes of formal workshops, collegial interaction, reading, observing others, and good feedback on practice, but all need some of each. No amount of district leadership, school autonomy, or budgetary control can compensate for an absence of opportunities to increase one's knowledge and skills.

It is hard for most educational professionals to hear the terms "in-service training" or "staff development" without negative associations. The combination of poor quality, faddish "spray and pray" workshops, and teachers' ambiguous motivations for attending ensure that they are generally a waste of time. Staff development in Poway and Jefferson County demonstrates the opposite qualities. There, professional development means a broad array of needed and interesting workshops, meetings, training sessions, and access to knowledge and resources that are directly connected to classroom practices. Their quality and connection to goals teachers share, combined with the new perception that being a professional means continuous learning, results in teachers and administrators seeking out professional development opportunities for the intrinsic satisfaction they offer rather than the usual extrinsic rewards (pay or course credit).

Professional development also encompasses induction of new teachers into the system: hence Jefferson County's professional development schools. Analogous to teaching hospitals, such schools provide on-the-job training for new teachers in settings that exemplify the best educational practices. Dade County frees experienced teachers part time so they can work with new teachers. Dade County's mentor teachers work with apprentice teachers, who are college graduates lacking education degrees; after eighteen months in the program, apprentices are qualified for certification.

How Districts Promote Professional Development. All three districts tackling structural change recognize the importance of professional development, although their resources for providing it vary considerably. At one extreme is Jefferson County, with an entire center and currently twenty-four schools built around professional development. The very existence of the Gheens Academy communicates to everyone in the school system the importance of the ongoing professional development of school staff. In Poway too, the superintendent has helped create a climate in which professional development is viewed as a valued resource for everyone associated with the school. Even clerical staff in the district office are trained to help them see how their actions contribute to the education of the district's students.

Jefferson County and Poway leaders have similar views on professional development. They believe it is important to: (1) create a climate in which ongoing professional development is viewed as desirable and even prestigious; (2) provide new knowledge and skills that teachers and administrators want and need, not the latest fad; (3) relate all professional development to student learning; and (4) invest substantial resources in such development. Even courses on management, leadership, and team building are designed to stimulate work and learning environments. More specifically, relating professional development to classroom instruction focuses the attention of staff on ways to engage students in learning to think, solve problems, and work in teams as well as for school staff members to interact as colleagues and grow intellectually.

In Poway, for example, school-district leaders required principals to participate in intensive training on clinical supervision and strongly urged them to attend workshops on instruction for their teachers. In fact, most principals attended several series of workshops on instruction in order to be present when different groups of their teachers participated. In this way, principals both demonstrated their support for instructional improvement and learned instructional skills themselves. Principals reported that the training in clinical supervision was invaluable; it changed the whole tone and effectiveness of their teacher evaluations by teaching them what to look for and how to deliver constructive feedback.

Poway school leaders also pride themselves on keeping up with the latest and best in professional development, drawing from both the world of education and the private sector. A young Poway teacher taking a graduate education course at a nearby university noted that for each new technique or practice introduced in her course, she had not only already heard about in her district but had been trained in it.

Jefferson County's professional development schools are being created now and will eventually function as education's equivalent for new teachers to teaching hospitals. Aided by the resources of the Gheens Academy, this goal provides an incentive for the schools to create exciting educational environments that can provide training grounds for new teachers; they are expected to be exemplars of teaching and administrative practices. Staff members from these schools have already participated in the development of a set of visions, goals, and standards for their schools.

Even in a climate in which workshop attendance, for example, is valued by teachers, there are limits to the amount of time and energy available for professional growth. Both Poway and Jefferson County's extensive offerings include provision for release time for teachers—time to attend training sessions, to review new materials, and to visit other schools. Dade County's new teachers' contract calls for joint management-labor task forces to develop a range of professional development programs including a professional leave bank and a school-based educational issues forum.

The Political Context: New Coalitions and New Conceptions of Accountability

Restructuring schools requires building new coalitions of support and creating new conceptions of accountability.

Building New Alliances. Restructuring requires new kinds of alliances, some between historical adversaries and others involving partners outside school districts in new ways. Because restructuring is comprehensive and long term, a superintendent needs the support of the school board, the teachers' union or other organization, and the community. Conversely, other district leaders who initiate restructuring are unlikely to succeed without the leadership and support of the superintendent. School boards must approve changes in budgeting processes and governance. Any significant changes in the roles and responsibilities of teachers quickly runs into conflicts with union contracts. Whether or not restructuring conflicts with union rules, district leaders recognize the need to both inform and gain the support of teachers before launching efforts to restructure.

The creation of new alliances and broad-based political support can be a partnership from the outset or a long, drawn out process of bargaining and negotiating. Whether the school board, superintendent, union leadership, advocacy group, or a foundation initiates the process, each should work to turn it into a cooperative venture. The parties should agree on goals so that efforts are not thwarted prematurely as a result of miscommunication, mistrust, or unrealistic expectations.

Collaboration between district management and teachers' unions creates trust among teachers that their interests have been protected. Dade County exemplifies a cooperative venture between districts and unions. The superintendent and union head of the United Teachers of Dade County jointly created the School-Based Management/Shared Decision Making program and negotiated details in advance, including a process for waiving contract provisions. The recently negotiated contract raises teacher salaries to perhaps the highest in the country and adds provisions for leave time for professional development. Poway is experimenting with a "trust agreement" between district and union management, based on a handshake rather than a hammered out legal agreement.

School boards have assumed a critical role in promoting restructuring, from hiring superintendents committed to restructuring to having board members sit on school-site councils. The trust and flexibility of school boards are essential to restructuring efforts. For example, the flexibility and schedule of school-based budgeting in Poway do not mesh well with the school board's annual budget preparation. If the school board did not have confidence in district and school staff, the process would fall apart, because schools cannot provide detailed data on expenditures to the board until the end of the school year, after the board has completed its budget for the following year.

Restructuring has brought new players into local educational reform. A number of private foundations—local and national—have become involved in restructuring activities in a variety of ways. Jefferson County presents a unique collaboration of the local Gheens Foundation, the superintendent, and the community. With substantial financial support from Gheens (reflecting the moral support of the business and civic community), district leaders established the JCPS/Gheens Academy. The growth in size and importance of the Academy, however, could not have happened with funds alone. It required district leaders to bring together the political support of the school board, teachers' union, and parents; it also required the willingness of district and union leaders to hire a strong reformer and educational leader to head the Academy.

The report of the Carnegie Forum's Task Force on Teaching as a Profession has had a visible influence; it was referred to in all three districts. The Matsushita Foundation has been playing a role behind the scenes providing assistance to restructuring districts, including Dade and Jefferson Counties, through a group of consultants and by establishing communication links between pioneering districts. Similarly, local business communities, universities, and parents are playing much more active roles in stimulating and supporting efforts in structural change.

The impetus for creating new coalitions need not necessarily come from the superintendent. In Jefferson County, for example, the impetus resulted from a combination of the superintendent and the opportunity afforded by the Gheens Foundation.

Restructuring districts also illustrate new kinds of cooperative ventures between local universities and school districts. The Dade Education Compact, a collaboration of Dade County, the teachers' union, and the University of Miami, has created a variety of innovative programs including an apprenticeship program for liberal arts graduates, tuition-free graduate work for teachers choosing schools where their race is in the minority, an adjunct faculty program, and a hotline for direct access linking the three organizations.

In Jefferson County, the University of Louisville has assigned nine faculty members part time to the Gheens Academy. The university offers courses through the Academy; for example, a course on action research that trains teachers to perform research in their classroom and publish the results. Cooperation between Jefferson County and the University of Louisville has been facilitated by the tenure awarded by the university to the position of Gheens Academy Director. The Academy and the university have also received federal and state grants for joint improvement ventures, including the creation of a center to support collaborative efforts jointly directed by the director of the Academy and the dean of the School of Education. Collaborations with other neighboring colleges and universities are also under way.

Restructuring Accountability. How can school districts tell if structural change is moving toward the goal set for it? Those involved in structural change realize that such efforts will die prematurely if their future is tied to immediate gains on standardized achievement tests. Yet people at all levels of a school system, as well as the public, want and need to know how well they are doing — all the more when they are changing the way they do things. Teachers experimenting with new approaches need to know they are successful, just as students need feedback on their progress toward learning goals. Because accountability is usually discussed in terms of schools and districts, it is easy to lose sight of the fact that these organizations are made up of people whose success determines the success of the system.

School districts recognize that a restructuring of schools to create more productive teaching and learning environments must be accompanied by a restructuring of accountability to reflect progress toward this goal. Not surprisingly, restructuring accountability recapitulates many of the themes of restructuring schools: the need for measures that match new goals, for involvement of teachers in creating criteria for success, and for the creation of measures that capture complex student outcomes and go beyond whether schools are complying with the rules.

Districts have taken the first steps to restructure accountability. They are striking new kinds of bargains with schools; in exchange for increased authority and flexibility at the school level, principals and teachers must demonstrate results. But such demonstrations rest more on a sense of professional responsibility than on paper-and-pencil measurements. Based on informed judgment, teachers and principals document what they are doing and what the results are. In Poway, for example, extensive training for principals in effective instruction and clinical supervision makes them better judges of good teaching practices.

New kinds of accountability are characterized by more flexibility than in the past: an emphasis on many measures including qualitative as well as quantitative, a shift from measures derived from filling out forms to on-site inspection of teaching practices, and, most importantly, a focus on the instructional goals and results of restructuring instead of on compliance with rules and procedures. The time frame for accountability is also being redefined more realistically — it takes far more than a year or two or even three to change people's skills and roles. Jefferson County and Poway leaders talk in terms of a ten-year period.

Leaders are not abandoning test scores and other traditional measures of results, but neither are they binding themselves to measure success solely on the basis of standardized test
scores. District leaders are willing to promise that test scores
will not go down over the next few years, but they are less willing to promise higher scores because the measures are so poorly
matched to the new goals they seek.

At the same time, district leaders are creating accountability mechanisms more suited to their restructuring goals. In
Jefferson County, for example, the first step to create such
mechanisms has been to create, with teacher participation, a
document that specifies the visions, beliefs, and standards for
the professional development schools. The document characterizes expectations for results in terms of the working environment, learning environment, and school staff roles, as well as
student roles and success.

When goals are explicit, results can be measured against
them. Jefferson County district leaders view the development
of assessment instruments and procedures for measuring progress toward these goals as integral to the development of professional development schools.

Jefferson County's approach, and that of other districts,
places accountability in a new light. Rather than a means of
external control, accountability is a vehicle for assessing progress of interest to all. This does not preclude district leaders
from rewarding success or penalizing failure; in fact, some
rewards and penalties are already built into the restructuring
process—for example, removing principals who are unwilling
to share their authority with teachers. But the emphasis is on
a sense of shared professional responsibility for success. In Dade
County, for example, pilot schools create their own formative
evaluation plans with the understanding that summative judgments including standardized tests will not be made or given
during the first three years. At the same time the district tracks
various school-level indicators, including grade-point averages,
detentions, teacher absenteeism, and staff turnover.

The districts are experimenting with a variety of accountability devices that rest on professional judgment. Poway is experimenting with peer evaluation for teachers, as well as educating

principals to make sound judgments and recommendations about instructional practices. School staff members also participate on teams that review schools in other districts (and are assessed themselves by teams visiting their own schools). Composed of teachers and administrators, school-review teams began as part of California's School Improvement Program in which each participating school draws up a three-year improvement plan. In response to the limited information derived from standardized tests and administrative compliance forms, these "quality review" teams now spend three full days visiting a school, observing classes, interviewing staff members and students, and reviewing documents.

Review teams conduct their review based on the school's own goals and plan for improvement. Their detailed report goes to the state, the district, and the school. The report contains an assessment of each curricular area, characterizing instructional techniques, materials, and content. It also includes assessments of planning and decision-making processes, school leadership, and staff development. Recommendations for improvement in each area are also presented. School staffs may not always agree with the assessments, but they appreciate being judged by peers. Moreover, those who participate on review teams (for which they are trained) gain tremendous perspective on their own schools.

Not incidentally, some aspects of restructuring have forms of accountability built into them. In Jefferson County's middle schools, every teacher is a member of a team, which makes his or her actions visible to other teachers, in contrast to the usual closed-door protection. Visibility provides a built-in incentive to maintain professional standards. Maintaining high standards and results is also reinforced by the ability of parents to move their children from one team (mini-school) to another. As Raywid argues in her chapter, the same principle applies when parents can choose among schools; schools that do not attract children will not survive.

Lessons from Pioneering Districts

Summary of District Actions. Restructuring school systems is a complex, time-consuming process. Districts leading these efforts are not taking short cuts; they are taking many-leveled reinforcing actions that fundamentally change relationships between schools and districts, and ultimately between teachers and students.

School districts in the process of restructuring accept the idea that the status quo is not working and that the current organizational structures of districts and schools stifles the development and exercise of the sound professional judgment necessary for productive learning. District leaders play powerful roles in articulating goals and visions for the future, devising strategies to achieve them, building alliances that support comprehensive change, and communicating ideas and images of effective teaching and learning environments to district and school staff and the community.

Leaders of restructuring efforts facilitate change through a combination of actions: devolving authority, relaxing regulations, encouraging experimentation, and directing resources and assistance to school staffs. In exchange, districts are asking schools to become more professional organizations where teachers and principals are responsible for creating the conditions that make more effective teaching and learning possible.

Districts differ considerably in which actions they take first. But they share the underlying philosophy that restructuring requires many complementary actions sustained over many years; there is no quick fix or single solutions. They must all have strong leadership, create new structures, and provide the support needed by teachers and administrators to change. Table 7.2, "What Restructuring School Districts Do," summarizes these actions.

As more and more districts initiate change, school-based management, narrowly defined, threatens to become the "quick fix" chosen by districts. Lessons from the restructuring efforts we have described argue for great caution. Productive learning environments require skilled, dedicated professionals who need supportive working environments and opportunities for growth to be effective. School-based management is only one of many components for achieving this goal; districts must also (a) involve teachers in school decision making, (b) relieve schools from restrictive rules, and (c) provide administrators and teachers

Table 7.2. What Restructuring School Districts Do.

Provide Leadership

Make long-term commitment to comprehensive change:
- Guided by goals not prescriptions
- Characterized by many reinforcing strategies and steps

Communicate goals, guiding images, and information:
- Create a language for change and a focus on student learning
- Have direct communication between schools and district leaders

Encourage experimentation and risk taking:
- Begin with schools that volunteer
- Support experimentation with waivers from constraining rules

Demonstrate and promote shared decision making:
- Involve all staff in developing educational goals and values
- Limit faculty meetings to items that require immediate action

Create New Organizational Structures

Participate actively in building new alliances:
- Make cooperative agreements with teachers' unions
- Create new joint ventures with foundations, advocacy groups, businesses, and universities

Devolve authority to schools and to teachers:
- Give schools authority over staffing and materials budgets
- Provide incentives for principals to involve teachers in school-site decisions

Promote creation of new roles, for example:
- Teachers as leaders, evaluators, curriculum developers, and facilitators of student learning
- Administrators as facilitators of teachers and as instructional leaders

Develop and demonstrate during the summer new models of:
- Restructured programs for staff and students
- Support for teachers to develop curriculum and educational materials

Create new forms of accountability that:
- Match the comprehensive nature and time line of restructuring
- Use many measures, including those defined by schools

Provide Support and Assistance

Provide a broad range of opportunities for professional development such as:
- On- and off-site assistance for teachers and administrators
- Development sessions that include techniques in management, clinical supervision, instruction, and content

Table 7.2. What Restructuring School Districts Do, Cont'd.

Provide time for staff to assume new roles and responsibilities:
- Time for planning, working with colleagues, and school decision making
- Release time for professional development activities

Seek supplementary sources of funding and assistance from:
- State and federal governments
- Local businesses, private foundations, and individuals

---

with access to new knowledge and skills, as well as the time and resources to put them to use.

Each school's teachers and administrators will vary in how much and what kind of assistance they need to create and judge new learning environments. Some schools will be able to create effective planning groups, assess their own weaknesses, develop new approaches, and mobilize staff to implement them with little more than access to professional development. Others will need help for one or more of these steps. Still others will need intensive on-site consulting assistance throughout the process.

Districts in the vanguard of restructuring are creating new organizational models for school policymakers as they experiment with balancing central control and school autonomy. They recognize that structural change will not occur in their schools without leadership, nurturing, and resources from district leaders. Nor will change dictated from the top effectively restructure schools unless schools are full partners in creating new teaching and learning environments.

Implications for State Action. The focus of this chapter is on the actions school districts take to restructure their schools; state influences on these districts were not investigated. However, there are clear parallels between actions districts take to promote restructuring and actions states can take. District leaders can inspire and support school change by communicating to school staffs goals and expectations for results coupled with giving staffs the authority, flexibility, and skills to reach them.

Similarly, state leaders can inspire and support district change through analogous actions.

States have a dual role in promoting structural change: (1) they can reinforce the goals and actions of restructuring districts, and (2) they can inspire and assist restructuring efforts in districts that do not have the leadership or capacity of those described in this report. Even the exceptional districts described here have depended on external help from foundations, advocacy groups, and others — sources that cannot possibly help all 15,000 school districts in the nation.

States can profoundly influence districts and schools by setting the tone, language, and terms of the discussion about educational change. The school districts we describe above are exceptional by definition — they are in the vanguard of structural change. Most district and school staffs are conditioned to think of education in terms of uniformity, standardized test scores, specific learning objectives, prescriptive rules, compliance monitoring, and discrete programs and approaches. These are concepts and terms that maintain the status quo and discourage thinking about new ways of organizing instruction and improving learning.

States can change the terms of discourse about education from these deeply ingrained concepts and terms to those of restructuring: schools as stimulating workplaces and learning environments, teachers as professionals responsible for the results of their teaching, students as problem solvers and conceptual thinkers, restructuring as a continuous process of incorporating new knowledge, flexibility in exchange for results, and shared responsibility for learning. In addition to language that communicates powerful images symbolically, states can promote restructuring by providing districts and schools with concrete images of effective learning environments and outcomes.

But language and images will communicate little if states continue to send messages on programs and accountability that contradict the goals of restructuring. States send strong messages to their districts about the core curriculum, accountability, and assessment, as well as categorical and other special programs. These signals need to be aligned with those of restructuring so that they together reinforce the same set of goals. If state curricular goals emphasize the achievement by students of basic skills and factual knowledge instead of problem-solving and conceptual skills, there will be little room for schools to change what they do.

States strongly influence what districts do through their choices of mechanisms for accountability and instruments of assessment. If these are not consonant with the goals and language of restructuring, they will influence district actions far more than language and imagery. The ways in which states judge districts and schools will have to expand to include more varied and performance-oriented measures of student outcomes and qualitative outcomes and a longer time frame for judgment if the measures are to match the goals of restructuring. Just as restructuring districts are helping schools create new ways of measuring progress, states may be able to help districts and schools institute them.

States communicate a vision of effective schools through the goals, requirements, and monitoring of categorical and other programs that they oversee. In the past, a multitude of special programs have sprung up in schools, often to compensate for weaknesses in the core educational program. States need to shift their focus from a fragmented approach to education that rests on enforcement of regulations to an approach that strengthens the core program and provides flexibility to districts and schools in the ways in which they adapt extra resources to meet their needs.

Obviously, there are limits to what states can change. Many school programs carry requirements from the federal government that states merely pass on to districts. (However, states can request waivers from the federal government as well as lobby for changes in legislative and regulatory requirements.) Of great importance, many such requirements are intended to protect the rights of children and guarantee that opportunities are not denied to disadvantaged or handicapped students. States, however, can greatly increase local flexibility without relaxing civil rights protections. In fact, states have an obligation to ensure that districts not overlook the schools at the bottom — typically those serving disadvantaged students.

States have a major role in providing resources to school districts. Aside from basic funding that maintains, and when possible increases, teachers' salaries to match their increased responsibilities, states can help districts restructure by providing access to training that districts may not have the motivation, resources, or capacity to provide. For example, states could offer training for superintendents and school board members in the concepts and goals of restructuring and in leadership skills.

States can also assist districts by providing information on research, policy, and experiences of other districts and by offering to provide on-site consulting experts to facilitate restructuring. Just as districts need to adapt their assistance strategies to the capacities of each school, states will need to provide training or on-site assistance in different ways to different districts.

Like districts, states face the challenge of creating an appropriate balance between central control and local autonomy — a balance between setting goals, standards, and expectations and providing districts with enough authority and flexibility to choose their own paths. States must avoid the trap of stifling change through shortsightedness, overly restrictive rules, and narrow measures of success. At the same time, states must ensure that schools and districts move in constructive directions, without penalizing students, as they experiment with new approaches to education.

Restructuring school systems to provide more students with the skills needed to function productively in society is a long-term undertaking. School districts that have embarked on restructuring have discovered the complexity of it and are not looking for quick solutions. If states do not take actions to support and reinforce the goals and actions of such districts, schools will be caught between conflicting signals and expectations and will be unable to change. If states promote and support the goals of restructuring through their actions, restructuring districts will be able to sustain their efforts. Similarly, just as very few individual schools are able to change significantly without leadership and support from their districts, most districts will need inspiration and assistance from state educational leaders to launch and sustain restructuring efforts.

References

Berman, P., and Gjelten, T. *Improving School Improvement: A Policy Evaluation of the California School Improvement Program, Volume 2: Findings.* Berkeley, Calif.: Berman, Weiler, 1984.

Carnegie Task Force on Teaching as a Profession. *A Nation Prepared: Teachers for the 21st Century.* Washington, D.C.: Carnegie Forum on Education and the Economy, 1986.

Casner-Lotto, J. "Expanding the Teacher's Role: Hammond's School Improvement Process." *Phi Delta Kappan,* 1988, *69,* 349–353.

Cuban, L. *The Managerial Imperative and the Practice of Leadership in Schools.* Albany, N.Y.: State University of New York Press, 1988.

David, J. L. "The Puzzle of Structural Change." Paper prepared for the Symposium on Structural Change in Secondary Education, National Center on Effective Secondary Schools, Madison, University of Wisconsin, July 1987.

David, J. L., and Peterson, S. M. *Can Schools Improve Themselves? A Study of School-Based Improvement Programs.* Palo Alto, Calif.: Bay Area Research Group, 1984.

Fullan, M. *The Meaning of Education Change.* New York: Teachers College Press, 1982.

Goodlad, J. I. *A Place Called School.* New York: McGraw-Hill, 1984.

Johnson, S. M. "Pursuing Professional Reform in Cincinnnati." *Phi Delta Kappan,* 1988, *69,* 746–751.

Kanter, R. M. *The Change Masters.* New York: Simon & Schuster, 1983.

Kirst, M. W., and Meister, G. R. "Turbulence in American Secondary Schools: What Reforms Last?" *Curriculum Inquiry,* 1985, *15,* 169–186.

Meier, D. "Success in East Harlem: How One Group of Teachers Built a School That Works." *American Educator,* 1987, 36–39.

Rodman, B. "Friendship and Trust: Unusual Keys to a Radical Pact." *Education Week,* 1987, *7* (4), 1.

Sickler, J. L. "Teachers in Charge: Empowering the Professionals." *Phi Delta Kappan,* 1988, *69,* 354–358.

Sizer, T. R. *Horace's Compromise: The Dilemma of the American High School.* Boston: Houghton Mifflin, 1984.

Timar, T. B., and Kirp, D. L. *Managing Educational Excellence.* New York: Falmer Press, 1988.

Wissler, D. F., and Ortiz, F. I. "The Decentralization Process of School Systems: A Review of the Literature." *Urban Education,* 1986, *21,* 280–294.

EIGHT

Key Issues Confronting State Policymakers

Michael Cohen

Despite the enormous number of state educational reform initiatives enacted since the beginning of this decade, there is a widespread belief among state educational policymakers that substantial improvement in the performance of the educational system is still required. There is also a growing belief that comprehensive and fundamental changes in the ways schools operate will be required in order to accomplish that goal. This is not because many policymakers believe that the reforms previously enacted have failed. Rather, it is because policymakers, along with many educational and business leaders, increasingly recognize that the demands on the educational system far outstrip its capacity to respond and will continue to do so as long as schools remain in their current form. Consequently, a bandwagon for restructuring schools is slowly taking shape, and it shows all signs of moving rapidly through the states in coming years.

"Restructuring schools" is frequently an ill-defined phrase, often connoting some mix of enhanced professional status for teachers or fewer regulations and more discretion for schools. For most state policymakers, however, the essense of restructuring involves altering authority and accountability systems (National Governors' Assocation, 1986). They view restructuring as trading off increased decision-making authority for educators in exchange for both significant improvements in and accountability for student performance.

This chapter provides an overview of issues on restructuring from a state-level perspective. It examines why state policymakers will increasingly direct educational reform initiatives toward a restructuring of the educational system, and what structural arrangements at the school and district level will require significant change. It analyzes the resources and tools available to states to lead this effort, as well as the limitations states will need to overcome in order to succeed. Finally, it suggests a strategy that states can take to accomplish this goal.

The State Context: Why Are State Policymakers Interested in Restructuring the Educational System?

State educational policymaking occurs in a national context. The publication of *A Nation Prepared* (Carnegie Task Force on Teaching as a Profession, 1986) and *Time for Results* (National Governors' Association, 1986) began to focus the attention of state educational policymakers on an agenda for restructuring schools. Subsequently, the findings of these reports have been reinforced by a series of other reports, conferences, projects, and other activities initiated by the national membership organizations serving state policymakers in education, as well as a variety of other organizations. These activities in no way reflect a national consensus about the purpose or details of restructuring. Their cumulative effect, however, is to make legitimate the need for continuing educational reform and to shape the nature of policy discussions within many states. The fact that organizations such as the National Governors' Associaton, the National Association of State Boards of Education, the Education Commission of the States, the National Conference of State Legislatures and the Council of Chief State School Officers are holding meetings and publishing reports about school restructuring is significant, for these organizations are frequently the most important information sources for state policymakers (Cohen, 1985). For state policymakers asking how to improve education, the answer provided by their primary national information sources is: "Restructure!"

Education has been on most state policy agendas for a

number of years. Yet conversations with elected officials suggest that they continue to see strong public support for educational reform. Further, policymakers now see education in a somewhat broader context than in the past. The same demographic, fiscal, and economic forces that continue to focus policymakers' attention on education also bring to the forefront issues such as childcare and preschool education, the treatment and prevention of substance abuse, adult education and worker retraining, teen pregnancy, and welfare reform (for example, National Governors' Association, 1987a). In short, educational reform is increasingly seen as part of a larger agenda of human resource development by states that is taking shape in the face of increased international economic competition, a shrinking pool of new workers, and a pressing need to break the negative effects on families caught in a continuing cycle of poverty. This has several implications for how policymakers view and define educational issues.

Policymakers recognize that these broader social and economic concerns are part of an interrelated set of long-term problems. While they approach these issues with a sense of urgency, they are generally not looking for quick solutions. Rather, education is seen as a critical part of a prevention system, one that must equip individuals with knowledge, skills, and enough experiences of success to engender healthy self-concepts and other attitudes. In this context, the educational system's relative effectiveness and ability to support effectively the efforts of other prevention programs such as preschool education or day care are increasingly being called into question. In addition, policymakers are coming to understand that successful social and human service programs, including education, depend upon local initiative and leadership, sustained and diffuse personal relationships between service providers and their clients, and the ability to tailor services and responses to the needs of individual clients and their families (Schoor, 1988). Such are generally not prominent features of state bureaucracies. Consequently, state policymakers inside and outside of education are increasingly receptive to ideas that propose trading flexibility for street-level bureaucrats in exchange for better results, which is a common theme of restructuring.

Budgets matter as well. From 1980 to 1987, state educational expenditures increased by $16.5 billion nationally, a rise in real terms of 26 percent (National Governors' Association, 1987b). While there is likely to be support for continued expansion of educational expenditures, there are also forces at work resisting such expansion. In many states policymakers are expressing increased concern over accountability, asking if investments made in previous years are paying off in terms of performance. Future increases are likely to be contingent upon at least the availability of a performance-based accountability system that can provide answers to this question, if not on demonstrable improvements in performance. Education will clearly be competing for additional state dollars with the other social-service, human-service and human-resource development programs mentioned above. Policymakers will be forced to choose among investments with some relatively immediate economic payoffs, such as job training and retraining; those with some medium term payoffs, such as elementary and secondary education; and those with some longer term payoffs, such as preschool education. In this environment, policymakers will be increasingly receptive to reform proposals that either are low-cost or promise large gains in productivity. Redistributing authority to make improvements (another common theme of restructuring) will, undoubtedly, be seen in some instances as a substitute for allocating additional dollars.

In short, the national dialogue about education and demographic, economic, and fiscal forces impinging on states are combining to create a "second wave" of educational reform around school restructuring. In order to better understand what this means for states and educational systems, a sharper view of the challenges facing the educational system is needed.

The Challenge for Public Education

The challenges facing the educational system today are fundamentally different from those addressed before, even in recent years. As recently as a decade ago, the overriding demand on schools was to increase the number of students who mastered basic skills such as reading and computing. Because of changes in the U.S. economy, maintaining a high standard of living in the future will increasingly require a workforce with greater intellectual competence and flexibility. These traits must be broadly distributed throughout the workforce; they will be important for line workers as well as for senior-level managers and executives.

While the precise nature of the connection between economic productivity and the skill level of the workforce is a matter of much debate, there are two lines of analysis that support the need for larger numbers of well-educated workers. One, typified by *Workforce 2000* (Hudson Institute, 1987), argues that employment opportunities for low-skilled workers are being eliminated, whereas jobs requiring higher skill levels are expanding. A second line of analysis (for example, Murnane, 1988) argues that, regardless of such labor market projections, a more highly skilled workforce will permit more effective forms of work organization and management, such as participatory management. These approaches can result in more efficient adaptation to and incorporation of new technologies into the production process and significant productivity gains. Both of these lines of analysis suggest a focus away from conventional notions of basic skills and toward a more rigorous conception of intellectual competence.

More specifically, students will need a substantial knowledge base as well as higher-order cognitive skills. Such skills include the ability to communicate complex ideas, analyze and solve complex problems, identify order and find direction in an ambiguous and uncertain environment, and think and reason abstractly. Because workers in the future will experience rapid changes in both work technologies and jobs themselves, students also will be required to develop the capacity to learn new skills and tasks quickly. This will require a thorough understanding of different subject matters and an ability to apply this knowledge in creative and imaginative ways, in novel contexts, and in collaboration with others.

Even dramatic improvements in the proportion of students who master routine basic skills would only result in a still-widening mismatch between the skills of the workforce and the skill demands of the workplace. Consequently, the demand on schools is now shifting from simply increasing the number of graduates with basic skills to both increasing the proportion of students who graduate and improving the intellectual capabilities of graduates.

Currently, only a small percentage of high school graduates have acquired and mastered the knowledge and higher-order skills they will need in the workforce. Because most high school graduates acquire only a rudimentary set of basic reading and computation skills, they are ill equipped to handle even moderately complex tasks in the workplace. For example, the 1984 National Assessment of Educational Progress showed that slightly more than 60 percent of seventeen-year-old students lack the ability to find, understand, summarize, and explain relatively complicated information, including information about topics they study in school (National Assessment of Educational Progress, 1985). Often, they do not have the reading comprehension skills needed in higher education or business environments. The same assessment showed that typically only 15 to 25 percent of eleventh graders could respond adequately to a writing task, depending upon the nature of the particular task. The overwhelming majority of eleventh graders could not write a brief passage well enough to accomplish their writing objective (Applebee, Langer, and Mullins, 1986).

While these low average performance levels are distressing enough, they mask large and persistent achievement gaps between subgroups of students. Students who are black or Hispanic, or who come from poor families or rural or disadvantaged urban areas, consistently perform less well than do others. For example, the average reading proficiency of black and Hispanic seventeen-year-old students is roughly the same as that of thirteen-year-old white students. And though approximately 45 percent of white seventeen-year-olds have acquired adept reading skills, the same is true for only 16 to 20 percent of black and Hispanic students (National Assessment of Educational Progress, 1985).

Further, roughly 25 percent of eighteen- to nineteen-year-olds and 15 percent of twenty-four-year olds nationally have not completed high school and presumably are considerably less skilled than most of their age cohort (Stern, 1987). These drop-outs are drawn disproportionately from the ranks of poor and minority youngsters. This suggests that the achievement gaps between minority and nonminority youth are even larger when the entire cohort of school-age youth, rather than just current students, is considered.

These achievement gaps are not new; they have been of concern for some time. What gives this issue more urgency to-day is that the percentage of students who are at risk of poor academic performance or dropping out altogether — those drawn from poor and minority backgrounds — represents an increas-ing share of both the school population and our future workforce. Thus, society cannot continue to write off this segment of the population; the future well-being of this country depends fun-damentally upon their educational success.

In short, the nature, level, and distribution of the educa-tional outcomes of students must change significantly. The power of schools to retain students must improve so that virtually all students at least complete high school. The proportion of students who master higher-order thinking skills must increase dramati-cally. In addition, it is not enough to raise the average perfor-mance levels of students; the proportion of students from poor and minority backgrounds who acquire higher-order skills must increase substantially as well.

There is the further problem that the required gains in student outcomes are proportionately greater than the likely in-creases in educational expenditures, even if funding increases continue at the pace of the past several years. Since 1983–1984, expenditures in education have grown more than 25 percent (National Governors' Association, 1987a). The state share of expenditures in elementary and secondary schooling now ex-ceeds 50 percent nationally (Stern, 1987). Investments also must be made in early childhood, higher education, and worker re-training programs, among others, to respond to the same eco-nomic and demographic challenges.

In consequence, the productivity of the education system must increase dramatically. Schools need to educate more stu-dents to considereably higher levels of achievement and need to use their resources more effectively in doing so.

Restructuring the Educational System: Critical Issues

Few would argue that so sweeping a challenge can be addressed adequately through incremental changes in schooling practices. Indeed, by calling for a fundamental restructuring of the educational system in reports such as *A Nation Prepared* and *Time for Results,* political, business, and educational leaders have recognized that the traditional structure and organization of schools are not well suited for the new demands they face. Typical instructional arrangements are more appropriate for teaching students basic skills than for helping them acquire more complex cognitive skills. Also, as currently organized, staffing arrangements and scheduling practices leave relatively little time for teachers to prepare for instruction, review student work, or engage in substantial, personal interaction with students. There is even less time and opportunity to develop collegial working relations among faculty members, relations important for both professional development and school improvement. Consequently, school improvement efforts initiated within the existing school structure, such as effective schools programs, may demonstrate some success in increasing basic reading and mathematical skills, but they cannot approach the productivity gains ultimately required.

This section discusses specific issues at the school building, local school district, and state levels that must be addressed and resolved in order to move from the rhetoric to the reality of restructured schools.

Two key assumptions provide the starting point for the following analysis. First is the assumption that the primary rationale for restructuring schools lies in the need to improve the productivity of the educational system in general, and, in particular, student acquisition of higher-order thinking skills. It should be acknowledged, however, that others advocate restructuring schools primarily to enhance other values, namely either teacher professionalism or parental and student choice. In this analysis, those issues are treated largely as instrumental considerations rather than necessarily desirable ends. The extent to which either one is promoted is dependent upon the contribution it makes to the overriding goal of improving the educational outcomes of students.

The second assumption is that improving educational productivity requires a restructuring of the entire educational system and not just the schools. The structure and process of governance and control at the state and local levels must be readjusted to accommodate and support necessary changes in the organization and management of instruction in schools and classrooms. Accomplishing this requires first an analysis of needed changes in instruction and then an examination of the educational system to identify further changes at the school, district, and state levels that also must be made.

Currently, most discussions about restructuring schools involve some mix of ideas about increased school-site management and autonomy, more flexibility and variability in the organization of schools, greater teacher participation in school decision making, decentralization of decision making, and deregulation of schooling. While each of these ideas, and others, properly belong in a discussion on restructuring schools, rarely if ever are they related in any clear way to improved school productivity or student acquisition of skills. Until such connections are made, it will be difficult to build political or policy support for initiatives to restructure schools and even more difficult to know how to go about doing so.

School-Level Issues

Helping all students acquire higher-order skills requires a curriculum that engages students in rigorous and challenging work. Particularly for students from disadvantaged backgrounds, who are prone to academic failure and dropping out, the curriculum also must be structured to provide opportunities for frequent success in order to enhance each student's sense of self-worth and competence. Further, schools must provide an environment in which students receive personal attention so that they feel that someone cares about them personally and consequently are able to form a positive attachment to the school.

The primary issues to be resolved at the school level have to do with identifying structural and organizational features of schools that need to be altered in order to accomplish this. Put somewhat differently, educators and policymakers alike need a map, or a vision, of what restructured schools might look like. This is especially critical when one considers that much of the work, and even more of the decision making, that will go into restructuring schools will be done by educators at the school level.

What features of schools need to be altered? A starting point are the conditions of instruction known to be related to student learning. These include educational goals, the structure of knowledge, instructional tasks and activities, instructional group size and composition, and instructional time.

Educational Goals. What students learn is at least partly a function of what schools are expected to teach them. To a considerable extent, instructional goals are determined by state and local school boards and the tests used to assess school and student performance. Because these measures continue to emphasize basic skills and minimize higher-order skills, instructional goals and student learning will fall short of what is needed. Therefore, state and local school boards must establish clear goals reflecting student acquisition of higher-order skills and invest in the development of assessment devices that both reflect and measure those goals.

Structure of Knowledge. The way knowledge is organized into school curricula has a significant impact on what students learn. For example, in many high school science courses, the curriculum emphasizes breadth over depth of coverage. Consequently, students may be exposed to what are little more than vocabulary lessons in thirty-four different units of physics, rather than concentrating on a half dozen or so concepts in a way that would enable them to learn how physicists approach and solve problems.

For a further example, elementary reading instruction is typically organized around discrete skills for decoding, acquiring vocabulary, or comprehension. The assumption is that skills are hierarchical in nature and that the curriculum must first help students master the simpler "basic" skills before they proceed to acquire "higher-order" skills. Therefore, youngsters who do not master the basic skills along with their peers are provided remedial instruction, generally in the form of additional drill and practice in the basics.

A growing body of research in cognitive psychology and related fields suggests that this mode of operation may be quite flawed (Resnick, 1987). In fact, studies demonstrate that skilled readers, even at the early elementary grades, are able to comprehend what they read not simply because they have acquired the basics, but because they intuitively and automatically rely on what we think of as higher-order skills. As they read, they actively draw on their own knowledge, and ask questions and make inferences about the printed text. According to this emerging view, improving the reading skills of poor readers requires far less in the way of drill and practice on the basics and far more in the way of experiences that cultivate students' thinking and reasoning skills.

Instructional Tasks and Activities. To a considerable extent at the secondary school level, and somewhat less in elementary school, instruction takes the form of lecture and recitation during which an entire class is focused on the same content and engaged in the same activities. This method effectively forces all students to move through the curriculum at the same pace, regardless of differences in their rates of learning. It encourages teachers to use question-and-answer strategies that emphasize brief and unambiguously correct answers from students, and limits student engagement in active learning (Bossert, 1979). Alternative teaching strategies that emphasize student choice between a selection of activities or cooperative small groups of students working on long-term projects can be more responsive to differences in student interests and achievement levels. At the same time they can provide opportunities for all students to become meaningfully engaged in reasonably complex and demanding learning tasks and gain practice working cooperatively with others.

Instructional Group Size and Composition. There is considerable evidence that student achievement is affected by the size and composition of each learning group (for example, Glass and Smith, 1979; Bossert, Dwyer, Rowan, and Lee, 1982). Grouping practices — class size, student assignment to classes, and the creation of instructional groups within classes — make a difference in student achievement. This is also true of tracking practices in secondary schools (Alexander and McDill, 1975; Oakes, 1985). They determine the curriculum, the social environment in which a student learns, the pace of instruction, and a host of other learning conditions. Further, the way instructional groups are typically formed in elementary schools — twenty-five students in a class, three to five ability groups per class — are neither the only forms of grouping nor necessarily the most effective. There is strong evidence that suggests that alternative forms, such as heterogeneous groups combined with cooperative reward structures and peer tutoring, can work well (Slavin, 1985). One can imagine a variety of arrangements that can be more effective, such as large lecture classes for some material balanced with small group projects for other material, individual student work on computers or other technologies, or extensive use of peer tutoring, which creates instructional groups of only two students and capitalizes on rather than eliminates variation in student achievement and ability levels.

Instructional Time. Time is a critical structural feature of schooling (Denham and Lieberman, 1980). It is perhaps the most important instructional resource. As a structural feature, time defines the basic organization of schools and instruction. The school year, the school day, the class schedule, the curriculum, graduation requirements, and even the progression of students from one learning opportunity or setting to the next, are all defined by fixed blocks of time and set by state or local policy or regulation. Consequently, time is treated as a fixed resource. All students are expected to learn at the same rate and complete their learning at the same time. Yet we know that students learn at varying rates. Within classrooms, treating time as a fixed resource means that some students are routinely bored while waiting for their classmates to catch up. Others must move on to the next unit before mastering the current material. Inevitably, these students fall further and further behind their peers. Treating time as a fixed resource means that some students, across courses and grade levels, experience the cumulative loss of opportunities to master needed skills. Consequently, by the time students complete or otherwise leave school, there is tremendous variability in their levels of knowledge and skills. In contrast to such organization of learning are outcomes-based education and mastery learning, in which student performance standards are treated as fixed but the amount of time and number of opportunities students have to reach standards can vary.

This is not a complete list of instructional conditions that affect student learning, but it does illustrate several points. First, it is possible to identify key aspects of the organization of instruction that affect pedagogical practices and student learning. Second, for each of these aspects, there is a basis in research and experience that can serve as a starting point for the design and implementation of new structural arrangements of education. Third, it is virtually impossible to change just one component at a time; they function integrally. Any substantial change to one requires — and permits — changes in the others at the same time. Therefore, improving school productivity and student learning demands that schools be restructured substantially.

Enough is known from research in effective schools to demonstrate that technical improvements in the organization of instructional and other school resources are necessary but not sufficient steps to realize the desired gains in student achievement (Purkey and Smith, 1983; Cohen, 1983). Schools, after all, are social institutions, and their culture, norms, expectations, and mechanisms for involving teachers and students in their work are critical to their success. Further, the circumstances of schools, even within a single district, vary considerably. Schools differ in their mix of students and staff, in the characteristics of the communities they serve, and in their past attempts at innovation and improvement. From this point of view, schools require considerable autonomy to allow for the most sensible fit between particular forms of instructional organization, current practices, existing staff capabilities, and student and community needs. Therefore, inventing a new set of structural arrangements to be applied uniformly in all schools would not suffice. Rather, schools must be able to form and adjust their own structures and processes as needed.

This approach has several implications. First, decisions about the most productive forms of instructional organization need to be made close to the act of instruction by teachers and principals at the school level. Second, if decisions about instructional organization are to be made at the school level, other related decisions must also be made at that level. These include, for example, staffing arrangements, decision-making processes, staff and organizational development needs, and curriculum selection and development. Allowing schools the leeway to make decisions in these areas requires that resources devoted to these activities be allocated to the school as well.

New instructional and organizational arrangements will mean new roles for teachers and new staffing arrangements. For example, creating smaller instructional groups, allowing variable time for student mastery and progress, or creating interdisciplinary curricula cannot readily be accomplished in schools in which a teacher's role is defined as responsibility for only a particular subject or for large groups of students. Rather, these new instructional arrangements will require greater use of team teaching and other forms of collaboration and coordination. Similarly, increased responsibilities for school staff in planning, decision making, professional development, and school improvement also will require new roles for and frequent interaction among teachers.

It will be critical to find time for teachers to assume these new roles and responsibilities. This will not be easy, given the way schools are currently organized. At present, schedules for teachers largely match the school day of students (though the teaching day is generally somewhat longer) and, despite the allotment of "preparation" time for teachers, rarely are there significant amounts of time during which teachers can interact with one another or with small numbers of students. Consequently, additional staff time, as well as new ways of organizing teachers' use of existing time, must be found.

In all probability, some of this time can be obtained only with additional resources for more staff, for a longer school day or year, or both. However, it may also be possible to find more effective ways to use existing staff resources, such as preparation periods, in-service training time, or the time of administrators such as department chairs or assistant principals. Further, it will be important to look for ways to use less expensive resources, such as paraprofessionals, volunteers, peer tutors, and instructional technologies, whenever possible so that each teacher's time can be used more productively.

School District Issues

The school district creates the context in which schools operate. In most instances, this context places primary emphasis throughout the system on the degree to which school practice complies with district policy. When district policy determines the allocation of instructional time, the amount of homework to be assigned, the number and length of teacher preparation periods, the curricular and instructional materials to be used, the number and timing of in-service days, and the like, some of the most important instructional decisions are being made at the district level. Teachers and building administrators then assume the role of implementing a set of procedures designed elsewhere.

At the heart of redefining the role of the local district should be a reorientation of schools toward performance, rather than procedure, in which the district provides enabling tools and resources rather than constraints. The primary orientation of school staff should be to make judgments about how to select, organize, and use available resources to achieve desired educational ends. In such an arrangement, interaction between the central district office and individual schools would focus mainly on whether schools are achieving district goals, rather than whether they are following district guidelines (Smith and Purkey, 1985; Corcoran, 1987).

Local district functions must be carefully examined and revised if needed change is to occur. The precise nature of these changes remains to be seen; it is reasonable to expect that new arrangements will differ widely depending upon district size and other characteristics. Nonetheless, it is possible to identify several broad issues that must be addressed by all school districts.

First, many functions typically performed at the central office level, uniformly affecting all schools, should be either delegated to or shared with individual schools. In most districts, responsibility for goal setting, curriculum development, textbook selection, grouping and tracking policies, personnel policies, and resource allocation are typically lodged with the school board and are uniform for all schools in the district. Legal authority for such policy decisions appropriately belongs with the school board. However, the standardization of these practices for all schools, without regard to variations in local circumstances, is often incompatible with the discretion required by schools in order to improve educational productivity. Consequently, districts and schools need to sort out which responsibilities and authority can be assigned to the individual school and which must remain at the central office level.

Moving in this direction will require districts to carefully balance competing pressures for centralized control and local autonomy. For example, though it is desirable for individual school buildings to have sufficient flexibility to select instructional materials well suited to their particular students and well matched to their instructional strategies, it is also desirable for students — especially in large districts — to be able to move from one neighborhood and school to another without finding entirely different textbooks and other instructional materials. Further, while the presumption is that increased school autonomy will result in instructional practices better suited to the needs of the school's clientele and therefore to higher performance levels by all students, in practice this will not always be the case. In some instances, educators may lack either the knowledge and skills to apply the best practices or the inclination to serve all students. Therefore, mechanisms will need to be established that both promote diversity and retain some common features among schools. Establishing districtwide goals and performance measures for which each building is accountable could be one such approach. However, developing assessment tools that faithfully reflect shared goals and, at the same time, permit varied curriculum materials will prove to be enormously difficult. Also, local school boards will need to develop intervention strategies for schools that fail to meet desired performance levels, without prematurely punishing desirable risk taking and experimentation. At present, no models exist for the new accountability arrangements that will be required. Therefore, districts will have to consider a number of strategies and arrangements to assure the proper balance between autonomy and centralized control.

For example, schools could be responsible for establishing annual goals within the context of district goals. Schools could have the authority to determine their own instructional policies, decide how best to group students for instruction, organize instructional time, select and use textbooks and other instructional materials, and control the resources required to perform these functions. The local school board and central office, in turn, might require the school to submit annual goals and plans for accomplishing them. The district would be responsible for reviewing and approving the plans, providing technical assistance and training to support the school planning process, monitoring implementation, and evaluating its effectiveness. This arrangement would require that responsibility, authority, and resources be given the schools, with the central office's responsibility shifting largely to supporting and evaluating school efforts and assuming a more directive role only where necessary.

School decision making and governance patterns must change as well. Providing greater discretion at the school level also should involve broader participation by schools in decision making, so that both teachers and parents participate meaningfully in shaping the school's program.

As indicated above, giving teachers greater discretion with respect to the organization of instruction is a key component of school restructuring. This does not mean more autonomy for teachers behind the closed door of the classroom. Teachers are interdependent. In order for schools to be effective, teachers must make decisions collegially. This is especially true when the task involves creating more flexible instructional arrangements and new roles for school staff; these are decisions that must be worked out by the staff as a whole. The challenge for school districts is to create organizational structures in which school-level decision making can proceed effectively and efficiently, and in which teachers can play a significant role in administrative and management decisions that have important instructional consequences. At the same time, teachers must retain a primary focus on classroom teaching so that their energies are not dissipated trying to manage the entire school.

One of the primary benefits of school discretion is the ability of the school, within the context of state and local goals, to shape a unique and coherent school mission and culture that responds to the needs of its particular clients. Providing greater discretion and empowering teachers to make decisions at the school level requires that parents and community members also be given a greater voice in school decision making (Raywid, this volume). The issue here goes well beyond the benefits of parental involvement for the academic performance of their children. Rather, it recognizes that the public — especially but not exclusively parents — must have a way of shaping decisions over the focus and mission of a school. In public agencies such as schools, it is not appropriate for questions about fundamental values to be resolved exclusively by the professional staff. While local school boards have historically performed this function, their capacity to serve as the exclusive method of lay participation in decision making will be diminished if a greater share of decision making is moved from the school district to the individual schools.

Consequently, school districts will need to establish school-level governance organizations, such as a school council composed of teachers, administrators, parents, and community members. Districts must determine the scope of authority for these organizations and help work out ways to make increased professional participation and greater community involvement mutually reinforcing.

Granting greater school autonomy and enhanced influence

to teachers and parents is only part of the changes required by the school district. When more autonomous schools take on truly distinct cultures and orientations, both students and staff will need greater choice in the school they attend or in which they work. In this way, the appropriate match of staff strengths, client preferences and needs, and school mission can be achieved. Therefore, districts also may want to consider altering traditional practices for assigning students and staff to schools. Rather than assigning students based on where they live, districts could permit students and their parents to select the school of their choice. Similarly, teachers also could have greater choice over their schools, to permit a better fit between each teacher's own style, skills, and philosophy and the school in which he or she works. Greater choice for both students and staff should create more widespread commitment to and support for a school's mission.

The nature of local district personnel policies and practices must change as well. Internship and induction programs for beginning teachers must be established to provide support and help them master both classroom and school roles. Teacher evaluation systems, which currently assess how well teachers demonstrate specific behaviors and instructional practices, should instead focus on how well they are able to make appropriate instructional decisions and judgments in order to accomplish results with their students.

The role of the collective bargaining process in promoting school restructuring needs to be examined as well. Evidence on the impact of collective bargaining suggests that unions have served to increase the extent of bureaucratic control by making the work of teaching more rationalized and more highly specified and inspected and by increasing the number and specificity of rules determining work roles and conditions (Kerchner, 1986). However, there are recent experiments, such as in Dade County, Florida, and Rochester, New York, in which collective bargaining has been used to promote greater flexibility in schools. In Toledo, Ohio, the teachers' union used collective bargaining to introduce rigorous peer review procedures in which senior teachers review and evaluate probationary teachers (Darling-Hammond, 1984).

The foregoing are illustrative of the range of current policies and practices that will need to be reviewed in order to promote school restructuring. Equally important is a reconsideration of local control and leadership. Over the past decade and a half, local school board authority has been eroded as a result of federal legislation, court actions, collective bargaining agreements, and, most recently, state initiatives. As a recent study by the Institute for Educational Leadership (1986) shows, local school boards frequently spend the bulk of their time on crisis management or operational details and engage infrequently in systematic planning, policy development, or oversight. Generally, local school boards lack strong connections to local government, political cultures, and business and civic groups.

These conditions, together with the demands made by restructuring schools, point to the need for developing new conceptions of local control and leadership. Successfully restructuring the educational system and providing greater discretion to individual schools must occur in a policy framework that establishes long-range goals, attracts and retains high-quality personnel, assures that resources are adequately targeted to students with greatest need, and generally makes success at the school level possible. Further, it requires ongoing oversight and assessment to determine whether goals are being accomplished and policies are having their intended effects.

Strengthened local leadership involves more than a proactive policymaking approach. It also requires development of mechanisms for strengthening ties to the local community and strong advocacy for education and youth. In addition, it requires the capacity to broaden the constituency and support base for education, promote widespread community understanding of the needs of the educational system, marshal needed resources for the schools, and establish linkages with parents and members of the community at large to support and strengthen the instructional program.

Implications for the State's Role in Education

Changes at the school and district levels will require changes at the state level as well. In part, this will entail the development of new policies as well as new strategies of influence. It will also require states to rethink their role and orientation toward local school systems.

Challenges to States

The primary challenge facing states is to decide ways to bring about the changes in local practices described above. While states have a history of attempting to influence local educational practices, most recently as part of the "first wave" of educational reform earlier in this decade, the challenge this time is quite different. Meeting this challenge will, in all likelihood, require changes in states' leadership roles, strategies of influence, and policy tools that cumulatively are at least as great as the changes required of practitioners and local policymakers. This is so for several reasons.

First, previous attempts by states to change local school practices have frequently taken the form of requiring educational services for new populations — such as special education, compensatory education, bilingual education — or higher standards for existing programs and services. In the case of services for new populations, the target populations have been reasonably well defined, and the desired responses have typically been the provision of additional services or programs, which could be grafted more or less readily onto the existing system. By now, state and local capacity in these areas are reasonably well defined. Local districts know how to design, administer, and implement such new programs, and states have experience with the policy tools required to initiate them, such as mandates and categorical programs (McDonnell and Elmore, 1987). These same state policy tools and local capacities also served, reasonably well, the "first wave" of educational reform in this decade, when states required additional course offerings or higher performance standards for students, teachers, and local school districts (Clune, 1989). However, mandates or financial inducements to provide new programs or services are not well designed to foster more fundamental changes in the management, authority structures, resource allocation patterns, or technologies of existing programs and practices, especially on the comprehensive scale involved in restructuring.

The limited evidence available based on the early experience of schools, districts, and states involved in restructuring (David, 1988; Elmore, 1988) suggests that restructuring at the local level requires new visions and beliefs about educational practice, high degrees of trust among local school boards, administrators, and teachers' organizations, and a willingness in these actors to take substantial risks together. It also requires a sophisticated strategy and a range of new practices for fostering staff involvement and participation, supporting and encouraging risk taking among educators at the school level, and working out new accountability arrangements. It requires a gradual redefinition of roles and responsibilities of virtually all actors in the system. Also, importantly, it requires sustained assistance and training for local educators to develop the talents and skills required in their new roles.

In short, the lessons from early restructuring efforts suggest that political will and organizational capacity for change at the local district level are critical preconditions for, and continuing ingredients of, successful restructuring. States can neither create nor support such will or such capacity simply through the development of mandates that require local compliance nor through the provision of resources to pay for the incremental costs of the change process. Rather, states will require policy tools and strategies of influence that are better suited to modifying the culture and capacities of local districts and the knowledge, skills, and talents of individual educators.

Political and organizational obstacles at the local level have parallels at the state level as well. While the impulses behind restructuring are attractive to state policymakers, marshaling support for needed changes will be problematical. This is partly due to the inherent complexity — and therefore ambiguity — of the concept of restructuring. The legislative implications of restructuring are particularly unclear. Beyond calling for the creation of pilot programs — which are already underway in Arkansas, Massachusetts, Maine, North Carolina and Washington state — advocates of restructuring have had a difficult time translating the radical changes called for at the local school-district level into equally ambitious initiatives at the state level.

I will indicate below a package of steps for a state agenda, but they are admittedly difficult to build a legislative package around. Further, the fiscal implications of restructuring are still unclear. Many of the costs are difficult to determine clearly, largely because the specific actions required at any level are difficult to describe in concrete terms (McGuire and Augenblick, 1988). The costs that are easiest to anticipate are continued increases in teacher salaries, partly to make teaching a more attractive profession and partly because political demands for salary increases would be present even without a call for restructuring. In the past, salary and other increases in educational expenditures could be achieved politically by linking them to readily understandable educational improvements, such as higher standards. Linking them now to vague notions of restructuring may be a far more difficult task.

States will have to confront limitations of organizational capacity as well. For the most part, the primary functions of state education agencies have been the administration of federal programs and monitoring local compliance with state regulations. The organization of state education agencies reflects federal policy priorities more than it does the administrative requirements of school improvement. Also, though data are difficult to find in this area, a good deal of the operating budget of state education agencies comes from federal funds. However, successful state leadership of restructuring efforts will require a far different orientation from that of current state education agencies. In particular, states will need to become far more sophisticated than most presently are in developing and using indicator and other information systems to both guide state policy development and stimulate and inform local improvement efforts (Kaagan, 1988; Cohen, 1988). They will also require enhanced capabilities for providing technical assistance to local districts and schools; capabilities oriented more toward helping local educators define problems and devise imaginative solutions than toward implementing proven practices or well-developed programs.

Operationally, this will require state education agencies to make better use of existing data, especially through the coordination of compliance monitoring and accreditation data with testing and other indicators of achievement. In many states, it will also require states to collect more data than they do now and to strengthen their evaluation, research, and policy analysis capabilities. States will also need new models for providing technical assistance and new ways of more effectively utilizing, or improving, the ability of existing agency staff to provide appropriate assistance to schools and districts.

Developing needed capacity for state education agencies will not be simple. In many states it will require some combination of internal reorganization, new staff capabilities, and additional resources. However, state legislatures, which frequently hold state agencies in low regard, will not easily agree to provide additional resources for what will appear to be the creation of an even larger bureaucracy. Also, in many states, local administrators will be equally unenthusiastic about strengthening an organization that is generally seen more as a source of headaches than of genuine help.

States' Advantages

While states face obstacles to effectively leading a restructuring of their educational systems, they enjoy some decided advantages as well. States cannot lead independently of, or clearly at odds with, other sources of influence such as local districts or the federal government. However, because of their considerable formal authority, resources, and the opportunities for influence available to them, state governments will remain in a dominant position in continuing efforts in educational reform. More specifically, states can capitalize on several advantages to change the policy and political environment within which education operates and provide visible examples of new structural arrangements and educational practices.

Because education is a constitutional responsibility of states, they have the authority to define the policy environment in which it occurs. States control entry into the educational profession through licensure requirements for teachers and administrators. They define the successful "product" of the educational system by establishing high school graduation requirements. Through the Carnegie unit, they establish the credits given a course. Through testing and assessment programs, states establish performance and accountability standards. Through accreditation and approval standards, they define required and acceptable programs of studies for students and professionals alike.

Without belaboring the point, state policies form a large part of the context of the educational system. States also provide a significant share of the resources for its daily operation. Presumably, through careful manipulation of the regulatory environment and incentive system in which education operates, states should be able to induce desired changes in local practice. This is far from automatic, however, and states still have a long way to go to understand precisely what policy and regulatory changes will in fact produce, or increase the likelihood of, such changes at the local level.

In addition to formal authority, states can also wield considerable influence with respect to the identification and formulation of problems in education as well as to the nature of needed solutions. Governors in particular have successfully used the bully pulpit to focus public attention and mobilize support throughout the decade. State education agencies are increasingly institutionalizing this role through the use of indicator and accountability systems through which data on educational performance are regularly released to the public. When indicating particular districts or schools, such data can begin to capture the attention of their communities in addition to the state as a whole. The point here is that states have the capacity to influence, if not alter, the political climate and culture of local school districts and increasingly direct attention toward the performance of local systems.

States also have the ability to support the creation of new models of schools, largely through the support of pilot programs. Such efforts can help make concrete ideas about what restructured schools might look like, draw attention to successful innovations, and provide support and encouragement to others inclined to make similar efforts.

Implications for State Action

In the context of both the challenges facing states and the resources available to them, state action will be required in three broad areas.

Setting Educational Goals. States must assume larger responsibilities for setting educational goals and defining standards for student outcomes. This is a critical precondition to providing greater discretion and flexibility to schools. Accomplishing this will require state action on several fronts.

State boards of education can begin by establishing long-range educational goals that adequately reflect the knowledge and higher-order skills graduates can be expected to need. Currently, few states seriously attempt to establish long-range educational goals. Historically, if educational goals were established at all, they were too vague to guide policy development or establish performance standards for schools and were forgotten soon after they were established. In many states, descriptions of desired student outcomes either take the form of vague prescriptions for youngsters to reach their full potentials or highly specified and lengthy lists of instructional objectives reflecting subject matter course requirements. There must be a middle ground.

States should institute a long-range planning and goal-setting process to establish educational goals to meet the broad societal needs schools must serve (Cohen, 1987; National Association of State Boards of Education (NASBE) Task Force, 1987). Desired outcomes must focus educators' attention and efforts on teaching important knowledge and skills while giving them the freedom to make curricular and instructional decisions about how best to accomplish these outcomes.

Setting appropriate goals is an important first step, but in order to have an impact on educational practice, goals must be linked to state testing and assessment programs. In many states, this will require replacing existing minimum competency tests, which focus exclusively on basic skills, with newly developed instruments for assessing higher-order skills.

In developing new assessment tools and procedures, several issues should be addressed. First, assessment systems can have powerful effects on curriculum and instruction, especially if such serious consequences as promotion or graduation depend on student performance (Resnick and Resnick, 1985). If tests are designed to be "taught to," as is the case with advanced placement tests, they can be powerful tools for shaping the local curriculum and making it more rigorous. They also can provide useful feedback to educators and incentives to students.

In order to work this way, tests should be linked to a specific program of study rather than assessing knowledge of a broad curricular domain. Further, tests must measure the depth of knowledge and higher-order skills required of students. If they continue to reflect only minimum competencies, they are likely to restrict what teachers attempt to do and thus lower educational standards and performance for all but the weakest students.

Second, assessment tools geared to higher-order skills may take different forms than those of most existing state testing programs (Archbald and Newman, 1988). Continued reliance on multiple-choice or short-answer questions is simply not adequate. Rather, assessment tools are needed that require students to synthesize, integrate, and apply knowledge and data to complex problems. They should present tasks for which no one answer is right but for which a range of solutions may be possible. These may take the form of essays, projects, or other demonstrations of competence, such as those called for in Theodore Sizer's Coalition of Essential Schools. Scoring systems that rely on expert judgment rather than simply checking for the correct answer are an essential part of these assessment tools.

Third, while states should develop assessment tools that effectively shape local curriculum and student preparation, they should also seek to ensure that the same measures do not overly restrict local curricular choices and instructional approaches, or else the benefits of increased school autonomy also will be restricted.

Fourth, states need to be wary of the danger that any particular assessment tool can have unintended effects on schooling

by overly narrowing the focus of educators to only those outcomes that are measured. This danger can be mitigated in part
by making sure that what is measured is truly valued, so that
teachers give attention to the most important educational outcomes. It also can be mitigated by developing a system of indicators that accurately reflect the many goals schools have. Not
only do we want average improvement gains, we also want to
ensure substantial gains for the lowest-achieving students. Although we want to improve cognitive skills, we also need to
reduce the dropout rate. And not only do we value students'
presence in schools, we also value their self-esteem, the degree
of satisfaction that they and their parents feel about their schools,
and the willingness of students to pursue a variety of learning
opportunities beyond formal schooling.

Stimulating Local Innovation. Improvement in educational productivity and the professionalization of teaching will
require new ways of organizing schools that allow more varied
instructional arrangements, greater collegial interaction among
teachers, and greater teacher involvement in decision making.
Although the need for restructuring is clear, notions of how
schools could be restructured are not yet well developed. New
concepts regarding restructuring must emerge through carefully
supported local efforts, where new ideas can emerge from and
be tested against the realities of schools and classrooms. Consequently, states must provide leadership by

- Articulating a vision of restructured schools
- Encouraging local experimentation with various forms of
  school organization
- Reducing unnecessary administrative and regulatory bar-
  riers to experimentation with promising approaches
- Providing ongoing implementation support and technical
  assistance to schools and districts trying new approaches
- Linking rewards and sanctions for schools to their perfor-
  mance
- Researching and disseminating results to other schools

Several states have already taken the initiative in this area by supporting pilot or demonstration programs at the school level. While this is an important first step, states will need to decide how to similarly encourage restructuring of entire local districts, altering the role of the local board and central office. They will also need to develop strategies for both institutionalizing and expanding the pilot program to other schools.

Rethinking State Accountability Systems. Successfully restructuring schools will require states to rethink the nature and mix of the accountability mechanisms on which they rely. States will need to fashion school systems that focus on educational outcomes and that provide strong incentives for improved results throughout the system by linking performance with rewards and sanctions.

Historically, states have regulated local educational practices largely by setting standards for inputs into the education system, for example, expenditures per pupil, availability of instructional resources, staff qualifications, program offerings, and the like. States rarely attempted directly to influence the nature of educational practices by regulating teaching methods or curriculum content. Nor have they collected or used information on educational outcomes — student performance — as part of their regulatory or accountability systems. With rare exceptions, states have not applied sanctions to schools or districts for failure to meet state standards, though they have had statutory authority to withhold funds or force consolidation of districts that did not comply. In short, states have relied on a set of bureaucratic regulations of educational inputs largely to provide legitimacy to an otherwise unregulated system (Meyer and Rowan, 1978).

In the past decade, states have begun to tighten and strengthen their accountability strategies. First, beginning in the mid–1970s, states have incorporated minimum competency testing into their policy frameworks. Thus, they began to specify and measure outcome standards. However, the standards were often set relatively low, focusing exclusively on basic skills performance. Typically, states did relatively little beyond collecting and reporting test scores, relying on their publicity to stimulate and inform local improvement efforts.

Second, several states have begun recently to incorporate into their regulatory systems the findings of effective schools research, which has helped them to establish standards for such educational practices as staff development, goal setting, the principal's leadership, and the like. Thus, in addition to regulating inputs and inspecting results, many states also have begun to regulate educational practices.

Third, there is renewed interest among states in developing appropriate sanctions for poor performance or noncompliance with state standards. For example, Arkansas forces school districts that fail to meet its revised accreditation standards to dissolve and consolidate with a neighboring district. And both South Carolina and New Jersey have developed procedures for the state to intervene to manage and/or govern local districts that fail to meet state standards. In New York state, schools with the lowest academic performance must participate in a school improvement program that receives state-sponsored technical assistance.

These developments in state accountability systems have occurred at a time when state attention has focused largely on improving the quality of the most poorly performing schools and districts in the state. In the past, state efforts were devoted to raising the floor of educational performance; as states turn their attention to raising the ceiling, they will need to rethink their approach to holding schools and districts accountable. More specifically, they will need to address several broad issues.

First, states must link the accountability system with the assessment system, so that accountability focuses primarily on how well schools produce desired results, framed in terms of school goals.

Second, states must fashion systems that focus on the school and the district simultaneously. Holding individual schools accountable for student performance recognizes that schools are the primary means for providing instruction and the basic building blocks for reform. It is consistent with the overall call for promoting greater school autonomy and acknowledges the often substantial differences in performance between schools within the same district. However, because schools operate under the direction, policy guidance, support system, and resource constraints of the local district, accountability systems must be designed to hold both schools and districts accountable for school performance.

Third, states will need to set appropriate performance standards for schools. There are three different standards of comparision the state can use to judge the adequacy of school performance: absolute standards, comparative standards, or improvement standards.

When absolute standards are used, the performance of each school or district is compared with some fixed, predetermined standards. For example, the state might require 85 percent of the students in every school to pass state tests, or it might set a goal of no greater than a 5 percent dropout rate for each school. Such an approach enables the accountability system to reflect state goals and targets equally throughout the system. However, it also means that such an accountability system will serve largely to distinguish upper middle class schools from those serving predominately poor students, since school performance and student body composition will be highly correlated.

In contrast, a comparative approach judges a school's performance only against those of schools serving similar student bodies. Such an approach offers several advantages. It is likely to be perceived as legitimate by educators, because it recognizes that socioeconomic and other resource factors influence school performance. Schools that serve predominately poor and minority students will have opportunities to succeed because they will be, essentially, competing against one another. At the same time, it reduces the likelihood that schools serving more affluent students will become complacent, because they, too, will be measured against similar schools. Thus, low-performing schools that seldom have opportunities to be recognized for success will find it possible to receive recognition for their efforts. Schools in affluent communities, for whom recogniton can often be a function of their clients rather than their effectiveness, will be challenged by the efforts of other schools with equally advantaged student bodies. However, this approach also has some disadvantages. It sets lower standards for schools with large concentrations of poor students. If these standards remain low, ultimately it will work to the disadvantage of the most at-risk students.

When improvement standards are used, a school's performance is judged against its own previous performance. Any school that shows significant gains, regardless of its starting point, is viewed as successful and deserving of reward. This approach makes it possible for virtually all schools to be successful (except those at the very top with little room for additional improvement). It increases the likelihood that low-performing schools will be viewed as successful simply because progress is easier to achieve when one starts at the bottom.

The three standards of comparison are not mutually exclusive. Each offers unique advantages and disadvantages. If carefully combined, they ought to provide rewards for outstanding performance and powerful incentives for continued improvement throughout the system.

A fourth accountability issue needs to be addressed: Once standards are set, states need to link rewards to performance. Although rewards may take a variety of forms, such as recognition and flexibility, there is reason to believe that discretionary dollars for the school should be an important feature of any reward system. The reason is not that additional dollars will motivate school staff to work harder. Rather, additional resources can powerfully underscore both the intrinsic satisfaction and the external recognition that comes with success. In addition, the school's decision about the use of additional resources can foster the sharing of problem solving among school staff members.

Finally, for schools that persistently fail to show improvement or meet performance standards, states must develop appropriate forms of intervention. State intervention strategies may involve a sequence of steps, including requirements for schools and school districts to develop and implement improvement plans, providing assistance in the development and implementation of such plans, specifying the steps the school or district must take in order to meet standards, or ultimately, some more forceful intervention, such as consolidation or state takeover of the district.

In moving toward performance-oriented accountability systems, states will need to review existing approaches to regulating educational inputs and practices. Greater emphasis on outcomes and performance must be balanced with the value of regulations regarding input for ensuring equality of educational opportunity, especially for students residing in rural, small, or poor districts, and with the potential of carefully crafted educational process and practice standards to effectively organize and inform local planning and school improvement efforts.

Aside from the need to sort out various regulatory arrangements, states also need to consider other possible accountability mechanisms. For example, a system that relies heavily on diversity and autonomy of local schools can accommodate, if not capitalize on, market mechanisms of control (for example, Elmore, 1986; Kearns and Doyle, 1988). Although this approach can take a number of forms, the underlying principle involves providing opportunities for students and their parents to enroll in the school or educational program of their choice. The assumption here is that if enrollment and funding levels are linked, schools will have an incentive to make themselves as attractive to students and parents as possible. Variability of educational programs among schools can allow for careful matching of school and student preferences and needs, presumably boosting productivity in the process.

Another approach to accountability relies on professional mechanisms of control. A professional control model essentially turns over decisions about appropriate educational practice to a self-regulating profession. It presumes that a well-developed knowledge base informs the training, certification, and evaluation of teachers, and that working conditions allow highly trained professionals to exercise judgment and employ the most appropriate instructional practices. One attraction of increased professional control is its potential to attract and retain highly talented individuals in the profession.

Within the educational system, few mechanisms are already in place that can form the basis of a professional system

of control. The National Board for Professional Teaching Standards, established by the Carnegie Forum on Education and
the Economy, is intended to be such a mechanism. It will enable
the profession to establish standards for the certification of high
levels of teaching competence. There are proposals to create comparable boards at the state level for the licensure of beginning
teachers as well. In most states, licensure responsibilities currently reside in lay state boards of education, which are expected
to act on behalf of the broad public interest. States must carefully
examine whether both licensure and certification should be controlled by the profession or whether licensure more appropriately
should be controlled by agents of the public.

To stimulate continuous school improvement, states must
analyze carefully and determine the most appropriate mix of
professional, market, outcome, process, and input systems of
educational accountability. They also must develop an appropriate set of incentives and sanctions attached to accountability
mechanisms. The task of states is not to select the single best
approach; rather, it is to sort out which mix of control strategies,
rewards, and sanctions will contribute most effectively to improvements of student outcomes according to each state's circumstances.

Conclusion

The preceding analysis has argued that the challenges facing the educational system are fundamentally different from
those it has confronted in the past, largely because of significant
changes in the economic and social fabric of the country. Responding to these new challenges will require a fundamental
restructuring of schools, especially of the way instruction is provided and the way staff roles and responsibilities are defined.
However, needed changes in schools cannot occur without corresponding changes in the way that local school districts and
state education agencies and programs operate. States and districts alike must find ways to create an emphasis on performance
and results throughout the educational system. Local districts
will need to find ways to shift greater decision-making author-

ity and responsibility to schools in order to enhance professional and parental involvement in decision making and ways to provide resources and other forms of support and assistance to individual schools. States, in turn, must significantly strengthen their efforts to set educational goals and assess school performance, provide rewards and sanctions linked to performance, and stimulate local diversity and experimentation. Only by making concordant changes at the school, district, and state levels will the educational system be able to respond to the challenges of the coming decade.

References

Alexander, K. L., and McDill, E. L. "Selection and Allocation Within Schools: Some Causes and Consequences of Curriculum Placement." *American Sociological Review*, 1975, *41*, 963–980.

Applebee, A., Langer, J. A., and Mullins, I. V. S. *The Writing Report Card: Writing Achievement in American Schools*. Princeton, N.J.: Educational Testing Service, 1986.

Archbald, D. A., and Newman, F. M. *Beyond Standardized Testing: Assessing Authentic Academic Achievement in the Secondary School*. Reston, Va.: National Association of Secondary School Principals, 1988.

Bossert, S. T. *Tasks and Social Relationships in Classrooms: A Study of Classroom Organization and its Consequences*. New York: Cambridge University Press, 1979.

Bossert, S. T., Dwyer, D. C., Rowan, B., and Lee, G. V. "The Instructional Management Role of the Principal." *Educational Administration Quarterly*, 1982, *18*, 34–64.

Carnegie Task Force on Teaching as a Profession. *A Nation Prepared: Teachers for the 21st Century*. Washington, D.C.: Carnegie Forum on Education and the Economy, 1986.

Clune, W. "The Implementation and Effects of High School Graduation Requirements." Research report RR-011. Madison: Center for Policy Research, University of Wisconsin, Madison, 1989.

Cohen, M. "Instructional, Management, and Social Conditions in Effective Schools." In A. Odden and L. D. Webb (eds.),

School Finance and School Improvement: Linkages for the 1980s.
Cambridge, Mass.: Ballinger, 1983.

Cohen, M. *Meeting the Information Needs of State Education Policy-makers: Report of a Survey of State Policymakers.* Alexandria, Va.:
State Education Policy Consortium, 1985.

Cohen, M. "State Boards in an Era of Reform." *Phi Delta Kappan,* 1987, *69* (1).

Cohen, M. "Designing State Assessment Systems." *Phi Delta Kappan,* 1988, *69* (8), 583–588.

Corcoran, T. B. "The Role of the District in School Effectiveness." In *Increasing Educational Success: The Effective Schools Model.*
Committee on Education and Labor, House of Representatives. Washington, D.C.: U.S. Government Printing Office,
1987.

Darling-Hammond, L. "The Toledo (Ohio) Public School Intern and Intervention Program." In A. E. Wise and others,
Case Studies for Teacher Evaluation: A Study of Effective Practices.
Santa Monica, Calif.: Rand, 1984.

David, J. "The Puzzle of Structural Change." Paper prepared
for the Symposium on Structural Change in Secondary Education, National Center on Effective Secondary Schools,
Madison, Wis., 1987.

David, J. *Restructuring in Progress: Lessons from Pioneering Districts.*
Washington, D.C.: National Governors' Association, 1988.

Denham, C., and Lieberman, A. *Time to Learn.* Washington,
D.C.: National Institute of Education, 1980.

Elmore, R. F. *Choice in Public Education.* Center for Policy Research in Education, Rutgers University, 1986.

Elmore, R. F. *Early Experiences in Restructuring Schools: Voices from
the Field.* Washington, D.C.: National Governors' Association, 1988.

Glass, G. V., and Smith, M. L. "Meta-Analysis of Research
on Class Size and Achievement." *Educational Evaluation and
Policy Analysis,* 1979, *1* (1), 2–16.

Hudson Institute. *Workforce 2000: Work and Workers for the 21st
Century.* Indianapolis, Ind.: Hudson Institute, 1987.

Institute for Educational Leadership. *School Boards: Strengthening
Grass Roots Leadership.* Washington, D.C.: Institute for Educational Leadership, 1986.

Kaagan, S. "State Education Agencies, Above or Beneath the Waves of Reform." Draft paper prepared for Council of Chief State School Officers. 1988.

Kearns, D. T., and Doyle, D. P. *Winning the Brain Race.* San Francisco: Institute for Contemporary Studies Press, 1988.

Kerchner, C. T. "Union-Made Teaching: The Effects of Labor Relations on Teaching Work." In E. Z. Rothkopf (ed.), *Review of Research in Education 12.* Washington, D.C.: American Education Research Association, 1986.

McDonnell, L. M., and Elmore, R. F. "Getting the Job Done: Alternative Policy Instruments." Educational Evaluation and Policy Analysis, 1987, *9* (2) 133–152.

McGuire, K., and Augenblick, J. "The Costs of Restructuring Schools." Draft paper prepared for National Governors' Association, Washington, D.C.: 1988.

Meyer, J. W., and Rowan, B. "The Structure of Education Organizations." In M. W. Meyer and Associates, *Environments and Organizations.* San Francisco: Jossey-Bass, 1978.

Murnane, R. J. "Education and Productivity of the Workforce: Looking Ahead." In R. E. Litan, R. Z. Lawrence, and C. L. Schultze (eds.), *American Living Standards: Threats and Challenges.* Washington, D.C.: Brookings Institute, 1988.

National Assessment of Educational Progress. *The Reading Report Card: Progress Toward Excellence in Our Schools.* Princeton, N.J.: Educational Testing Service, 1985.

National Association of State Boards of Education (NASBE) Task Force on State Board Leadership. *The Challenge of Leadership: State Boards of Education in an Era of Reform.* Alexandria, Va.: National Association of State Boards of Education, 1987.

National Governors' Association. *Time For Results: The Governors' 1991 Report on Education.* Washington, D.C.: National Governors' Association, 1986.

National Governors' Association. *Bringing Down the Barriers.* Washington, D.C.: National Governors' Association, 1987a.

National Governors' Association. *Results in Education: 1987.* Washington, D.C.: National Governors' Association, 1987b.

Oakes, J. *Keeping Track: How Schools Structure Inequality.* New Haven: Yale University Press, 1985.

Purkey, S. C., and Smith, M. S. "Effective Schools: A Review." *Elementary School Journal* 1983, *83* (4), 427–452.

Raywid, M. A. "Restructuring School Governance: Two Models." Draft paper prepared for the Center for Policy Research in Education, 1987.

Resnick, D. P., and Resnick, L. B. "Standards, Curriculum and Performance: A Historical and Comparative Perspective." *Educational Researcher,* 1985, *14* (4), 5–20.

Resnick, L. B. *Education and Learning to Think.* Washington, D.C.: National Academy Press, 1987.

Schoor, L. B. *Within Our Reach: Breaking the Cycle of Disadvantage.* New York: Doubleday, 1988.

Sizer, T. *Horace's Compromise: The Dilemma of the American High School.* Boston: Houghton Mifflin, 1984.

Slavin, R. E. *Cooperative Learning.* New York: Plenum, 1985.

Smith, M. S., and Purkey, S. C. "School Reform: The District Policy Implications of the Effective Schools Literature." *Elementary School Journal,* 1985, *85* (3), 353–390.

Stern, J. D. (ed.). *The Condition of Education: A Statistical Report 1987 Edition.* Washington, D.C.: Center for Education Statistics, U.S. Department of Education, 1987.

✻ · NINE

Conclusion:
Toward a Transformation
of Public Schooling

Richard F. Elmore

This book has presented an analytical view of the major themes underlying school restructuring. It has examined school restructuring from the perspective of the individual school, examining alternative conceptions of the core technology of schools, conceptions of teachers' work, and relations between schools and their clients. Also, it has examined school restructuring from the perspective of the broader political system, examining policy options at the local and state levels. Its main message is that school restructuring has a number of possible meanings and may have a number of possible consequences for the organization and effectiveness of schools, depending on the specific proposals, the conditions under which restructuring occurs, and the political stakes of the different actors involved.

In this brief conclusion, I would like to speculate about the issues policymakers and practitioners will confront as they undertake school restructuring and about the political prospects for restructuring reforms. It is risky to speculate about anything as complex as school restructuring, so I will hedge my predictions by considering three possible scenarios rather than an estimate of the likely outcome of restructuring efforts. The three scenarios define a continuum extending from the maximum to the minimum effects to be expected from such efforts. They provide a way of sorting through the possible consequences of school restructuring.

Scenario 1: Transformation

One possible scenario is that the current interest in restructuring schools signals a major transformation of American schooling, from a traditional bureaucratic form to a completely different form that is not yet fully specified. This new form of organization would attach much less importance to standardization, central bureaucratic control, and externally imposed rules as means of controlling the performance of schools, and more importance to school inquiry and problem solving, school autonomy, professional norms, and client choice.

What might schools look like after this transformation? The content, pedagogy, and technology of instruction might shift in the direction of what Rowan (in this volume) has called a "diagnostic" perspective. This shift would place significantly greater responsibility on schools and teachers to develop clearer strategies for dealing with student diversity and closer connections with the school's clients. A change in the technology of instruction would necessitate a change in the definition of teachers' work, as Sykes, Gideonse, and Moore Johnson (in this volume) suggest, entailing more flexible use of teacher time, more teacher-initiated inquiry, greater reliance on teacher judgment in the construction of the curriculum, and greater teacher participation in evaluation of their peers. Likewise, changes in instructional technology and teachers' functions would necessitate major changes in the organization of authority and the responsibilities of schools, as Raywid (in this volume) suggests, with emphasis placed on decision making at the school level and on the substitution of process controls and client choice for standardized output measures.

Transformational changes of this type imply the presence of certain political and social conditions. For example, broad changes in the core technology of schooling would require reform of state and local policies on curriculum, research, development, and professional education and their alignment around a common conception of what schools should do. Institutionally, this alignment would involve actors with diverse roles and interests. State and local curriculum specialists, professional development specialists, university teachers and researchers, and the like, would have to orchestrate their interests around a common set of purposes. Likewise, major changes in the definition of teachers' work would require alignment of teacher educational programs, certification policies, collective bargaining agreements, and management practices in local school systems. The major actors would be teacher educators, teacher organizations, and teachers in local schools. Finally, major changes in the governance structure of local schools would require changes in state and local staffing policies, curriculum and testing policies, and training and support for school-level personnel, and a major outreach to parents. The major actors would be local school boards and administrators, state and local testing and measurement experts, community leaders, and school-level personnel.

This quick inventory suggests that the transformational scenario is not very likely to occur, for at least three reasons. First, the alignment of political and institutional interests necessary to produce the required changes in policy and practice is so extensive and complex that the likelihood of its occurrence over a broad scale is slim. This is not to say that something approaching this alignment will not occur, or is not already occurring, in a few local settings, as Jane David (in this volume) suggests. But, as we shall see in a moment, this type of movement leads to a different set of outcomes.

Second, the alignment of political interests required to produce change on the scale required by the transformational scenario is inherently unstable. These interests cut across almost every major institutional, jurisdictional, and professional boundary in education, including teacher/administrator, school/district, state/local, university/school, and researcher/practitioner boundaries. The closest historical analogy to the kind of change suggested by the transformational scenario is the progressive era in the United States. For a relatively short period of time, the political, administrative, and educational progressives were aligned around a common ideology that produced a large volume of reform, both inside and outside education. While these reforms resulted in extensive changes in many settings, it was not long before political and administrative versions of progressivism, with their heavy emphasis on managerial expertise and rational administration, developed tensions with the educational version of progressivism, with its emphasis on spontaneity, diversity, and discovery. A common ideology, in other words, failed to resolve important individual and institutional differences.

Third, there is at least one glaring inconsistency in the idea that school restructuring would create a transformation of American education. One of the key insights behind restructuring schools is the idea that the overall improvement of American education depends on getting individual schools to operate more effectively as organizations. Those who propose school restructuring have a bias toward changing the system by changing individual schools; according to them, systemwide change will occur by lodging greater responsibility with people who work in schools. If this really is the central insight of school restructuring, then it seems contradictory to argue that all schools will or should change in the same way as a result of school restructuring, since to do so, schools would all have to arrive spontaneously at more or less the same solutions to highly complex problems of content, pedagogy, technology, organization, and governance. Lodging a high degree of discretion with schools is, in other words, inconsistent with broad uniform effects.

While the transformational scenario is a useful thought experiment for understanding the conditions necessary to produce school restructuring on a broad scale, it is an unlikely result of the present reforms. Two other possibilities are more likely — adaptive realignment and cooptation.

Scenario 2: Adaptive Realignment

While it is highly unlikely that political and institutional interests will spontaneously align themselves around a new transformed understanding of schooling, it is much more likely that significant shifts of alignments of key interests will occur in response to changes in the political and social environment of schooling, and that these realignments could have significant and enduring effects on the way many schools operate.

For example, important changes are presently occurring in the labor market for teachers. Whether or not a "teacher shortage" is imminent, the labor pool from which teachers will have to be drawn is changing, as is the range of opportunities available to the pool from which teachers have been drawn in the past. These changes in the labor pool will drive some school systems to compete for teachers by offering them significantly different working conditions, in addition to the traditional salary inducements. The demography of metropolitan areas is also changing, with larger concentrations of the extremely poor and the affluent and an erosion of the traditional middle class constituency for the public schools. These changes could produce pressures for urban and suburban school systems to become more responsive to differences among student populations and to develop more self-conscious strategies for attracting and retaining middle class and affluent parents in public schools characterized by greater student diversity.

Also, the balance of power between federal, state, and local jurisdictions has shifted significantly in the past decade, with significant shifts in both financial support and authority for key domestic educational programs from the federal and local levels to the states. The increasing amount of regulatory and financial responsibility for education borne by the states is already provoking a reconsideration of the relationship between states and school districts and a search for ways to decentralize decision making.

The point of these examples is that there are forces in the social and political environment of schooling that could push schools in the direction of restructuring. But these forces are not uniformly distributed, nor is the interest and capacity of policymakers and educators to engage in restructuring as a response to these forces. Hence, a likely scenario is that a significant number of states and school districts will take major school restructuring initiatives as a response to pressing social and political problems and pursue the initiatives as long as pressures persist. How much restructuring occurs, then, will be a function of how pressing the problems are, how well school restructuring responds to those problems, and how ingenious school practitioners and researchers are at grafting school restructuring onto a broader political agenda.

Changes in the content, pedagogy, and technology of schooling can, for example, be grafted onto the broader issue of responding constructively to the increasing social diversity of metropolitan areas, changes in the working conditions of teachers onto the issue of attracting and retaining a middle class workforce in cities, and changes in school governance onto the issue of improving the responsiveness and efficiency of urban public services. These issues could significantly realign established political and institutional interests, since specific gains could result from specific changes. Public schools can gain increased enrollment by appealing more effectively to specific constituencies, teachers increased autonomy and better working conditions by putting themselves in the role of solving pressing and highly visible problems, and parents and teachers more control over schools by using improved responsiveness and increased effectiveness as arguments for changes in governance.

Specific changes in the organization of schools — some of them potentially far-reaching — are possible, then, if the changes are seen as solutions to pressing social and political problems and if they have tangible pay-offs for key constituencies. But the underlying dynamics of this process are adaptive rather than transformational. The formulations of the problems and the array of political interests aligned around these problems will vary significantly from one setting to another. The range of organizational solutions will likewise vary from one setting to another. School restructuring, then, will become a series of strategic responses to a set of pressing problems, organized around a certain set of themes, rather than a comprehensive template for the transformation of schools. It is also worth noting that adaptation is not necessarily synonymous with incrementalism. If the problems of metropolitan areas are as serious as they seem, some solutions might be quite bold.

There is already significant evidence that this process of

adaptive realignment is happening in places like Dade County, Florida, Rochester, New York, and Jefferson County, Kentucky. So this scenario seems to conform better to initial experience than the transformational one.

There are, however, two major problems with this scenario. The first and most obvious one is that if school restructuring is simply an extension of Tip O'Neill's famous dictum that "all politics is local," then the likelihood is high that it will become a scattered collection of isolated experiments without any coherent set of themes. While it seems more plausible to think about school restructuring as driven by immediate and tangible problems and interests, the result of this process, left to its own devices, is much variation that can only be explained by local variables over which no one has much control.

The second major problem with the adaptive realignment scenario is that there is no guarantee that the restructuring it produces will change the conditions of teaching and learning for teachers and students. There are a variety of ways for educators and politicians to appear to be responding to pressing political and social problems without doing much about the content, pedagogy, technology, working conditions, or governance of schooling.

In order for adaptive realignment to produce any broad, significant change of the key aspects addressed by restructuring, specific restructuring efforts in specific settings have to be informed by a broad agenda that puts the conditions of teaching and learning at the center of restructuring and also creates political and professional networks with an interest in reinforcing that agenda that transcend states and localities. If there is not major emphasis by national networks of educators and policymakers on the basic message of restructuring, which is that the rationale for changes in structure and governance is changing the conditions of teaching and learning, then it is highly unlikely that adaptive realignment will produce anything more than a series of interesting prototypes. One of the features that seems to distinguish the current interest in restructuring from other recent reform initiatives is that it is being adopted by both educators and policymakers.

Scenario 3: Cooptation

The most pessimistic scenario, of course, is that states and localities will embrace school restructuring as a label for what they are already doing and discard the substance. Large public school bureaucracies, the argument goes, typically adopt the rhetoric of reform without seriously altering their organization or modes of operation. As noted in the introduction to this book, there is much evidence to support the proposition that the daily realities of teaching and learning in schools were set long ago by enduring social and institutional forces and that periodic attempts to reform schools have never succeeded in changing these realities in anything more than superficial or short-lived ways. Indeed, in the absence of external political pressures like those outlined in the previous section, it seems unlikely that school systems will be obliged even to adopt the rhetoric of school restructuring, much less the substance.

The major flaws in the cooptation argument, however, are twofold. First, large bureaucracies do not persist in existing procedures and practices just because they want to; they do so because it is functional. Stable processes and organizational structures are functional in that they both hold individuals with potentially divergent interests together and generate predictability and support from the political environment. When conditions change both inside and outside large bureaucracies, they change, often by way of the kind of adaptive responses outlined above. Sometimes they change in major ways. So it is not accurate to say that the only response of school bureaucracy to innovation is cooptation. School systems could respond by significantly changing content, pedagogy, technology, working conditions, and governance if they perceive such changes to be functional in maintaining themselves as organizations and in solidifying their relations with the political, social, and economic environment that supports them.

The second flaw in the cooptation scenario is that it presents school bureaucracies as unitary, value-maximizing units when, in fact, school systems are more accurately portrayed as collections of loosely coupled interests. When one looks at school systems as loose collections of interests, one can see it is possible that many of the pressures for restructuring will come from within the systems themselves. As it becomes more difficult for some systems to recruit and retain good teachers and administrators, for example, it is plausible to believe that they will use their key position to change the way the system works. As pressure mounts for more attention to results at the school level, it is possible that school personnel and parents could form alliances to extract more authority and resources from the system at large in return for better performance on measures central administrators consider important. In other words, the possibilities for diverse political alignments within a seemingly monolithic bureaucracy are many.

While cooptation is an appealing point of departure for predicting the likely effects of school-restructuring reforms, then, it is in many ways as problematical as the transformation scenario. Both views attribute a kind of uniformity to schools and school systems that seems on its face to be suspect.

Overview

What this quick review of alternative scenarios demonstrates, I think, is that the fate of school restructuring is in large part a function of how actively various political interests use restructuring to solve educational and social problems and the degree to which they are willing to orchestrate their actions around a common agenda that takes the conditions of teaching and learning seriously. The weaker these factors, the more likely it is that school restructuring will drift toward the cooptation scenario. The stronger these factors, the more likely it is that school restructuring will result either in adaptive realignment around significantly different types of schooling for significant numbers of children or in a fundamental transformation of public schooling.

Index